THE ENCLOSURE MOVEMENT

How to reduce all sorts of grounds into a square for the better measuring of it.

A seventeenth-century land surveyor at work
(from Norden's *Surveior's Dialogue*, 3rd edn. 1617)

THE ENCLOSURE MOVEMENT

W. E. TATE

WALKER AND COMPANY
NEW YORK

Copyright © W. E. Tate 1967

Library of Congress Catalog Card Number: 67–23645

First published in the United States of America in 1967 by
Walker and Company, a division of Publications Development Corporation.

Printed and bound in Great Britain.

'—Ne voyez-vous pas, mon fils, s'écriat-il, ce furieux qui coupe avec ses dents le nez de son adversaire terrassé, et cet autre qui broie la tête d'une femme sous une pierre énorme?

—Je les vois, répondit Bulloch. Ils créent le droit; ils fondent la proprieté; ils établissent les principes de la civilisation, les bases des sociétés et les assises de l'État.

—Comment cela? demanda le vieillard Maël.

—En bornant leurs champs. C'est l'origine de toute police. Vos Pingouins, o mâitre, accomplissent la plus auguste des fonctions. Leur œuvre sera consacrée à travers les siècles par les légistes, protégée et confirmée par les magistrats.'

Anatole France,
L'Ile des Pingouins, 1907.
(Livre II, Chapitre III.)

PUBLISHER'S NOTE

W. E. Tate, B.Litt., F.S.A., is the author of *Nottinghamshire Parliamentary Enclosures, His Worship the Mayor, The Parish Chest, English Inn Signs, A Domesday of English Enclosure Acts and Awards,* and joint-author of *British Institutions* and *A History of Yorkshire.*

He has been sometime: Village Schoolmaster of Sutton Bonington in the County of Nottingham; Secretary, Sutton Bonington Labour Party P.D.C.; Chairman, Sutton Bonington and Normanton-on-Soar Branch of the National Union of Agricultural Workers; later G. W. Medley Senior Research Scholar in the University of Oxford. He is at present Reader in Historical Sources in the University of Leeds.

His great-grandmother was the last proprietor by inheritance of the cottage selions *Short Lythe* and *Sandbeds* in the open fields of Haxey, in the Isle of Axholme, Parts of Lindsey and County of Lincoln.

CONTENTS

8   CONTENTS

See below, p. 203, for a note on the Frontispiece.

The quotation on the title page is from the Rev.
Francis Trigge (below, p. 145, fn. 9). The 'horne' is,
of course, the horned sheep, the 'thorne' the thorn hedge.

LIST OF TEXT FIGURES

* Mr. Lear has also been responsible throughout the book for minor amendments to the illustrations when these were called for, and for the re-drawing to new scales and/or projections of such maps as needed this. I am anxious that he should receive full credit for his neat and accurate work.—W. E. T.

LIST OF PLATES

A seventeenth-century land surveyor at work (from
Norden's *Surveior's Dialogue*, 3rd edn. 1617, by courtesy
of Mr. G. E. Fussell)   *(Frontispiece)*
facing page

PREFACE

THE STORY OF the English Village makes a fascinating study, and the history of enclosure is an important part of it. In this work, those who are interested in the countryside will find an elementary account of enclosure, the main factor in the change which converted the mediaeval village to the village as we know it today. The subject has, however, more than merely historical and antiquarian interest—it touches also upon agriculture, law, sociology, economics and politics.

The work does not profess to contain, save perhaps in Chapters 4, 8, 9 and 10, a great deal of original matter. In the main the material in it, with a great deal more of the same type, is to be found in the standard authorities set forth in the book-list. To these works also the reader may be referred for more detailed bibliographical notes upon various aspects of the movement at different periods.

It will, I hope, be apparent to him that this brief introduction to the study of a wide-ranging subject is the fruit of many years' interest in the group of topics dealt with, and many years' pursuit of inquiry into them. In this I have been helped at various times by many friends, known and unknown, and it is my very pleasant duty to say so here. Taking my benefactors in a rough chronological order, the first of them is certainly the late A. A. Kidson, of King Edward VI Grammar School, East Retford. He implanted in me a passion for history—especially local history—which for half a century or so has given me a major interest. Retford School is quite near to the famous open-field village of Laxton, and Kidson it was who described the place to my school-fellows and me, piqued our curiosity about it, and persuaded us to include it among the local places of interest which we visited in out-of-school hours. For this reason I dedicated to him my first book on enclosure; in gratitude to his memory I name him here as first among those to whom I owe acknowledgement.

When, at the age of twenty-three, I was appointed as head-master (indeed, sole master) of a tiny village school, I had some very interesting and most exciting experiences on leaving south

Yorkshire where the non-statutory bodies wielding most
influence locally were such concerns as the Yorkshire Miners'
Association and the 'Barnsley British' Co-operative Society, for
the south Nottinghamshire-Leicestershire border. Here they
seemed rather to be such establishments as the Junior Imperial
and Primrose Leagues, the South Notts. Hunt, the Belvoir and
the Quorn. The influence of all this may well be still dis-
cernible in an unconscious personal bias in my treatment of the
social and economic issues involved in the historical inquiry
with which I am here concerned. If so, it is for the reader to dis-
count this and to correct me, if he can. Certainly I have tried
to be as dispassionate as possible in treating of matters which
for centuries have been the subject of controversy, and which
seem likely to remain so as long as this aspect of English
economic and social history remains a subject involving the
heart as well as the head. Perhaps the reader may be interested
to know how I came to be involved in it.

Like every other master of a one-teacher or two-teacher
school, I had to be something of a polymath—I even 'taught'
needlework, if my single girl assistant teacher needed a day's
holiday. So when I discovered that my top class, in working
through my predecessor's history syllabus, had reached 'The
Enclosures—their Causes and Consequences', I was quite happy
to carry on where he had left off, depending for my facts on
vague recollections of Laxton, and on an adolescent reading of
the Hammonds' *Village Labourer* (during which, I remembered,
I had almost choked with indignation). Seeking, like any
teacher worthy of the name, to make my lesson as interesting
and attractive as possible to my half-dozen pupils, I decided to
illustrate it by use of the local enclosure award. With some
difficulty I borrowed from the parish council their copies of the
two local awards (why two? I wondered), 1775 and 1777, and
pored over these, trying to make head or tail of them. They
seemed to differ substantially from one another (and both from
what the Hammonds had led me to expect). I then borrowed
from the county library 'two good books on enclosure'—as it
happened, Curtler and Slater (Appendix 2 below). They
appeared to contradict one another, and both disagreed with the
Hammonds. I visited one or two neighbouring villages: the
award for Normanton-on-Soar to the south of us was dated
1771, and both it and its authorizing act seemed to differ very
much from the corresponding sources for Sutton. At West

Leake, bordering us on the west, there were two acts, of 1742 and 1754, but no awards had ever been made under them—I wondered why. Kingston-on-Soar, which marched with us on our north, had neither act nor award—it had been enclosed in the reign of Henry VII. Again I wondered how, and why, and by whom? Ratcliffe-on-Soar, the next village, had been enclosed without Parliamentary consent at some time unknown before 1700. 'Why', I asked myself, 'should this apparently have been possible at Kingston and Ratcliffe, but not done at Sutton Bonington or Normanton?' Clearly the situation called for another visit to the county library (which I paid as soon as I could spare the necessary two and tenpence!). And so on. . . . Without originally intending anything of the kind, I was lured into a most elaborate and lengthy historical and archival investigation.

All this happened rather more than forty years ago, and I never gave my lesson—at any rate, in the form, and with the content and to the audience I originally intended it for. I still cannot answer with any degree of assurance some of the questions I set myself in 1925, but I have spent much time very enjoyably for many years in pursuing inquiries into them. Perhaps I was all the more active in doing this as I became interested in the social make-up of my village and its like, and as I became convinced—I still am—that this had a historical origin, since enclosure was at the root of many pressing rural social problems of today. I owe my thanks also, then, to my tutors at Westminster College, who taught me how to teach, and, if only indirectly, to my pupils at Sutton Bonington School, for whose benefit my investigations first began.

When, in rather later adult life, I began to devote myself seriously, though still as an enlightened amateur, to historical pursuits, I was much helped by the encouragement of professional historians having the technical knowledge and training which I then lacked. Outstanding among these were Professor J. D. Chambers, of *Nottinghamshire in the Eighteenth Century* and joint author of *The Agricultural Revolution, 1750–1880*; the late Professor G. D. H. Cole; the late Mrs. Barbara Hammond, of *The Village Labourer*, etc. etc.; the late Dr. C. S. Orwin, with Mrs. C. S. Orwin, of *The Open Fields* and the late Dr. Gilbert Slater, of *The English Peasantry*. (When, many years ago, I ventured to suggest that this last should be either thoroughly revised or, perhaps better, replaced, by a work taking into account some of the mass of research in the subject published since 1907, Slater was good enough to say he would gladly see me undertake the work: hence the present volume. I owe my thanks also to the late Dr. J. A. Venn, of Queens' College, Cambridge; to Professor M. Postan of Peterhouse, who for many years has been very kind to me; and perhaps most of all, to that great historian and great and good man, the late R. H. Tawney.

As a village schoolmaster without any very specific academic status, I found some difficulty in completing the forty-two detailed studies of enclosure in the English counties and the dozen or so essays on various aspects of agrarian history which lie behind the work now offered. My self-imposed task was beginning to encroach rather heavily on leisure which anyhow was already somewhat restricted. I discovered also that the costs I must meet in supplying myself with a minimum of necessary reference books, and in travelling, however inexpensively, to such local county record offices as were then accessible, were substantially more than my very modest means would allow. I could and did meet the second need by a variety of expedients—night school teaching, the training of rural pupil teachers, freelance journalism (on topics ranging from local history to, what was then rather more remunerative, 'Aunt Philippa's Personal Problem Corner', and the preparation of articles and pamphlets on the history of local inns and the heraldry of their signs). The further demands which this made on my leisure exacerbated, however, my first problem. My dilemma was resolved when in 1943, after due inquiry of my academic friends, the Leverhulme Research Fund awarded me a modest annual research stipend for two years, so enabling me to discontinue activities which, useful enough and certainly interesting, were distracting me from what I had come to regard as my main undertaking. It is fitting, then, that I should repeat here the acknowledgement, made long ago, of my indebtedness to the Committee and their Secretary, the late Dr. L. Haden Guest, M.P.

With the aid of the Leverhulme Fund I was able to complete and to see into print several of the county sections mentioned above (and referred to below as parts of the *Domesday of Parliamentary Enclosures* . . .). Consequently when my Oxford friends suggested that I might go up and take, rather late in life, the formal research training in historical sources of which clearly I stood in need, I was able to produce a fair amount of published work in support of their efforts on my behalf. I have to thank the Houblon-Norman Research Trustees for their generosity in giving me a research fellowship, so enabling me to do this without neglecting what were by now fairly heavy family responsibilities. For help and encouragement of one kind or another, received then and later, I have reason to feel very much indebted to the late Humphrey Sumner, the Warden of All Souls; the three successive Masters of Balliol, the late Lord Lindsay, Sir David Keir, and Mr. Christopher Hill; the then Warden of Nuffield, the late Sir Henry Clay, and Professor L. Elvin, then Principal of Ruskin. I am—indeed I must needs be—eternally beholden to my College, Balliol.

For three years, while I was employed elsewhere, the Oxford G. W. Medley Committee awarded me a Senior Scholarship, and I am grateful indeed to the Committee members for this. In the last few years when my work has lain in Leeds, first as Lecturer then as Reader, the University authorities have been very understanding and sympathetic employers, especially considering that the work for which they engaged me in the first place, though specifically historical and archival, related to one of my subsidiary historical interests rather than to my main one. I owe them my thanks for their generosity, and for many kindnesses which they have shown me. I am particularly grateful to them for giving me a lengthy period of sabbatical leave in 1963–4, and for meeting the expenses involved in my re-visiting, for longer or shorter periods, every county record office in the country.

I have to thank also the fifty-odd county archivists in charge of these. Both during my visits, and often in lengthy and voluminous correspondence before and after these, they have shown me every courtesy, though my demands must often have encroached heavily on their limited time, and strained their exemplary patience. Both before and after I began work on the present book I have been in close touch with Mr. E. P. Thompson, formerly of Leeds University and now of the University of Warwick, and with Mr. Rex C. Russell, then W.E.A. Tutor in Lindsey, now of the University of Hull. Both have done much work on my subject and on topics related to it. Both have read the book in typescript, and in its present form it owes much to their friendly and helpful criticism. It is but just to add that responsibility for any remaining errors of fact, and for all expressions of opinion, is mine alone. I shall be happy indeed to hear from any reader able to correct the one, or inclined to contradict the other.

Finally, I have to thank for help of various kinds Dr. B. Swann of the Commons Society, and my present or former colleagues at Leeds, Professor M. Beresford, Mrs. W. Digby, Mr. G. Hunter, Mr. W. H. Long and Mr. W. B. Thompson. I owe very sincere thanks also to a succession of patient and hard-working secretaries, usually appointed in the first place for less interesting but much less demanding work. In addition to discharging their primary duties—and seeing to it that I did not neglect mine—they have also acted in some measure as research assistants. My work, both in the major undertaking and in this condensed summary of and guide to it, owes much to their loyalty, their energy and their devotion. In this connexion I must name especially Mrs. D. Proctor, Mrs. M. Oddy, the late Mrs. H. Pickup, Mrs. K. McManus, Miss L. Smith, and Mrs. M. Atkins.

Part of Chapters 1 and 2 is based upon my work in *The Parish Chest*,[1] and part of Chapter 4 on the Introduction to my *Nottinghamshire Parliamentary Enclosures*.[2] I am obliged to the Cambridge University Press and to the Thoroton Society Record Series and its editor, the late Mr. T. M. Blagg, for permission to use this matter. A good deal of Chapters 8, 9 and 10 incorporates some part of articles of mine in *The English Historical Review*, *The Economic History Review*, *Economic History* and the (American) *Journal of Modern History* and *Agricultural History*.[3] I am indebted to the editors and publishers of these: Dr. Previté Orton and Messrs. Longmans, Professor Postan and Messrs. A. and C. Black, the late Lord Keynes and the Royal Economic Society, Professor S. W. Holperin, and the University of Chicago Press, Mr. E. E. Edwards and the Agricultural History Society for sanction to use this part of the text. Part of Chapter 4 originally appeared in *The Church Militant*,[4] and I owe my thanks to the editor, the Rev. H. O. Mason, for permission to reprint this. The final paragraph of Chapter 16 is taken almost *verbatim* from

[1] Cambridge 1944 and edns.   [2] Nottingham 1935.
[3] Respectively *E.H.R.* LVII, 1942, 250–63; LIX 1944, pp. 392–403; *Econ. H.R.* XII 1 & 2, 1944, pp. 68–75; *Econ. Hist.* LIV Apr. 1944, pp. 75–79, *J.M.H.* XXIII 2, 1951, pp. 137–145; *Ag. Hist.* 23.3, 1949 pp. 213–20.
[4] 'The English Church and the Agrarian Problem' in *C.M.*, Dec. 1936–Sept. 1937.

The Open Fields,[5] by the late Dr. C. S. Orwin and Mrs. Orwin. I
am obliged to the authors and to their publishers, the Oxford
University Press, for allowing me to use these paragraphs. I
have to thank the late Mr. T. M. Blagg also for permission to
use a paragraph on p. 81. This is from his editorial introduction
to my book above cited.

W. E. Tate

[5] Oxford 1938.

INTRODUCTION

This book attempts to fill a triple role. Its first purpose is that of giving to the general reader a reasonably objective account of an important phenomenon in English social and economic history. I hope it may appeal specially to the Englishman who loves England—especially her countryside—and who would gladly know a little more of the past which lies behind and explains much of her present. It may perhaps on occasion be of value also even to the professed student of history whose interests lie primarily in other historical fields. Secondly, I very much hope that it may be useful to the history teacher who thinks, as I do, that history should take some notice of the school environment, and that local history especially should be largely an out-of-doors subject, rather than one wherein the children sit patiently in rows, while their teacher chalks and talks. It is also intended for the benefit of the local historian generally.

In the story of the English village, and for that matter in the earlier story of many of the English towns, an understanding of the agrarian basis, on which until of late society rested, is necessary to any serious study of the development of that society. In much of the countryside particularly, the great historical change from the mediaeval organization of society to the modern one is closely connected with the technical agrarian change from the semi-communal organization of open-field agriculture to the modern system of land ownership, tenancy and cultivation 'in severalty', that is, the great change that was brought about by Enclosure.[1] Thirdly then it may, I hope, be of value to the political or social philosopher, the sociologist and their fellow scholars.

In the 'normal' English village—if indeed there is any such place (perhaps it would be better to say 'in a great many villages of the English Midlands')—this change took place under parliamentary authority in the later part of the eighteenth

[1] The student new to the group of subjects dealt with is asked to note that, throughout the book, I have rarely interrupted my text in order to gloss or define a technical or archaic term when using it for the first time. I have been at some pains with the Glossary, pp. 185–92, and I hope that the reader will use it whenever he has occasion to do so.

century, or in the first years of the nineteenth. There were of course enclosure movements in earlier years—in the first chapters there is a little about them—but the eighteenth-century change is generally taken as the enclosure movement *par excellence*. The greater part of the book is devoted to it, the movement taking place in, roughly, the reign of George III, say very approximately from the years about 1760 to those about 1820. In general, apart from the account in a few introductory pages, we leave on one side the origin and development of open-field agriculture in the place with the English settlement. Similarly we shall not concern ourselves a great deal with mediaeval attempts to adjust agriculture to meet the needs of an increasing population, with, one hopes, rising living standards. All this is well worth looking into, but it is not our special business here.

We must say a little of enclosure in mediaeval, Tudor and Stuart times, but our more detailed inquiries will begin no further back than a couple of centuries ago, when the needs aroused by the Industrial Revolution in the more urban areas at once demanded a corresponding Agrarian Revolution in the countryside, and tended to encourage its development. In each of these great changes, economic progress was achieved at the cost of social dislocation. But eighteenth-century landlords and farmers were not vastly more concerned by this than were eighteenth-century merchants or millowners or ironmasters. (And of course eighteenth-century politicians had other things to think of!)

Much of the story, not altogether a happy one, is fairly plain to make out. But even so the story will lack beginning, middle and end. Obviously for a 'typical' eighteenth-century Midland enclosure, the story should begin with the gradually growing discontent of the leading proprietors in the place with the rigid and inelastic open-field system, which prevented them from modernizing their methods of husbandry as they wished. Doubtless this was followed by informal discussions held among themselves. Then came tentative inquiries as to the cost of an attempt at enclosure (these made of the local attorneys, who were beginning to find a profitable line in specializing in this class of business). Probably often this was followed by a visit to the neighbouring township which had recently been enclosed, or by long discussions with its proprietors in the farmers' 'ordinary' at the local inn, in the interval of business on market day. Then followed the ceaseless propaganda in favour of the scheme among the smaller and more conservatively-minded landowners. There was much insistence upon the benefits that could be expected to accrue from the introduction of new crops and new methods, and the abolition of outworn customs which it would make possible. Farmers would benefit by the enormous increase of productivity which was confidently predicted. The lord of the manor would receive a sufficient compensation for his not-very-valuable interest in the soil of the common. The incumbent could have his tithe commuted at a handsome valuation. The highways might well be improved while the enthusiasm for progress lasted. The deserving poor would find small plots in severalty, or small pasture closes, more useful than scattered scraps in the open fields, and vague grazing rights. Certainly they would be no worse off without the largely illusory advantages of the common, and the very real temptations to idleness which its presence entailed. The undeserving poor, especially the insubordinate squatters, living in riotous squalor in their tumbledown hovels on the common, would prosper morally and economically if they were compelled to do regular work for an employer. Everyone in the parish would gain by the increase of employment in hedging, ditching, fencing, draining, and by the fall in the rates which was confidently expected as soon as the common had ceased to form a constant attraction to all the beggars, wastrels and drunkards in the district.

Then the story should deal with the methods used to induce the smaller freeholders at length to give a reluctant consent. Then it might cover the gradual buying-out of those who proved recalcitrant to the last, until finally the promoters had the necessary *quantum* of consent in support of their proposal. Of all this, however, the greater part of the records—if there ever were any—have perished, and the tale can but be pieced together from casual and fragmentary references. It is clear, however, that this, or something very like it, must have happened before ever the enclosure petition was drafted by the local attorney to be presented to the House by one of the county members.

The missing middle of the story would tell how, when, and where the commissioners met, how they regulated their proceedings, dealt with the infinity of claims, just, unjust, and dubious, submitted to them and tried to harmonize conflicting interests. It would be most useful to know exactly how they reduced what they regarded as the unbusinesslike chaos of the open-field area to something more in accordance with their conception of what a reasonably well-ordered parish should be. All this, however, can hardly be discovered without the aid of the commissioners' working papers. It is very doubtful whether many of the commissions kept any records at all (there was no statutory rule that they should do so); and when commissions were businesslike enough to keep proper working papers, only a proportion even of the minute-books are known to survive.[2]

The end of the story is not yet. Nor will it arrive until the much discussed 'Land Question' shall finally be settled, if indeed any such settlement is possible, in a fashion which shall be just as well to the landowner, the tenant farmer and the farm worker, as to the community at large, whose vital interests are so largely concerned in it. Did enclosure tend to land monopoly, as is often alleged? What was its effect, in the long run, upon the productivity of English land? Did it actually result in the 'high farming' advocated by the pioneers, or was its outcome at the last, at any rate in some parts of the country, the reversion to something almost approaching prairie methods, bringing rural depopulation and unemployment in their train? Were the smaller occupiers actually maintained in the possession of their holdings, or fairly compensated if they lost them? If they were dispossessed, can enclosure be fairly blamed for their disappearance? If it can, was the dispossession a sequel to the enclosure, or was it not often rather a necessary preliminary thereto? What prospects had they of attaining the somewhat precarious dignity of each a farm tenancy of his own? Did they rather swell the ranks of the new urban proletariat, whose development brought with it problems, social, political, economic and moral, some of which are still with us?

These questions and many like them are not unworthy of attention. It is only by study of the enclosure movements that they can receive it. This present work is intended not only as a historical essay, but also as an introduction to such study.

W. E. TATE

[2] There were some 4,200 separate commissions. Since I became specially interested in their records in 1940, I have seen or obtained references to some 230 surviving minute-books. Doubtless a few more will turn up in the course of time, but it seems unlikely that these exist (? or ever have existed) for more than a small proportion of the remaining 4,000-odd occasions.

CHAPTER I

THE PARISH AND THE
VILLAGE COMMUNITY

THE ENGLISH VILLAGE is sometimes considered to be an institution of immemorial antiquity. There are certain features apparent upon a superficial study of it which lend colour to this view. The main thesis of this book is, however, that in its essentials—in its social structure, in its economic basis, and even to a great extent in its mere physical form—the village as we know it is an affair of relatively recent development. It will be apparent that I think this development has not been always and everywhere a healthy one. There is more than merely a cheap paradox in the assertion that the village as it exists nowadays, and as it has been perhaps for the last couple of centuries, is a growth indeed, but actually in certain respects perhaps a morbid growth.

Let us consider for a time the village as it now stands, comparing it in several respects with the same village as it existed say three or four or five centuries ago. A fifteenth-century villager who came back to life in his old haunts would find probably only the parish church still remaining of the physical structure of the village as he knew it. This church is no longer the religious home of the entire community. A great part—and often alas the more active and enlightened part—of the villagers find spiritual solace more to their mind in the red-brick or galvanized-iron Bethel which is to be found in the high street. Even today, when the priest is often materially worse off than many of his people, his dwelling also is not as theirs—nor are his cultural and social standards. The snug Georgian rectory or vicarage, which replaced the old priest's house, is the mark of a class society, in which the gulf between shepherd and flock had become far wider and deeper than it was in mediaeval times, a gulf which to a considerable extent still remains today.

The manor house is the orbit of a still more exalted luminary —and too often of one even more divorced from the day-to-day life of the place. And unlike their mediaeval predecessors, both these dignitaries—the spiritual guide to and the secular lord of the local community—are now, and every day are becoming more completely, severed from the land and all that has to do

with it. The rector lives mainly on tithe rent-charge, instead of
tithe, and in many instances no longer farms his glebe. In
many villages there is no longer any glebe to farm. The rector
is then a *rentier*, or if there is a vicar he is largely the beneficiary
of the various societies which supplement his somewhat exiguous
stipend. With this augmentation he may dwell modestly in a
corner of the huge parsonage with which his eighteenth- and
nineteenth-century predecessors have endowed him (and for
which he and his wife curse them daily). Above all, he is the
dependant of the Church Commissioners, the great administrative organization formed by the amalgamation of the Ecclesiastical Commissioners and the Governors of Queen Anne's
Bounty. Eventually it is even possible that he may lose his
cherished freehold and become their mere employee.

Similarly the squire, though often of course he still retains
the home farm, is but rarely a practical farmer. He tends rather
to be a new capitalist entrepreneur from the town, whose
farming, if it exists at all, is a somewhat expensive hobby, the
(real or alleged) losses on which he may persuade H.M.
Commissioners of Inland Revenue to set against his receipts
in interest and dividends, at any rate now (1967) for five
years in succession. His 'farming' may well be not much
more than the conventional accomplishment of one who
occupies the social rank which he holds—or hopes his grand-
children may hold. Certainly, and fortunately for all concerned,
it is rarely the main source of the foodstuffs on the manor house
table.

Next in the social scale come the larger farmers, no longer
resident in the picturesque but somewhat inconvenient houses
of the 'town street', but each occupying a substantial Georgian
or later farmhouse in the middle of its own farm lands, perhaps
a mile or more from the centre of the parish. A few of these
farmhouses are the descendants of mediaeval sub-manors, but
most of them are a legacy from one of the enclosure movements.
In open-field conditions a farmhouse could not be sited in the
midst of its own lands, for these were scattered in minute parcels
throughout the entire parish. The town street was the best and
most central place for a farmhouse. (The old houses, when they
still remain, have fallen in the social scale. Now they are
partitioned to form the dwellings not of farmers but of farm
workers, though evidently they were originally designed for the
occupation of persons of rather higher social and economic

status.) Even in days of farming prosperity, these farmers rarely own their own lands, save under the handicap of heavy mortgages. Their real landlord may be the squire, or it may be the bank or some other financial corporation. What is more to the point is that the farmers produce not for use but for profit. A cash economy has replaced the old subsistence agriculture, a production for sale, one for eating, or using or wearing. And naturally the crops produced are those which the farmer hopes will bring the best cash return. Only two or three centuries ago in many districts there were far fewer large farmers but many more small ones, and large and small alike produced largely for consumption, perhaps only secondarily for sale or exchange.

Next in the social scale comes perhaps the village school-master, neither employed nor paid directly by the villagers. He is of a class now, alas, rapidly becoming extinct because of the 're-organization', i.e. decapitation, of the village schools, and the transfer of all their senior scholars to the new county secondary or comprehensive schools in the very large villages and in the market towns. Years ago the schoolmaster—if there was one—also was much more closely connected with the land than he is now. Sometimes he was paid partly by an endowment of land, which he would work in his spare time. Very often indeed he carried on such activities as land surveying, will making, keeping accounts, running the local 'sick and divide' club, acting as parish clerk, etc., in order to supplement the somewhat meagre salary attached to his primary office. In earlier times still the schoolmaster—where indeed the village rejoiced in the possession of such a luxury—had often been the chantry priest. His school was quite usually, until relatively recent years, a porch room or a spare aisle or transept in the parish church.[1]

The other more usual public servants were essentially the villagers themselves, elected directly or indirectly by their own fellows, or 'serving the office' when the turn of their farm or cottage came round on the rota. The churchwarden discharged a host of duties now entrusted to other functionaries, from that of censor of morals to that of rat destruction officer. The overseer of the poor did the work now carried out by the social welfare officers of the County, or of the Ministry of Social Security. The constable was a parish constable, not a (county)

[1] One example, of hundreds which could be adduced, is at Normanton-on-Soar, Notts.

policeman. The surveyor of highways was a temporary, usually unpaid, servant of the parish, not a permanent salaried officer of the county. And in serving most of these offices every inhabitant householder took his turn, it may be often very reluctantly, and frequently no doubt with a complete absence of the paper efficiency dear to the heart of a modern bureaucrat.

In a modern village, above or below the schoolmaster according to the tradition of the place (in the north of England the schoolmaster's status is high, in the south generally not so high), come the local shopkeepers—in a fair-sized village the grocer, often the butcher and the baker, the alehouse- or innkeeper and so on. A couple of centuries ago there was little scope for these—save of course the last. Such manufactured goods as were needed were bought on market day or at fair time in the neighbouring borough. Meat was largely home-fed and home-killed, and bread was usually (as it still is quite generally in some parts of the north of England) home-baked, often then from flour locally milled from home-grown wheat or maslin. Much beer was home-brewed. (Despite metal salvage drives in two World Wars, a fair number of quite small farmhouses still retain their ancient brewing 'coppers'—copper 'coppers', not cast-iron ones.)

Now, of course, the village shopkeepers are largely the mere distributing agents for Dutch cheese, New Zealand butter, Danish or Irish bacon, American 'cereals' and the like, West Indian sugar entering the country by Liverpool, Virginian tobacco reaching them via Bristol, Indian tea coming through the Port of London, and so on, with such home-produced luxuries as cakes from Kensington, chocolate from Birmingham and soap from Birkenhead. The shopkeeper, of course, makes none of these, but despite the competition, of late, of the 'supermarket' in the neighbouring town, he gains a comfortable livelihood by purchasing them at one price and retailing them at a considerably higher one. Even the innkeeper—formerly often a village artisan or smallholder, who brewed his beer and managed his smallholding in his slack hours—is now in his ('tied'), 'tenanted' or 'managed' house the dependant, often indeed the mere employee, of a brewery company perhaps a hundred miles away.

A few independent and semi-independent artisans still survive. The cobbler is very generally found, the handloom weaver and the stockinger, the thatcher and the basket-maker, often still remain in special districts. Usually the blacksmith —where there is one—is an independent worker also. In late years he has often blossomed forth into a garage proprietor. The village carpenter-cum-builder-cum-undertaker is still to be seen here and there. But, as well as making his product with the traditional tools of his craft and by its traditional techniques, often he is largely an agent for factory-made doors and window frames, chestnut pale fences and chicken-houses, clothes horses and clothes-line props (and even, on occasion, ready-made coffins).

Socially and economically, beneath all the dignitaries and personages mentioned, at the very foundation of rural society is the farm worker. He is—even now—sometimes badly housed, often in a 'tied' cottage. Until quite lately he was ill-educated and abominably paid.[1] His trade union was pathetically feeble, compared with the efficient and sometimes rather truculent organizations which defend the miner, the textile worker, or the engineer. Often he is still too timorous, too niggardly, or too ignorant to join it, and to take an active part in its management. He owns neither house nor land, and he has but the remotest prospect of ever owning either. His children after him will be farm workers like him, save in the rare instances when he is lucky and clear-sighted enough to get them away to the town. There they will benefit by the better educational opportunities available, and by the better social services generally. Then, especially since the introduction of wage-related social welfare benefits, having acquired wives and families of their own, and having done a period of service in an appropriate industry, they may well be eligible during sickness, or unemployment for rates of benefit considerably exceeding the normal wage of a skilled farm worker. Only three or four centuries ago, when the village was in its hey-day, throughout some shires, at any rate according to very reputable historians, it was the exception rather than the rule for the employed farm worker to be entirely landless.

The village has changed physically less than socially, and the countryside still carries on its face plain marks of the open-field system by which the old peasant economy was supported.

---

[1] While this book is in the press, after a good deal of controversy the minimum wage has been raised to £10 16s. In my active N.U.A.W. days, not so very long ago, the local rate, not the lowest in England, was £1 11s. 6d., and the employers sometimes engaged in the most ingenious 'fiddles' in order to avoid payment of it.

The broad highway, it is true, a couple of centuries ago was an ill-defined and unmetalled dirt track (unless of course it was important enough to have been subject to the activities of a turnpike commission. Legally a road is still rather a right of passage than a strip of land. Unless it is a major highway, and as such has been lately rationalized by the county authority or the Ministry of Transport, it still wanders circuitously across the countryside, zig-zagging as though constantly changing its mind as to where it is making for. This is not for the reason alleged by G. K. Chesterton, that it was set out by 'the rolling English drunkard'. It is in truth because our twentieth-century road is still making its way, as by long usage, from balk to headland and from headland to balk amid the old open-field furlongs and selions, although these vanished perhaps a couple of centuries ago. It is narrow and tortuous in the village centre, because there its borders have been built up for centuries. It may widen to a sixty- or forty-foot road on the outskirts of the village, because there its course has been laid out by the enclosure commissioners of the eighteenth century.

In the old grass fields of the place which centuries ago have been arable, the ⌒⌒⌒⌒⌒ sectioned ridges often mark out the former arable selions. That they are older than the present hedgerows may be seen by the fashion in which these cut them, often transversely. That they were laid out by an ox plough may be judged from their curvature; in plan they are very much the shape of an elongated and almost straightened out inverted letter S ⌁.

There are still in many villages so-called 'commons', 'carrs', 'heaths', 'moors' and 'marshes' now entirely privately owned. Here and there may still be seen the meerstones of the old common meadows. The Ordnance map of today has place-names innumerable, reminiscent of the old primitive communal system of land tenure, which preceded the modern system of individual ownership and cultivation. The pound, or pinfold, is a mark of the old system, when hedges and fences were rare. There is little need for a pound when the farmer hedges, or fences or walls his closes, to keep his own stock in and other people's out.

This is the crux of the matter. The hedge, the fence and the wall are the makers of modern rural England. And the process by which open land became fenced, hedged or walled—to keep one's own stock inside a private pasture close, or the stock of

I An eighteenth-century surveyor at work on enclosure, at Henlow, Beds., enclosed 1795–8; *see p. 203*

II Grazing fields at Crimscote, Warws..

others outside a private arable close, is enclosure. Enclosure is cast as the villain of the piece. Enclosure has had much to do with making the English village a class society of clearly de-marked possessors and dispossessed. It is partly due to enclosure that throughout much the greater part of England we have no longer a landed peasantry. It may well be due to enclosure that the village nowadays is the abode of an assembly of disconnected individuals and classes, rather than that of a well-knit and finely graded community, with class distinctions, it is true, but these much more blurred than they became in later times, and often still remain. In the open-field village each class tended to shade off into its neighbours above and below, rather than to be divided from them by clearly-ruled boundary lines which only a rather exceptional individual might pass, and this with some difficulty.

In the open-field village as it existed towards the end of the Middle Ages, in some instances well into the eighteenth century (and in a few even into the nineteenth), neither county justices nor central government normally had much concern with the everyday conduct of village affairs. The parish priest and the nominated-and-elected churchwardens supervised the moral welfare of the community. The care of the poor was in the hands of the elected overseers, that of the highways was entrusted to the elected waywardens, law and order were enforced by the elected constable. Other elected officers, or sometimes the entire parish, assembling in a kind of miniature parliament, the vestry meet-ing, regulated the use of the commons and open fields, which were economically the foundation of rural life. This vestry meet-ing in most villages had succeeded in the sixteenth or seven-teenth or eighteenth centuries to most or all of the governing duties of an earlier administrative body, the (manorial) court baron. It was in effect the parochial parliament-cum-cabinet of the self-governing village community.

Chapter 2

OPEN FIELDS AND COMMONS

THE OPEN-FIELD VILLAGE was then essentially a self-contained social and economic organization originally based upon production for subsistence, not for market. It was not, of course, peculiar to England—or to Europe. Probably whenever and wherever man first reached the stage of settled cultivation, some form of open-field agriculture was adopted, at any rate for a time. We are concerned here especially with the village in its English form—itself a product of many centuries of evolution. It may be profitable then to consider for a short time a 'typical' Midland open-field village, though the word typical is something of a misnomer, for the village community in very fact did not, of course, conform to the neat definitions and generalizations of the textbooks. To produce the three main necessities of life, bread and other vegetable foods, beer, and flesh meat, the husbandman must grow the cereals, wheat or rye for bread, barley for bread and beer and for his stock, oats also for his stock, and the pulses. He must have pasture for the use of his stock in summer, and meadow for the production of a supply of hay to last him through the winter. Considering the last *desideratum* first:

The Meadow

The quantity of natural meadow land was strictly limited, and there was little possibility of creating extra meadow in the days before the use of artificial phosphates. The fact is reflected in the high valuation which is placed upon meadow in mediaeval surveys—meadow alone is measured by the acre in *Domesday* —and so on. The management of this meadow was carried out after a very primitive fashion. Possibly enough the occupancy of the arable lands had originally changed from year to year (though there is little record of this in historic times in England). Much of the meadow, on the other hand, until quite recent times, was subjected to a periodical—generally annual—re-allotment. Apparently it was too valuable ever to become purely private property. The internal divisions in it were ideal

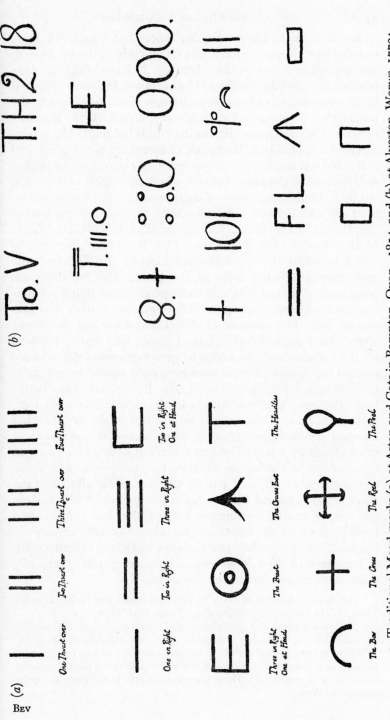

1. Traditional Mead-marks (a) at Aston and Cote in Bampton, Oxon., 1854, and (b) at Alveston, Warws. 1772;

see p. 196

rather than real. They were not fences but imaginary lines, running from posts or meerstones on one side of the meadow to corresponding marks on the other side. At haysel the lines were trodden out, and the traditional lots so demarked were allocated by lot or rotation, or some combination of the two, among the proprietors claiming rights. Originally, no doubt, the meadow rights had been in proportion to the arable holdings. The system survived until lately at Bampton, Oxfordshire, and a good deal of it is left—it remained more or less in its entirety up to 1938—at Yarnton[1] in the same county, where allocation was carried out by balloting with thirteen cherrywood balls, bearing names most of which have been identified as those of mediaeval proprietors in the place, William of Bladon, Gilbert, Walter Molly, Walter Geoffrey, etc. The Bampton distribution, which lasted until 1854, was carried out by the 'Sixteens', the customary governing body of the place. The meadow was permanently shared into sixteen large divisions styled layings-out, each of these being subdivided into four further divisions named sets. The customs of Aston and Cote (in Bampton) were 'based upon the principle of justice and equity between all the commoners'. In order to give everyone a fair chance of securing a plot of good meadow, each tenant or group of tenants had a traditional mark, the frying pan, the 'hern's foot', the bow, the 'two strokes to the right and one at top', and so on. Four of the tenants were called forth, each bearing his mark cut on a piece of wood. These were cast into a hat and drawn forth by a boy. The first taken out entitled its owner to have set one in the laying out then being disposed of, and the proprietor went off, and cut on the turf of his allotment the mark which signified his possession for the year.[2] The custom was not, of course, confined to Oxfordshire, but variants and modifications of it appeared in almost every county in England.[3] And elsewhere, as at Aston and Cote, the aftermath of the meadow after haysel was a common pasture, generally open to all proprietors in the township.

[1] The classical account of Pixey Mead, West Mead and Oxhey Mead in Yarnton is by Gretton, R. W., in *Econ. Journ.*, Mar. 1912.

[2] This is a rather free paraphrase and condensation of the account given by Giles, J. A., *History of Bampton*, pp. 75–82 (p.p.) Bampton, 1848.

[3] Often the meerstones are still to be seen, especially in a former common meadow now (technically) enclosed, but in fact still in the joint occupation of two or three proprietors. There is a good example in the Ham at Upton-on-Severn, Worcs.

The Open Arable Fields

The open arable land was arranged after a fashion less primitive, but still archaic and on the face of things vastly inconvenient. It may well represent a transitional stage when the scattering of estates in small parcels still persisted, but any annual re-allotment had been abandoned. For the arable lands of the place were divided into two or three (very much later, and rather exceptionally, sometimes four) large 'fields', properly so styled. The rotation they followed was often merely wheat or rye, barley, fallow—the three-course rotation and the three-field system; or wheat-or-rye-and-barley, fallow,—the two-course rotation and the two-field system. The field was subdivided into more or less rectangular areas styled furlongs or shots, each made up of a number of long narrow selions. And as the proprietor of meadow usually had sets in more than one laying-out, so the same man in his capacity as the holder of arable might have land in every furlong in the parish.

He *must* have land in each field, and for this reason. The method of allowing the land to regain its fertility was the ancient practice of fallowing; sometimes a fallow was given every other year, sometimes a 'rest' of one year in three would suffice. Since there were no permanent hedges or fences inside the fields, every man's land lying cheek by jowl with every other's, the entire field[4] or furlong must be under the same crop at the same time. Sowing must be carried out more or less simultaneously, for the stock remained on the land until sowing time. So must reaping, since it was readmitted to pasture after harvest. (The only exception was that a few unfortunates held

[4] On furlong see below p. 37 and Glossary. It may perhaps be helpful to note here, after this necessarily brief summary of the main features of open-field husbandry, an interesting fact, first pointed out by the late Sir William Ashley, *The Bread of our Forefathers* (Oxford, 1928), notes appended to Chap. II, p. 57: 'The masque which occupies most of the first scene of Act IV of *The Tempest* [?1611/1623] begins with an invocation of 'Ceres, most bounteous lady . . .', with her:

'. . . rich leas
Of wheat, rye, barley, vetches, oats and peas;'

It is to be noted that this is not a chance collection of words; the colloquation is entirely correct from the point of view of contemporary agricultural practice, wheat and rye being the two winter and bread corns, the others being the spring 'corns', and barley being put first, of course, as the national drink corn.'

headlands or selions which served as means of access to other men's land, so therefore any crops thereon must be sown a day or two after those of others, and reaped a little before.) Any proprietor having land in only one field of two, or two of three, would have found himself without bread or beer for a whole year once every two or three years. Moreover, for obvious reasons, he must have approximately equal areas in each of the three fields—at any rate in the days when open-field cultivation was the basis of rural life, and when there were few if any arable closes.

Like the meadow after haysel, the arable fields after corn harvest and the fallow field throughout the greater part of its fallow year served as common pasture for the beasts of the township. Grazing rights were often held more or less in proportion to arable holdings, measured according to acreage, or yardlands, or oxgangs. The arable fields then were made up mainly of roughly rectangular patches of diverse proportions and areas, each again composed of long, narrow strips, doubtless every one of them originally an 'acre', a day's work, in area, and perhaps on an average something like ten times as long as they were broad. If an individual strip was about forty poles, a furlong (furrow-long) in length, and four poles in breadth (220 yards by 22) it would contain somewhere in the region of what we know as a statute acre of land. It is to be noted that, although this is the ultimate origin of the statute acre, with its curious area of 4,840[5] square yards, in historic

[5] The superficial area of the 'acre' as a unit of measurement depended on the length of the pole; from the arithmetical point of view it varied as the square of the length of the pole [Edmund Gunter and his 22-yard chain date only from the early seventeenth century]. An areal acre was—indeed still is—the equivalent of a rectangle four poles by forty poles. But the length of the customary pole varied not merely from county to county, but sometimes from village to village—the customary pole of Sutton, Notts., differed in length from that of the interspersed vill of Bonington! Walter of Henley (*fl. c.* 1250) sets forth that ploughing an acre, 'as measured by the King's perch of 16½ feet' i.e. what we know as a statute acre, is on the average a fair day's work, but admits that this ideal is not always attained 'because', as he rather plaintively remarks, 'of the malice of ploughmen'. In our period the 'acre' strips or selions might contain anywhere from about a rood to as much as an acre and a half. I have thought it well to go into this in some detail, for historians, both amateur and professional, have often confused both themselves and their readers here. (Understandably enough, since the present-day ridges are often an indication of former open-field selions, and the selions are sometimes styled 'rigs', just as sometimes they are termed 'acres', the terms ridge, selion and acre are sometimes to be understood as

times the 'acre' of the selions seems rarely to have contained much more than the equivalent of about half a statute acre.

The breadths of the 'furlongs' were conditioned mainly perhaps by the slope of the land. (What surface drainage was possible was based on the-selions-in-their-'furlongs'.) Their lengths depended largely on its nature. In a fairly light soil, a furrow of something like 220 yards meant fairly heavy work for a yoke of oxen, before turning on the headland to plough another furrow in the opposite direction would, incidentally, give them a brief respite from their labours. However the furlongs varied in other respects, they were always composed of (widely varying) numbers of selions, these last being, ideally, 'acre', in fact more usually (more or less) half-acre, strips. The roughly rectangular nature of furlongs and selions, each furlong following the slope of the land, meant that in the corners between them, there must be many odd scraps (often known as fothers, pightles, gores, etc.) and triangular or approximately so in shape. Many of these were used as rough pasture for the community at large. Others were allocated from time to time to meet regularly recurring charges levied upon the community, or for the salaries of communal officers. Pinder's Pieces, Swineherd's Balks, Constable's Gores, Bellrope Pieces and even Apparitor's[6] Headlands appear quite commonly in terriers of open-field land.

It is reasonable to suppose that the first furlongs had been set out by the earliest settlers when the land was originally taken into cultivation. Often this was done with careful consideration of the lie of the land, so that some simple scheme of land drainage could be followed. Later on, with the pressure

synonyms. Often, however, they are not. In any event the word 'acre' is, at the least, ambiguous).

The simplest way to inquire into this matter in any specific instance is:

ridges and *acres*: pace out the ridge breadth in yards, from crest to crest, or better, from furrow to furrow, and its length from headland to headland. Reckon its area as that of a rectangle having the same dimensions (always bearing in mind the statute acre equivalent of any local acre).

ridges and *selions*: transfer the data from any available terrier (or better, field map) to a modern Ordnance Survey 25-inch plan covering the same land. On this last, because $25 \times 25 = 625$, and there are in a square mile 640 statute acres, for all practical purposes every square inch may be taken as representing a *statute* acre. The point is that '625' is virtually equal to 640. In fact the '25-inch' plan is really to the scale of $\frac{1}{2500}$—25·34". So the approximation is even closer than might at first sight appear, for $(25·34)^2$ is 642.

[6] See Glossary.

of population on the means of subsistence as the settlement developed, the fields must for centuries have been subject to a process of gradual enlargement, by the taking into cultivation —whether by individual villagers or the community as a group —of further patches of wood or waste or moor or marsh suitable for arable cultivation. The process might end only when it could develop no further without unduly encroaching on the pasture required to meet the needs of the community. Or it could cease when the process of expansion brought the group into contact with the reclaiming pioneers of another neighbour group, expanding in like fashion towards whatever boundary had been agreed on, or could be arrived at. A study of *Domesday* seems to suggest that in much of England this must have happened at various dates unknown, but many of them well before the Norman Conquest. The limits of these early townships are many of them the boundaries of English rural parishes today. The arable fields themselves have of course survived very rarely until the present. There are, however, good examples still to be seen at Laxton and at Eakring in Nottinghamshire and less typical specimens in the Isle of Axholme, in Lincolnshire. Until a century ago they remained extensively, albeit often in a somewhat vestigial form, in half the counties of England.

The Common and the Waste

Outside the open meadow and the common arable land lay the unredeemed waste, not yet taken into cultivation, and stretching often to the limit of a corresponding waste belonging to the next township or parish. Some portions of this or of other land near the village might be set aside as Cow Pasture or Horse Common, but the greater part of it was often simply a vast area of rough grazing—very rough grazing. Common rights on it might be exercised according to a carefully-worked-out scale, specific pasture rights attaching to each plough-land or oxgang, or to the site of each ancient messuage (stinted common), or the common might be open to all who cared to turn on their beasts (unstinted common). Or some common might be set on one side for plough cattle, other left open for such undesirable creatures as geese, swine, or donkeys, legally speaking having no common rights at all. Other parts of the waste might be reserved as sand- or gravel-pits, as turbary for the cutting of turf or other fuel, or wooded portions might be subject to common of estovers (the taking of timber for use as fuel, or for the repair of farmhouses or of implements of husbandry).

Wastes and commons still remain, of a very considerable gross acreage, in many English counties.[7] Often they are to be found in old corporate towns, where a few still provide valuable perquisites to the freeman. Sometimes in boroughs or county boroughs, for example at Doncaster, Newcastle-on-Tyne, and Pontefract (Yorks. W. R.), they have been converted in whole or in part into municipal parks or racecourses. Sometimes, for example at Nottingham and at Newcastle-under-Lyme, Staffs., a part has been let on building lease or otherwise disposed of, and the freemen of the borough may still draw a modest annual dividend in recognition of their rights. Sometimes these rights descend from the most remote antiquity, even greater than that ascribed to them by their possessors, as for example at Malmesbury, Wilts., where the freemen claim under a charter from King Athelstan! A rural parish had, of course, no freemen, no incorporated governing body, and (as such) no representatives in Parliament, so it was less able to make its voice heard or its influence felt when proposals were put forward for the enclosure of its common.[8] It is not surprising then that, as G. K. Chesterton says:

> 'The village green that had got mislaid
> Turned up in the 'squire's back-yard.'

The Origin of Open-field Agriculture

Numerous theories have been put forward in the effort to explain the origin of the system outlined above. Sometimes it is alleged that the main idea behind it was that of a rough and ready equity—a desire to give each proprietor some good land and some bad, some over-wet and some over-dry: then, whatever the seasons might be in any particular year, each cultivator would at any rate be assured of a return at subsistence level. Modern work on the matter appears to suggest it as much likelier that the land was thus allocated when it was first taken into

[7] The most recent account of these is in the *Report* of the Royal Commission on Common Lands, 1955–58 (Cmnd. 462, 1958), with, based on this, the Appendix, pp. 245–350 to Hoskins, W. G. and Stamp, L. D., *Common Lands of England and Wales*, 1963. See also, below, p. 182.

[8] The reader interested in this aspect of the matter should see below Glossary, *Gateward's Case*, and references thereunder.

cultivation from the unredeemed wastes. The partners in the co-operative enterprise shared the fruit of their activity in much the same fashion as children distribute a packet of sweets, or as the dealer hands out a pack of cards. It might—or might not—be more logical to divide the dividend by the divisor, allocating to each party the quotient, but there are practical reasons in favour of the more archaic method. The theory that this is how the scattered ownership arose is perhaps borne out by the fact that in some places, within living memory, the incumbent's glebe and the lord of the manor's demesne were also composed of scattered strips. (Though, of course, in many other villages these influential personages early contrived to secure their land in extensive, compact, more easily managed plots.) Still stronger is the argument that many early field terriers and maps show plain traces of a systematic and symmetrical allocation of selions, ABCDE, ABCDE, ABCDE and so on.

The origins alike of common meadow and common waste probably date back to an even earlier period than do those of open arable field. There is hardly space to deal with them here, save perhaps to note the anachronism of the legal theory which ascribes their origin to the sufferance of the lord of the manor. They have certainly existed since long before the time of manors, and the Anglo-Norman legal theory was quite mistaken. The point is worth noting, for much enclosure from the Statute of Merton[9] (1235) onwards has been based on an incorrect legal interpretation of a historical fact.

The classic quotation bearing on the origins of the English open-field system is earlier than England itself, a famous mention of it in Tacitus' *Germania*, dating from the later part of the first century. The reference is not, however, very clear, and the two most celebrated codices of Tacitus have variant readings of the passage.[10] These lend themselves to different

[9] See below pp. 60–1. The reader is asked to note especially that, throughout the book, dates and brief particulars of all acts of Parliament referred to are set forth in the Table of Statutes, pp. 193–5.

[10] Agri pro numero cultorum ab universis in vices (ab universis vicis) occupantur, quos mox inter se secundum dignationem partiuntur. Facilitatem partiendi camporum spatia praestant. Arva per annos mutant et superest ager. (*Germania* XXVI). I follow Church, A. J. and Brodribb, W. J., *The Agricola and Germania of Tacitus*, in translating this as 'Land proportioned to the number of inhabitants is occupied by the whole community in turn, and afterward divided among them according to rank. A

interpretations of what Tacitus is describing among the Germans, so, by analogy, of the type of agriculture one may reasonably suppose to have been originally practised by their Anglo-Saxon kinsmen. It seems to be generally accepted that Tacitus is depicting an early 'field-grass' husbandry such as would develop naturally in a primitive society, where there were still extensive areas of land not taken into cultivation. Its people grew corn on the same land continuously until it would no longer yield a fair crop; then when the natural fertility of the soil was exhausted, the community as a whole moved somewhere else. The soil would in due course recover, by a natural fallow, until at some date in the more or less distant future it could again be taken into cultivation by the same or some other body of occupiers. This is presumably the type of agriculture which began with the beginning of farming in Neolithic times, and which persisted, without any very fundamental change, to the Bronze Age. Something not wholly dissimilar to it remains among a few very primitive folk today.

Clearly such a system was practicable only when there was a huge surplus of cultivable land, which could be tilled without the expenditure of great effort in drainage, tree-felling, etc., and when the primitive communities were highly mobile. Neither of these conditions seems to have been prevalent in Britain at the time of the Anglo-Saxon immigrations, settlements and conquests. It is likely then the first English farmers followed an open-field system which had developed to a further stage. Moreover, in some parts of England it is quite clear that there was the most marked contrast between their agricultural usages and those of their British predecessors (with whom we are not here concerned). In others the contrast is not nearly so marked. It is at least possible that at the time of the English arrival in England they had developed, or were developing in their homelands an agricultural system evolving from some such primitive arrangements as Tacitus seems to refer to. This more elaborate development from the original simple

wide expanse of plains makes the division easy. They till fresh fields every year, and they still have more land than enough . . .'

Clearly the former reading lays stress on the occupation of land 'by the whole community in turn', the latter simply 'by whole communities'. The second phrase accentuates the common tenure, the first one an annual shifting, such as is again referred to in the phrase 'arva per annos mutant'. This again seems to refer to a primitive field-grass husbandry, not to a regular alternation of crop and fallow.

husbandry had come inevitably as surplus land had disappeared
with the growth of population.

In this the (now not-so-primitive) community, having
determined the boundaries of its territory, would by trial and
error hit on the expedient of dividing its cultivable land roughly
into halves, to be tilled in alternate years. As centuries passed
by and population grew still further, the community might be
faced with the necessity of tilling two-thirds or ultimately even
three-quarters of the land each year, leaving only a third or a
quarter fallow.[11] However, much of the land was thoroughly
exhausted even by one crop. Therefore a fallow of one year in
two, or at least one year in three, was the minimum needed if it
was to retain or recover any great proportion of its fertility.[12]
Perhaps mainly for this reason, though in much of England the
two-field system at a quite early period developed into a three-
field system, this rarely evolved further into a four-field system.
There are plain references to (two-field) agriculture in Old
English[13] times. There is clear archival evidence of a change in
some villages from two-field to three-field arrangements in early
mediaeval days.[14] In a few counties, especially perhaps Oxfordshire, the further development took place.[15] Usually, however,
there was no thought of this until the introduction of the

[11] But on this see Dr. Thirsk's recent work, below, App. 2, p. 179.

[12] Both the fallow itself and the droppings of the stock grazing on it
helped materially in this. It is for this reason that our ancestors developed it
not, as is alleged to have been set forth in her essay by the young lady
student 'doing' the open-field system as part of the economic history in her
economics course in the technical college. She asserted that the one-in-three
fallow was necessary 'because manure had not yet been invented'!

[13] Much of it is set out in Gray, H. L., *English Field Systems*, Cambridge,
Mass., 1915, pp. 50–62 and 82.

[14] Gray, *op. cit.*, pp. 62–81, and his App. 2, pp. 450–509.

[15] For evidence of the change from two-field to three-field arrangements
in mediaeval times, the best source is the extents of *inquisitiones post mortem*,
especially, for some reason which is not apparent, those from *c.* 1270–*c.*
1370. Many indications of the later changes from three-field to four-field
arrangements, especially after 1571–1604, are to be found in the glebe
terriers of various parishes still remaining in open field. (These were
prepared in accordance with *Canons*, 1571, No. X: *Patroni et Proprietarii* . . .
'Episcopus curabit ut justum inventarium quodque vocant terrarium . . .',
etc., with another canon to much the same effect in the current *Constitutions
and Canons*, those of 1604, No. 87.) Thus in my own parish of Sutton Bonington St. Anne's, Notts., a terrier of 1764 gives the place as in three fields;
at the enclosure of 1774–5 it was certainly in four. So the creation of the
fourth field plainly took place at some time during the ten years 1764–74.

Norfolk four-course rotation, which came in the seventeenth century, but was not widely adopted until the eighteenth. By then, of course, the abolition of open-field agriculture rather than its reform was the goal. Usually at the time of enclosure it was a three-field, or more rarely a two-field village that was enclosed.

All this, however, is highly theoretical, and the evidence for much of it is scanty and conflicting. What lies beyond all dispute is that, from the earliest times of which there is any reliable record, agriculture, throughout most of England, was carried on under the so-called open-field system. This normally involved the existence in each township of two, or three (or more rarely and in much later years four or more) of the great open arable fields above referred to and described. The holdings of each proprietor or occupier were widely scattered in small plots in each field, and appended to them was the use of common meadow and common pasture, arable meadow and pasture alike being subject to some degree of communal control and management. The replacement of these holdings by individual hedged or fenced closes and farms, and the replacement of communal control by that of persons pursuing policies of 'enlightened self-interest' is the process technically known as enclosure.

CHAPTER 3

THE DISADVANTAGES OF THE OPEN-FIELD SYSTEM: EARLY METHODS OF ENCLOSURE

THE OPEN-FIELD SYSTEM had evolved to meet the needs of a stable society, based on subsistence agriculture. It was seen later to have major disadvantages. It did not lend itself to agricultural experiment and progress. It was not always, of necessity, but it certainly could be on occasion, hideously uneconomic in labour and in time.[1] The very evident inconveniences and extravagances often involved in it early led to efforts to modify it. The wastes were the first varieties of land to be attacked. In 1235 and 1285 the Statutes of Merton and Westminster II gave powers to manorial lords to approve (enclose) such portions of the still remaining waste as were not needed by their free tenants. This power was very generally used, though apparently but rarely for the enclosure of any very considerable area of land. In general, action under these statutes seems to have been accepted as reasonable, though there are a few records of very violent protests against such operations. It is easy to understand how there may have been wide differences of opinion between lord and free tenants as to what was the 'sufficient' common which the lord was to leave still open.

Early References to Enclosure

In the latter part of the fifteenth century, however, enclosure is first referred to as a substantial grievance. The first recorded protest is that of John Rous, c. 1459–86.[2] From then until the end of the sixteenth century, and even later, there is an endless flood of propagandist literature, alleging that enclosure

[1] It is perhaps worth noting that 'townee' historians and economists whose knowledge of agriculture has been entirely theoretical have often been very scathing in their denunciations of open-field husbandry. On the other hand, one or two scholars who were also skilled practical farmers have seen many merits in it. Perhaps the best instance is the late C. S. Orwin (*The Open Fields*, cited below, *passim*). Orwin, Estates Bursar of Balliol and Director of the Oxford University Institute for Research in Agricultural Economics, was skilled alike in the history, the economics, the theory and the practice of farming, and he took a much more favourable view of open-field agriculture than many city-bred historians have done.

[2] Below, pp. 63, 143, 167.

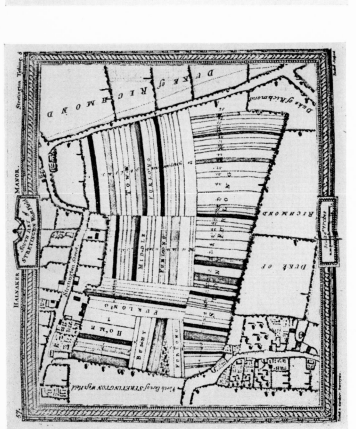

III(a) Survey of open-field selions, part of
Strettington, West Sussex, 1781; *see p. 205*

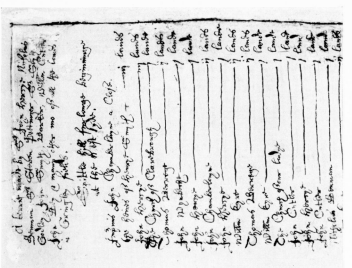

(b) The first folio of a terrier of open-field
selions in Little Gringley, Notts., 1547 or 1548;
see p. 206

IV (a) and (b)
Two 'lost villages',
Middle Ditchford
(now in Blockley),
Glos., and Martins-
thorpe, Rutland; *see*
pp. 206–7

for emparcation or for the making of several pastures meant the conversion of arable to pasture, and the rearing of deer, sheep, or cattle rather than men. It was being followed by the depopulation of rural England, and if persisted in it could not but bring about the complete ruin of the commonwealth. Sir Thomas More's *Utopia*,[3] which appeared in 1516, contains a famous passage in which he brings to the notice of the authorities his complaints as to the neglect of the interests of the small proprietors by manorial lords, both laymen and clerics, and presses for measures to be taken to check the agrarian revolution then in full swing. A commission set up in 1517, which has been described as an honest attempt to protect the peasant, appears to have been a direct result of More's appeal. Certainly it began its labours in the year following the publication of his book. There had previously been statutes forbidding enclosure: this was an effort—a vain one—to secure by administrative and judicial action that enclosures should be thrown open again, and lands converted to pasture restored to their former arable use. In the returns to this commission there are one or two indications that the peasantry themselves were not averse to enclosure, sometimes as individuals, each anxious to use his land to the best advantage, very occasionally as an organized group, in the interest of the rural community generally. Instances of this last are recorded, for example, at Winfarthing, Norf., where twenty-five acres were enclosed by 'the whole Vill', at Whitcott, Salop, and at Aldborough, Yorks, W. R. Other proprietors great and small were involved in enclosure proceedings, lay freeholders, and, as More notes with indignant irony, 'yea and certayn Abbottes, holy men no doubt'.

Enclosure by the Court Baron/Vestry Meeting[4]

Usually it is clear that enclosure at this time was carried out rather by what, perhaps, we may style 'unilateral action' on the

---

[3] Below, pp. 65, fn. 4, 156, fn. 5. *Utopia* was published in Latin at Louvain in 1515–16. Wolsey's Commission was issued 28 May 1517. The returns to it were edited by I. R. Leadam in *Trans. R. Hist. S.*, N.S. VI, VII, VIII (1892–4) from (sometimes incomplete) transcripts in the British Museum of the documents relating to eleven counties. Leadam edited also from the original Chancery returns in the Public Record Office two separate volumes which he styled *The Domesday of Inclosures*, published by the same Society in 1897.

[4] As set forth elsewhere, the Court Baron as a rule seems to have evolved into or coalesced with the Vestry Meeting.

part of the lord of the manor, without the approval of, and often in the face of very keen opposition by the tenants, In later years and in some manors it was on occasion alleged that the custom of the manor permitted enclosure on the part of anyone, lord or tenant, provided he surrendered common rights upon the land still remaining open, and regularized the whole process in advance by obtaining the sanction of the court. The central authorities, however, made it clear that whatever might be the manorial point of view, the administration regarded enclosure, at any rate enclosure of open-field arable, as contrary to public policy. As we shall see later, successive Governments periodically made not very successful efforts to check it.

Probably the total area of the land enclosed in England by manorial lords, with or without the sanction of their manor courts, was a very considerable amount. In the very nature of things it is, of course, quite impossible to furnish any reasoned estimate of how great this area was.

Enclosure by Chancery or Exchequer Decree

However, by the seventeenth century, it was felt that a more formal legal way of effecting the change was desirable. This was found in the use of decrees issuing from the Chancery or the Court of Exchequer.[5] These seem to have developed as a means of confirming enclosure agreements by a decree of the court, following a collusive action. In many cases, no doubt, the decree was simply a matter of recording a decision come to by quite genuine agreement upon the part of the proprietors interested. In other instances, however, it seems certain enough that the menace of an expensive and lengthy Chancery suit was used in order to extort acquiescence in enclosure from persons who were in reality strongly opposed to it.

When once a decree had been obtained, confirming the allotments to those interested, this seems to have been taken as giving the necessary security to all persons concerned in the proceedings. It is alleged that sometimes it was held also, (quite unjustly, and it appears also illegally) as preventing

[5] There is no comprehensive study of the enclosures carried out in this fashion. Gonner's book (App. 2, below), pp. 168, 181, gives some references to them, and Leonard, Miss H. M. 'The Inclosure of Common Fields . . .' in *Trans. R. Hist. S.* XIX, 1905, has several interesting examples. See also below, pp. 54, 124.

other persons, not parties to the suit, from disturbing the division of the land concerned, or exercising pre-existing common rights upon it. Sometimes, indeed, it seems that these other persons may have been in complete ignorance of the proceedings until after the suit had been ended and the decree obtained. On the other hand, often in enclosures of this kind it seems to have been felt that the poor as such had [? both legal and] moral claims upon the lands to be enclosed. It was therefore quite usual in these seventeenth-century enclosures, though very unusual in the parliamentary enclosures of the next century, for the local poor to be given in the decree special allotments, or for it to make other specific concessions to them.

How much land was enclosed by Chancery or Exchequer decree no one can say. It is not known exactly for which parishes such decrees exist. Certainly, however, many thousands of acres in almost all the counties of England were enclosed in this fashion. In the County Palatine of Durham, a great many very similar decrees issued from the Chancery of the Palatinate. Here, in fact, a much larger acreage was enclosed by this means than under the enclosure acts of the next century. It is likely enough that much enclosure in Lancashire and in Cheshire (where also there are relatively few eighteenth-century enclosure acts) may have been carried out by rather similar means. Here, apparently, data are lacking.

The procedure on enclosure of this kind is interesting.[6] In enclosure by Chancery decree, usually the first stage was the summoning of a meeting representing the interests affected. At this the commoners appointed two commissioners to act for them with another two, representing respectively the lord of the manor and the incumbent. A survey was made, sometimes by a field jury, and an award drawn up. The result of this is set forth in the 'plott book' which is sometimes to be found with the decree. Next came the collusive action, say by the tenants against the manorial lord. They petitioned the court, setting forth the terms of the agreement and the award, and stated that 'all is duly performed but the lord of the manor refuses to consent'. The defendant admitted the terms of the agreement and the award, but denied the refusal to consent. The court thereupon decreed the enclosure.

The whole business is curiously reminiscent of those quaint old legal devices the Fine and the Common Recovery, and

[6] *Cf.* p. 54 §(b).

was probably developed for very similar reasons. Its legal use seems to have been that the court could enable trustees and guardians who consented to bind their successors and wards, and could even commit dissentients. The procedure under Exchequer decree was less complicated. Here, as a rule, the actual division was made by commissioners, acting under a commission issuing out of the Court of Exchequer. Exchequer decrees seem to have been used especially for the enclosure of wastes. It was doubtless uncertainty as to the exact limits of the powers of these two courts that caused a bill to be brought forward in 1666 to legalize all enclosures made within the last sixty years. This failed, and from this time enclosure by Chancery decree gradually became disused, although there were some enclosures of this kind as late as George I's time, and one (by the Durham Chancery) in 1766.

It is perhaps significant that in a later era several of the first enclosure acts for Leicestershire, a county where enclosure of this kind had been much in vogue, were passed in order to confirm enclosures carried out by Chancery decree half a century or a century or more earlier. Apparently it was felt that this method of enclosure was far from satisfactory in giving a secure title. In the later part of the seventeenth century no less than eight bills concerning enclosure were introduced into either Lords or Commons. At least two or three of these were intended to confirm 'inclosures made by decrees in Courts of Equity'. All the bills, however, were dropped. Enclosure by quite informal private agreement went on side by side with that by Chancery decree. Again, no one knows how many tens or hundreds of thousands of acres were enclosed in this way in the late seventeenth century, throughout the eighteenth and in the early part of the nineteenth.

CHAPTER 4

THE LATER HISTORY OF ENCLOSURE

HERE BOTH ENCLOSURE acts and awards are considered in general terms. There is a rather more specific treatment of each of them, with some suggestions as to where they may be found, etc., in the tail-notes to Chapters 9 and 10 respectively.

The Evolution of the Enclosure Act

Enclosure by private agreement was clearly a long and difficult business. Its operation was much too tedious for the enthusiastic eighteenth-century agricultural reformers. So the next stage was to confirm the agreement by act of parliament instead of by court decree, and the earliest enclosure acts for lands in most English counties are acts confirming (usually recent but sometimes much earlier) agreements. In the East Riding of Yorkshire, for example, of fifteen enclosure acts before 1760, certainly nine, possibly more, confirm pre-existing agreements. The final step was for the act to ordain the appointment of (usually specially qualified) commissioners who should survey the parish and re-allot the open lands in it, with due regard to equity, and to the quality, quantity and situation of the lands concerned. Their decisions were to be set down in a carefully made and legally executed award. In effect the act confirmed in advance the adjudgement the commissioners should make. From about 1760 the usual means of effecting enclosure came to be by private act of parliament.

The promoters of the act nominated in it the commissioners, at first sometimes a dozen or more, later usually three or five, to visit the parish. Under their direction it was surveyed by a professional surveyor. The commissioners heard all the claims of those having either open land or common right, and then they allotted to all proprietors who had made good their claims an equivalent in land, or very occasionally in cash, for the rights they were to surrender. The land was allotted in severalty, after the modern fashion, entirely discharged from common right and other ancient obligations of almost every kind. Manorial incidents[1] were occasionally commuted—such ecclesiastical

---

[1] The most interesting manorial incidents are those connected with copyhold tenure, many of which remained until 1922 (see Table of Statutes). The copyholder was the remote successor of the mediaeval villein and had

dues[2] as tithes very often so. The commissioners' decisions were set forth in the award, which was proclaimed in the parish church, when it became final and legally binding. In much of England the enclosure award is the foundation charter of the modern village.

From the legal point of view it was quite natural that enclosure by act should develop in an age when the power of the legislature was rapidly overshadowing that of the monarch and that of the judicature. Both the Chancery decree and the private act are essentially the answer by the monarch to the petition of the subject, the former when the petition is addressed to the king in his Chancery, the latter when the petition is submitted to the king in his parliament. Lord Ernle[3] sums up the question neatly when he says that after the Restoration the jurisdiction of Chancery was first supplemented, then ousted, by the private act of parliament. The eight earliest enclosure acts in England are usually held to be those for Radipole, Dorset, 1603, Marden, Herefs., 1606, Malvern Chase, Glos., Herefs. and Worcs., 1664, Horton, Glos. 1668, Hameldon (Hambleton), Rutland, 1692, Salford, Oxon., 1695, Ropley, Hants., 1709, and Farmington, Glos., 1713.[4] After 1760

therefore, charged upon his land, financial and other obligations to his lord. These normally remained after enclosure (and often until *post*-1922). Conversely, the lord might have primitive obligations towards his tenants, e.g. in maintaining the pound or supplying a bull to serve the tenants' cows. Such obligations also were often discharged at enclosure, the allotment of the lord as such being slightly reduced, and those of the copyholders correspondingly increased.

[2] For the history of tithe see below, chap. 14, and/or any work on parish history generally, e.g. my *Parish Chest*. It was a matter for the promoters of any bill whether they should or should not include in it provisions for the partial or complete commutation of tithe in the parish. If so, it was usually done by the allotment to the tithe owner(s), clerical or lay, of a rent charge (often a corn rent, see below, Glossary), or of an area of land in compensation. The other ancient ecclesiastical dues were normally Easter Offerings, and mortuaries; these were almost always excepted from the commutation of other ancient dues. Mortuaries have now been replaced by [? absorbed in] burial fees. Easter offerings were regularized and restricted by statute in 1548, and were normally commuted under the Tithe Act of 1839; 'they' are still, however, quite voluntarily paid by an Anglican to his parish priest at Easter.

[3] Ernle (App. 2 below), pp. 162-3, Scrutton (App. 2 below), p. 133.

[4] This excludes a rather interesting series of (1530-84) acts for draining and enclosing marsh lands in Kent and Middlesex, along the Thames, for reclaiming heath land near London and for enclosing and cultivating waste

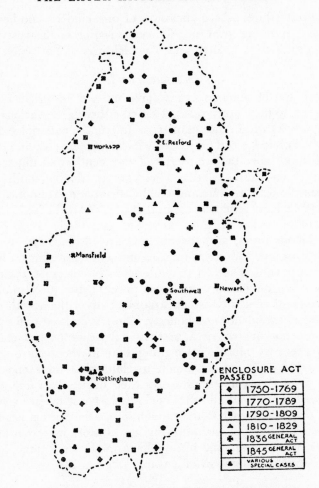

2. Parliamentary enclosure in Nottinghamshire
1743–1868; *see p. 196*

altogether there were about 5,400 enclosure acts and enclosures
under general acts, covering, it is estimated, more than seven
million acres—say a fifth of the area of England.[5] Before 1760
the total number of acts was but 259, more than half of which
related to lands in Warwickshire, Northamptonshire and

lands within twenty miles of the Scottish border. All these are dealt with
briefly by Scrutton (App. 2 below), pp. 94–95. The first three of the eight
acts mentioned are in fact in the 'Public' category. On the distinction
between Public and Private acts see below, p. 104.

[5] *Cf.* p. 88.

Gloucestershire, where enclosure of one kind or another had been a standing grievance for centuries, or in the vast waste moorlands of the North and West Ridings of Yorkshire.

Enclosure Awards

There are, of course, a great many series of historical records relating to the countryside preserved either in the various local repositories within the counties, or among the national archives in the Public Record Office. Few if any of these rival in interest and importance the long series of eighteenth- and nineteenth-century enclosure awards. These are invaluable, both as to 'agrotechnical' matters and on the social and economic problems which are so closely connected with them. There is a great difference between this extensive, systematic and almost continuous series, and the often scanty, fragmentary records which are our sources of information as to agrarian problems in earlier ages. The fact that the series of enclosure awards is almost a complete one makes it possible, too, to summarize its contents, and to base an argument upon them with some degree of confidence and honesty. There is no need to fear that records not quoted because they have disappeared contain evidence very much outweighing that in the records cited. Therefore, it is not too much to claim that these enclosure awards of Georgian times are in their evidential value much more weighty than all other enclosure records taken together. It is surprising, then, that although so much attention has been given to individual enclosures by local historians, few students of social and economic history have made any attempt at a large-scale investigation of a whole series of the awards.

The Primary Purpose of Enclosure Awards: Other Data Given

The first purpose of the awards was to achieve and to record the change from the ancient methods of husbandry to the modern system of individual land ownership and cultivation. The awards, however, do much more than this. They are a valuable source of field- and other minor place-names. They record incidentally the courses of ancient highways and watercourses. The existence of footpaths and rights of way is evidenced by them. So are the courses and breadths of the main land drains. The liability to maintain these, and the ownership of fences and hedges are often recorded in these same invaluable documents. Titheable lands are often distinguished in them

V Frontispiece of Blagrave's *Epitome* . . . (1669), and *New Additions* . . . (1675); *see p. 208*

To the Right Honourable the Lords Spirituall and Temporall of the House of Lords in Parliament assembled

The humble Petition of Thomas Hunter and Robert Hunter both of Medomsley in the County of Durham Gentlemen Charles Collinson Clerk and Cuthbert Johnson gentleman both of Medomsley aforesaid

Sheweth That your Petitioners Thomas Hunter and Robert Hunter are seised to them and their heires of and in the Antient Mannor of Medomsley in the said County and also of and in severall Messuages Lands Tenements hereditaments and large Rights Comons and Moors lying and being within and part and parcell of the said Mannor within the Parish of Lanchester in the said County of Durham And that they and all those whose Estates they have and in the said Mannor and premises have severally held and enjoyed and ought to hold and enjoy Comon of pasture and other Rights and privileges within and upon a large Comon or Fell called Lanchester Fell part of the Mannor of Lanchester aforesaid And your said Petitioners Charles Collinson and Cuthbert Johnson are also severally seised to them and their severall heires of and in—

VI A successful anti-enclosure petition, for Lanchester, Co. Durham, 1721

from lands non-titheable. (In many places the tithe award is less useful a source of information about tithe than is the enclosure award, since throughout whole counties more tithe was commuted under enclosure acts than under tithe acts.) They record allotments of lands for public purposes, and the endowments of ancient village schools and other charitable foundations. They contain much information as to the nature and distribution of land ownership and holding in rural England one to two centuries ago. They serve as ultimate evidence of title to no inconsiderable proportion of the countryside, from the rector's glebe and the lord of the manor's home farm, to the parish council's 'allotments' staked out on the site of the old parish gravel-pit.

The Evidential Value of Enclosure Awards

Accordingly, the enclosure awards are invaluable sources of historical information, to the historian, the antiquary, the economist and the administrator, to the steward of the great estate, and to the social reformer with a ready-made prescription for Utopia. It is no wonder then that individual enclosure awards are more often consulted than members of any other record series in the county repositories. Many awards, it is true, have disappeared, but the estimate of those missing— a third of the total—given before a royal commission in 1915 is grossly excessive. In any case it will be clear from what is said below, 'Enrolment' p. 118 and fn. 15, that normally awards were executed in duplicate, after 1845 in triplicate (while a great many unofficial copies have been made at different times by various people for divers purposes, and many of these are now in public or semi-public custody). Of all the parishes subjected to parliamentary enclosure, there are few then for which the award is not available somewhere-or-other, even if it is not in its original place of deposit, the parish chest. A reasoned estimate suggests that the 5,400[6] awards under private act and under the general acts relate to lands in perhaps 5,000 parishes, say half the (ancient) parishes of England.

Types of Enclosure Award: Enrolment of Awards

Enclosure awards fall into five main classes:[7]

[6] See App. 3.

[7] There is no large-scale survey of the documents in categories (a) and (b), and the likeliest place to inquire about them is the appropriate County Record Office. Those in classes (c), (d) and (e) are indexed and tabulated in my *Domesday of English Enclosure Acts and Awards*, now almost ready for

(*a*) Early agreements and awards under private agreement of the parties affected. A sub-group of this class are the memoranda of enclosure agreements, which turn up occasionally in court rolls and vestry minutes. These agreements and awards are often to be found in the parish chest, or failing this, in the county record office.

(*b*) Enclosure awards under Chancery or Exchequer decrees, mainly in the latter part of the seventeenth century. A few of these are found in the parish chests or county record offices. Others are still with the records of Chancery or the Exchequer, now in the Public Record Office; others again are known to be in private possession. These are very difficult to turn up, and when found, not easy to interpret. The complications of Chancery procedure often make it hard to determine whether the record is of a genuine suit or a fictitious one.

(*c*) Awards made by parliamentary enclosure commissioners acting under private and local acts. These normally exist in duplicate, the original copy now with the incumbent, the parish council or the county record office; the enrolment usually among the county records, or occasionally in one of the Courts at Westminster—these last now in the Public Record Office.

(*d*) Awards made without any reference to parliament under the General Acts of 1836 and 1840. These were always made in duplicate, one copy for the parish (as above), one for the county authority.

(*e*) Awards made under the general acts of 1845 *et seq.*, many after reference to parliament, and a few without such reference. These were made in triplicate, a copy for the parish (as above), one for the county authority (as above), and one for the Inclosure Commissioners (see pp. 136, 186) who ultimately were absorbed by the Ministry of Agriculture. This third—as it were the 'original copy'—is now in the Public Record Office.

Enclosure by private act and by commissioner's award was, however, the result of a long process of historical evolution. Before we deal with it in the further detail which its importance demands, it will be well for us to consider briefly the means of enclosure which had been adopted in earlier years, and which led ultimately to this method.

publication. See below, p. 107 *et seq.*, and App. 3, pp. 183–4, which are especially concerned with awards in categories (*c*), (*d*), (*e*).

CHAPTER 5

MEDIAEVAL ENCLOSURE MOVEMENTS

CLEARLY THE OPEN-FIELD system of farming as outlined in Chapter 2 lent itself to a stable system of agriculture, and the maintenance of a conservative order of society, but it was ill-adapted to agricultural progress. Probably from very early times, then, the history of agriculture in England has been largely that of change from semi-communal usages to a system of severalty, under which each individual owner or tenant could cultivate his specific plot or plots of land in such fashion as best pleased him. It does not appear, however, that in very early times there were many attempts to enclose open fields. The prevalent tendency was rather to take into cultivation further areas of the vast extent of unreclaimed waste which existed all over the country. As indicated above, usually in the first place each tiny settlement had been at first divided from its neighbours by such a border of waste land, often inter-commonable to the stock of two or more villages. Early agricultural improvement consisted largely of the reclamation of this waste.

The Early English Village and the Waste

Some other agricultural progress there was, no doubt, even within the limits of open-field agriculture. It seems clear that two- or three-field husbandry itself had evolved in the first place as a technical improvement on a 'field-grass' husbandry (above, pp. 40–1). This seems evidently a method of agriculture which would only be adopted completely among tribes in a nomadic or a semi-nomadic stage. The shift among the two or three great fields of the typical mediaeval English village community was clearly an enormous advance upon this, and probably one which took several centuries to complete. It has been suggested that perhaps the change may have been taking place about the time of the English conquest of England.[1] Little is known of the details of agricultural technique among our early ancestors, but what little there is suggests an open-field

[1] On this point see Orwin C. S. and Mrs. C. S., *The Open Fields*, chap. 2, orig. edn. 1938, pp. 49–58; new edn. 1958, pp. 30–52.

system of some kind. Perhaps it is safe to argue by analogy from Germany, where it appears likely that the three-field system was well known in the eighth century. Many scholars would assert, however, that it is not. Probably the most one can say with safety is that on the face of things it seems not unlikely that an extensive husbandry was practised by our early ancestors. This evolved (perhaps through a one-field system early abandoned because it so rapidly exhausted the land) into a two- and a three-field system. These last two were in fairly general use in England nine hundred years ago. As Archdeacon Cunningham puts it, though in a rather different connexion, 'By the time of the Confessor the social organism had embodied itself in a territorial shell.'[2]

Two-field and Three-field Husbandry

It has been suggested above that the curious primitive usages associated with the occupation of common meadow land may ? perhaps be survivals of the days when land was occupied for one year only by any individual proprietor. There have been in Yorkshire and elsewhere local customs of husbandry which may also have been survivals of one-field usages. The marks of the two- and three-field stages are written deeply upon the whole face of the English countryside. It is rarely known at what time cultivation in any particular township passed from a two-field to a three-field plan. The matter was first investigated in detail by the American scholar Howard Gray, and most later work on it is based ultimately on his.[3] Sometimes it is known with rather more certainty when a fourth (or sometimes even a fifth, sixth or seventh) great field was introduced, and this was often in the sixteenth and seventeenth centuries, before the introduction of the Norfolk four-course rotation. There were, however, some counties where a two-field system was generally prevalent until the eighteenth century, and others where it disappeared in very early times indeed. Attempts have been made to correlate the prevalence of the two systems with racial factors, but these have not in general met with the acceptance of scholars. As two recent writers say: 'A two-field system of alternate corn and fallow was the first step in the evolution of farming from its more primitive forms,—the three-field system was an evolution of the two-field system, proceeding variously, and

[2] Cunningham, W., *Growth of English Industry and Commerce*, var. edns.
[3] Cited above, p. 24, fn. 12. See especially his Chap. 2.

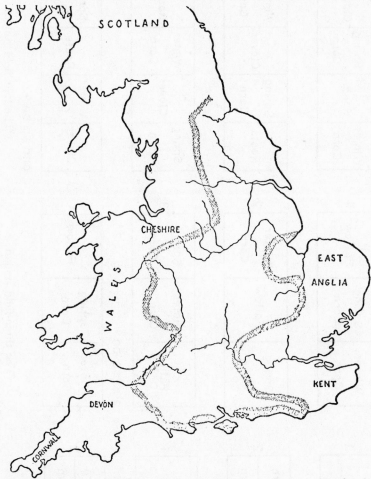

3. The main area of 'Germanic' open-field agriculture in England;
see p. 197

see p. 197

carried to different stages of completion in different places.'[4]

The differences between the two systems is mainly that in the
one a half, in the other only a third of the land is 'wasted' every
year. Under a two-field arrangement as under one of three
fields, two corn crops were necessary, wheat-and-rye, and
barley-and-oats-and-beans. No doubt, as a rule in a two-field
system some half of the cultivated field each year was devoted
to winter corn, the other half to spring corn.

Diagram 4 will illustrate the point.

[4] Dr. and Mrs. Orwin, above, chap. 4, fn. 4.

The two-field system

1st Year

Field 1: Winter Corn / Spring Corn — Fallow

Field 2: Winter Corn / Spring Corn

2nd Year

Field 1: Fallow

Field 2: Spring Corn / Winter Corn

and so on:-

3rd Year

Field 1: Fallow

Field 2: Spring Corn / Winter Corn

4th Year

Field 1: Fallow

Field 2: Spring Corn / Winter Corn

The three-field system

1 — Winter Corn | Spring Corn | Fallow

2 — Spring Corn | Fallow | Winter Corn

3 — Fallow | Winter Corn | Spring Corn

and so on:-

1 — Winter Corn | Spring Corn | Fallow

The four-field system

1 — Winter Corn | Roots | Spring Corn | Clover

2 — Roots | Spring Corn | Clover | Winter Corn

3 — Spring Corn | Clover | Winter Corn | Roots

4 — Clover | Winter Corn | Roots | Spring Corn

and so on:-

4. Diagram: Two-, three- and four-field systems: two-, three- and four-course rotations; see pp. 39–43

The great agricultural writer of the thirteenth century, Walter of Henley, makes it clear that in his time both systems were in use:

'If your lands are divided in three, one part for winter seed and the other part for spring seed, and the third part fallow, then is a ploughland nine score acres. And if your lands are divided in two, as in many places, the one half sown with winter seed and spring seed, the other half fallow, then shall a ploughland be eight score acres.'[5]

At the same time as some villages were changing their husbandry from a two- to a three-course rotation (making desirable though not quite necessitating a three-field system instead of one of two fields), others were modernizing their husbandry in other ways. Often the lord's demesne or the incumbent's glebe, both of which seem in general in early times to have been held in acre strips interspersed with the acre strips of the other proprietors, were quite early withdrawn from the general intermixture, and held as compact blocks in severalty.[6] Presumably, where this happened, the advantages secured to the proprietors would not be lost upon the other people of the village, and would often tend to cause a demand for enclosure of their own holdings by at any rate the more prosperous of the other landholders. There is ample evidence too that the mediaeval village was for centuries pushing out its frontiers into the waste by which it was surrounded. Often, land reclaimed was added to existing open fields, careful regulations being adopted for its distribution amongst the persons who had shared in the enterprise. Very frequently 'New Fields' and 'Breeches', i.e. 'Breaks or Brecks', or 'Intake Furlongs', contain in their names evidence that this process has been in operation. In other instances, however, it is clear that arable land, reclaimed from the waste by individual private enterprise, was from the beginning held in severalty. (It is reasonable to suppose that the evident advantages of this to the proprietors would tend to encourage a demand for the enclosure of other lands, nearer the heart of the settlement, which had from time immemorial been in open field.) It is in connexion with this reclamation of the waste that enclosure first appears in the Statute Book.

[5] Ed. Lamond, Miss E., R. Hist. S. 1890, pp. 7–9.
[6] On this as on many other matters of agrarian history, Tawney, R. H., *The Agrarian Problem in the Sixteenth Century*, 1912, is a mine of information. It contains several maps illustrating this point.

The Statutes of Merton and Westminster II

In the thirteenth century there are to be found records of free-hold tenants proceeding against their lord upon the ground that he had enclosed part of the common, and thereby robbed them of their rights of pasture, etc. By the Statute of Merton in 1235, it was, in effect, ordained that the lord of a manor might enclose the common at discretion, provided he left a 'sufficiency' of land open to meet all the common rights of the free tenants. The onus of proving the sufficiency, and ensuring that the tenants had access to the land, was to rest upon the lord. This statute, re-enacted in 1550, remained on the Statute Book until 1952, though in its last few years enclosures under it might take place only with the consent of the Board, latterly the Ministry, of Agriculture (i.e. virtually not at all). The statute was extended by the Statute of Westminster II in 1285, which enabled lords to enclose against their neighbours in wastes, etc., commonable to two or more manors.

These statutes at once limited and confirmed the seigniorial powers over the waste. It is uncertain how far before them the manorial lord as such had any legal powers over it. After these statutes, it was legally vested in him, his tenants retaining merely limited rights of user over the surface. Both before and after, the manorial lords were not slow to 'make their profit' of the waste. Often no doubt they interpreted the needs of their tenants somewhat narrowly, and their own rather generously. The classical county histories—Blomfield, Bridges, Dugdale, Thoroton, and the rest—contain numerous references to the free tenants bringing an *assize of novel disseisin* against their lord for 'straitening' the pasture, or to the lord and the tenants entering into an agreement for a limited amount of enclosure to take place upon certain specified conditions.

Enclosures on the Berkeley Estates

The whole matter can be followed up in the annals of the great baronial house of Berkeley.[7] Thomas I, d. 1243, a few years before the Statute of Merton, reduced great quantities of ground into enclosures by procuring many releases of common land from freeholders. His successor Maurice I, d. 1281, less observant of legality, converted a common wood into a private park,

---

[7] Smyth, J. (1567–1640), *Lives of the [first twenty-one] Berkeleys*, first published 1821, *passim*.

to the indignation of his tenants. They fell in with his plan while he was alive, 'but later fell upon his sonne with suits'. Maurice also consolidated much of his demesne land, throwing together scattered strips, and exchanging those that lay farthest from his manor house for others lying close to it. Evidently he was trying to get 'the home farm into a ring fence', as we might put it nowadays. Thomas II, 1281–1320, carried on the same policy, 'to the great profit of his tenants and himself', so that for the compact estates, instead of the scattered strips, he was able to secure an increased rent of 1s. 6d. per acre, compared with fourpence or sixpence previously. Other noblemen and gentlemen great and small acted in the same way. It is to be feared that the example of Maurice I was followed oftener than that of Thomas I.

The Two Types of Enclosure

It will be seen that there were at least two quite distinct enclosure movements going on side by side, though each of them acted on and was reacted on by the other. The one was a movement for the reclamation and possible bringing into cultivation of the remaining waste. Sometimes it was desired for imparking rather than for arable cultivation. The Towneleys of Whalley in Lancashire [? a county where there had never been many open fields] were prominent in this aspect of the movement, especially perhaps Sir John Towneley, fl. *temp.* Henry VII. A tradition lingered among the peasantry for centuries that Sir John's ghost was doomed to wander for ever in Horelaw Park (which he had filched from his poorer neighbours) crying

'Lay out, lay out,
Horelaw and Hollinghey Clout.'[8]

The other movement was one to rationalize open-field agriculture by gathering together the scattered selions of open land, and often cancelling the pasturage and other rights upon them.[9]

Either of these changes would involve the loss of pasture

[8] Whitaker, T. D. . . . *Whalley*, 1801, edn. 1872–6, II, p. 53.

[9] It is noteworthy that in many early enclosures by agreement (e.g. Welcombe, Warws. *temp.* Jac. I., Kinwarton, Warws. 1722), though I think in few if any later ones of any class, the arable land might still lie open as grazing after harvest.

and other rights, and each was often carried out very high-
handedly without any proper compensation being made for
rights lost. From the social point of view, the latter movement
was the one about which there was most public concern. The
soil of the open fields was often exhausted by continuous
cropping. It might be profitable on enclosure to convert it to
pasturage for the rearing of sheep (or more rarely of cattle). If
this happened, however, without other land being taken into
cultivation, the corn acreage would be diminished. There
would be a shortage of employment (since the same area gave
much more employment when it was under the plough than
when it was in grass). Small proprietors, copyholders and
others might be thrust out of their own because of some real or
alleged invalidity in their titles. Their houses would be pulled
down and their villages depopulated. The church would be
robbed of the tithe which it had formerly enjoyed from a
prosperous and self-supporting community of what had been
virtually peasant proprietors. The former villagers might be
expelled from the place and driven into vagrancy. If as vagrants
they begged, they were liable to be whipped and branded, and
if they stole they might suffer death under the Draconian legislation of the Tudors. Statements that enclosure and depopulation
of this kind actually happened became very frequent after
about 1480. The social and economic displacement involved by
an agrarian revolution of this nature could not but be accen-
tuated by the price revolution which was taking place about
the same time. Doubtless the economic upheaval caused by the
dissolution of the monasteries made its effects still more disastrous. It is easy to see then how especially in the early- and
mid-sixteenth century, enclosure became a major social and
political issue of the day.

CHAPTER 6

ENCLOSURE MOVEMENTS IN TUDOR TIMES

John Rous

WE HAVE NOTED above that complaints as to the process of enclosure appear as early as *c.* 1459–86. John Rous, a chantry priest of Warwick, had petitioned Parliament on the subject of depopulation in 1459, and in his *History of the Kings of England*, written at some time between that year and 1486, he returned to the charge with a detailed account of enclosure and depopulation in his own county of Warwick.[1] He gives a list of some sixty-two townships, hamlets, manors and parishes, mostly in South Warwickshire and within thirteen miles or so of Warwick, all of which he says had been decayed and depopulated in whole or in part by enclosure. Some villages, for example Compton Scorpion, had totally disappeared, and their very churches were in ruins. In others the population had been reduced by as much as ninety per cent. A writer of a century later says 'enclosure began to be more frequent, whereby arable land, which could not be manured without people and families was turned into pasture, which was easily rid by a few herdsmen. This bred a decay of people.'[2] Or in the words of a contemporary petition to Parliament, 'sheep and cattle drave out Christian labourers'. It was in response to complaints of this kind that the Government passed the not very effective legislation of 1488, 1514, and 1515, elsewhere referred to.

More and Wolsey

Complaints of wholesale enclosure still occurred, and the cause of the poor was taken up by two very influential men indeed, Thomas More, then a rising court favourite, and Thomas Wolsey, Cardinal, and Archbishop of York, Lord Chancellor of

[1] Rossi, Johanni, *Historia Regum Anglie*, ed. 2da. Oxon. (ed. Hearne, T.), 1745, pp. 122–3. Apparently no copy of the petition has survived, but Rous's book is readily accessible, though in a somewhat corrupt version. For a corrected text of this part of it, made by the present writer with the help of Mr. P. Styles of the Warwickshire *V.C.H.*, see *Birm. Arch. Soc. Trans.* LXV 1943/4, pp. 57–63.

[2] *History of Henry VII*, 1622. I cite Joseph Davey's edn. of 1874, pp. 359–61.

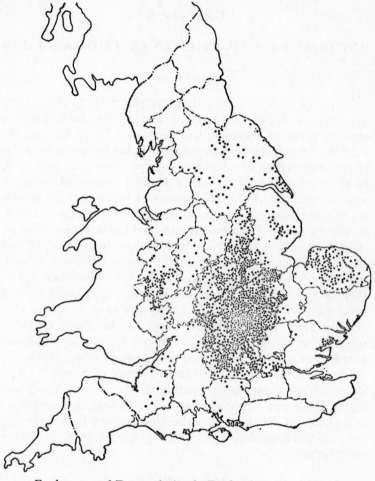

5. Enclosure and Depopulation in England *c.* 1485 (*sic*)–1607;
see p. *197*

England. More's celebrated *Utopia* appeared in its Latin form
in two books in 1516 and 1517 (the first English version was not
published until 1551).[3] In *Utopia* More offered a most powerful
and effective criticism of the agrarian change then taking place,
and a very moving plea for the peasant:

'There is an other (cause of stealing), whych, as I suppose, is
proper and peculiar to you Englishmen alone . . . your shepe that

[3] *A frutefull pleasant, and wittie Worke* . . . , trans. Robynson, Raphe (2nd
edn. 1551), ed. Sampson, G., 1914.

were wont to be so meke and tame, and so smal eaters, now, as I heare saye, be become so great devowerers and so wylde, that they eate up, and swallow downe the very men them selfes. They consume, destroye, and devoure whole fields, howses, and cities ... nobleman and gentlemen: yea and certeyn Abbottes . . . leave no grounde for tillage, thei inclose al into pastures: thei throw doune houses: they pluck downe townes, and leave nothinge standynge, but only the churche to be made a shepehowse . . . that one covetous and unsatiable cormaraunte and very plage of his natyve contrey maye compasse aboute and inclose many thousand akers of grounde together within one pale or hedge, the husbandmen be thrust owte of their owne, or els either by coveyne and fraud, or by violent oppression they be put besydes it, or by wronges and injuries thei be so weried, that they be compelled to sell all: by one meanes therfore or by other, either by hooke or crooke they must needes departe awaye, poor selye wretched soules, men, women, husbands, wives, fatherlesse children, widowes, wofull mothers, with their yonge babes . . . Awaye thei trudge, I say, out of their knowen and accustomed houses, fyndynge no place to rest in . . . And when they have wandered abrode tyll that be spent, what can they els doo but steale, and then justly pardy be hanged, or els go about beggyng. And yet then also they be cast in prison as vagaboundes, because they go aboute and worke not: whom no man wyl set a worke, though thei never so willingly profre themselves therto. For one Shephearde or Heardman is ynoughe to eate up that grounde with cattel, to the occupiynge whereof aboute husbandrye many handes were requisite . . . Caste oute these pernicyous abhominations, make a lawe that they which plucked down fermes, and townes of husbandrie, shall reedifie them, or els yelde and up-render the possession therof to such as wil . . .'

The 1517 Commission

As a matter of fact there was such a law, but it was little heeded.[4] More's appeal fell on very sympathetic ears, and in 1517, under his inspiration and that of Wolsey, the King himself set up a commission to inquire into depopulation, conversion and enclosure in all the counties of England save the four most northerly ones. Its returns are still largely extant as originals or abstracts, and very interesting they are. They confirm the existence of the evil as alleged in the statements of Rous and

[4] For the Act of 1489, see below, Table of Statutes. The Act of 1515 was made permanent in 1516. The first part of *Utopia* was published in 1515, the second part in 1516.

More, and those which were made a century later (but as to this period) by another Lord Chancellor of England, the great Francis Bacon, though they suggest that the King's efforts to check it had met with some degree of success:

> 'Enclosures at that time became to be more frequent . . . this bred a decay of people . . . there ensued withal upon this a decay and diminution of subsidies and taxes . . . [and a lack of good infantrymen for] . . . to make good infantry it requireth not men bred in a servile or indigent fashion but in some free and plentiful manner. In remedying this inconvenience the King's wisdom was admirable, and the Parliament's at that time . . . (which did) . . . much advance the military power of the Kingdom.'[5]

There are, however, a great many instances of the legislation being ignored or bypassed. To take one at random: at Stretton Baskerville in Warwickshire (not one of the villages referred to by Rous) Thomas Twyfoot in 1489 decayed four messuages and three cottages whereto belonged 160 acres of arable. He sold the place to Henry Smyth. Smyth enclosed another 640 acres in 1494, decaying twelve more messuages and four cottages, and expelling eighty people, who were reduced to poverty and misery. The parish church was in ruins, and brute beasts profaned it, and grazed on the graves of departed Christians in the churchyard. Another 160 acres were enclosed by 1549, and [an unspecified number of] houses were decayed and persons expelled. Stretton is still an [ecclesiastical] parish [of about one thousand acres], but its ancient parish church of All Saints has disappeared, there is no village, and the present-day population of the entire parish is given as fifty-eight, much less than it was in 1450. Of other similar villages the very sites are identifiable only with difficulty; the churches have disappeared, leaving no trace, and the places have been entirely obliterated.[6]

Henry's action on the commission's report was prompt, but less effective than had been hoped. His administrative measures

---

[5] *loc. cit.*

[6] Of late years much attention has been given, especially by Beresford and his co-workers, to these lost villages, depopulated either because of enclosure or for other reasons. See e.g., Beresford, M., *Lost Villages of England*, 1954, and his *History on the Ground* (especially chap. 4, 'A Journey among deserted Villages'), 1957. There is a Deserted Mediaeval Village Research Group (address c/o 67 Gloucester Terrace, N.W.1).

to deal with the problem continued at any rate until 1527: they have been dealt with elsewhere. Enclosure still developed, however, and the literature of the period is full of complaints of it. It is clear that the legislation on the subject had been evaded, often because its administration was put into the hands of the magistrates, belonging of course to the very class which had most offended. Half-way through the century it was said that a house might be pulled down, but a single room left for the occupation of a shepherd or a milkmaid. A solitary furrow drawn across a pasture field was held to satisfy the law that it should be restored to tillage. The number of sheep to be owned by one man was limited, so the ownership of flocks was fathered upon sons or servants. Sir Anthony Fitzherbert in 1523 tells how the action of the lords pressed on the poorer classes:

'(The lords) have given license to divers of their tenants to enclose part of their arable land, and to take in new intakes or closes out of the commons . . . so that the common pastures waxen less, and the rents of the tenants waxen more.'[7]

William Tyndale in 1525 says:

'Let them not take in their commons neither make parks nor pastures, for God gave the earth unto men to inhabit, and not unto sheep and wild deer.'[8]

In the revolts of 1536 and 1549, enclosure played an appreciable part among the rebels' grievances, though in the later ones of 1554 and 1569 there was perhaps less element of agrarian motive. There were enclosure uproars in Oxfordshire in 1596, and again in the Midlands in 1607 agrarian grievances led to something approaching armed revolt.[9] For well over a century the literature of the time gives much information as to the causes and consequences of the changes taking place. Thomas Starkey in his *Dialogue between (Cardinal) Pole and Thomas Lupset* in 1538 represents Lupset as complaining, 'There

[7] Fitzherbert, Sir Anthony (?qu. or his elder brother Sir John), *Boke of Husbendrye*, 1523, 1534 etc., *Surveyinge*, 1523, 1539. There is a convenient reprint of 1767 which includes both works. The *Husbandry* alone was reprinted, ed. Skeat, W. W., by the English Dialect Society in 1882.

[8] Tyndale, W., *Doctrinal Treatises*, Parker Society, edn. 1848, p. 202.

[9] Gay, E. F., 'The Midland Revolt and the Inquisitions of Depopulation of 1607' in *R. Hist. S. Trans.* N. S. XVIII, 1904, pp. 195–244.

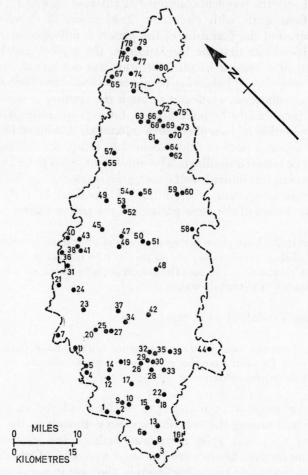

6. Deserted villages of Northamptonshire (after Allison,
Beresford and Hurst); *see p. 198*

KEY TO NUMBERING
Deserted Villages of Northamptonshire

post 1086	9, 41 *2*
c. 1125–*c.* 1350	49 *1*
c. 1350–*c.* 1450	13, 15, 24, ?26, 31, ?50, 51, 55, 61, 63, ?76, 67, 71, ?77 *?14*
c. 1450–*c.* 1700	1, 3, 4, ?5, ?6, 8, ?10, 11, 12, 14, 16, 17, 19, 20, 22, ?23, 25, 28, ?29, 30, 32, 33, ?34, 35, 37, ?38, 39, ?40, ?43, 44, ?45, 47, 52, 53, 54, 56,

57, ?58, 65, 68, 69, 70, 72, ?73, 74, 75, ?76, ?78, ?79 ?49

After c. 1700   2, 18, 27, 30, 42, 46, 48, 64, 80 9

Of uncertain date 7, 21, 59, 60, 62 5

Total: 80 Two places not identified. Grand total: 82

The numbers themselves are tabulated with those of other midland counties on p. 20. Summarized, the county statement amounts to this:

Early desertion (*post* 1086)	2
(Plus not identified)	2
Deserted c. 1125–c. 1350	1
Deserted c. 1350–c. 1450	14?
Deserted c. 1450–c. 1700	49?
Deserted *post* c. 1700	9
Deserted, date uncertain, at present	5
Total: 80 Grand Total:	82

It will be noted that the great majority of the villages disappeared c. 1350–c. 1450 and, still more, c. 1450–c. 1700, the classical period of depopulating enclosure.

is no man but he seeth the great enclosing in every part of arable land, and whereas there was corn and fruitful tillage, now nothing is but pastures and plains, by the reason whereof many villages are destroyed'. *Rede me and be nott Wrothe* in 1527 speaks of the greedy step lords who 'occupy a dosen mens lyvingis', and the complaint recurs in the sermons of popular preachers like William Tyndale, Thomas Becon, Hugh Latimer and Thomas Lever, in the works of such pamphleteers as Simon Fish and Henry Brinkelow, and in the rhymes of such versifiers as Sir William Forest and Robert Crowley. Becon calls enclosing landlords 'caterpillars of the common weale, unchristian landlords', Tyndale speaks of 'the unsatiable cormorants who let two or three tenantries to one man, take in commons, and make parks or pastures of whole parishes'.[10]

Latimer's opinion on the same question and the action taken, presumably under his inspiration and that of his party, to check

[10] Most of the dozen or so works cited are to be found in the *Harleian Miscellany* or in the Extra Series of the Early English Text Society, one or two in the publications of the (defunct) Ballad Society and Spenser Society. Sermons of the time are printed in various volumes of the Parker Society. There are more readily available texts of Lever's in Arber's *English Reprints*, 1901 and of Latimer's in Dent's *Everyman* Series, 1906.

the movement are dealt with elsewhere. Here it may be sufficient to note that, in response to the prevalent agitation, and because of the revolts of 1548-9, another commission was set up to check the movement. The secretary was John Hales, a leading anti-enclosure propagandist. For a variety of reasons, the commission came to little. Few of its records are now extant. Probably most of them were destroyed, when on the Duke of Somerset's (first) fall in 1549 the triumphant opposition reversed his policy, re-enacted the Statute of Merton, and exploited and oppressed the peasantry more mercilessly than ever in the two or three years during which they remained in power. Even so another depopulation act was passed in 1552, though this seems to have been without any result.

The wave of anti-enclosure propaganda broke out again in Elizabeth's reign. According to Thomas Bastard in 1598:

> 'Sheepe have eate up our medows and our downes,
> Our corne, our wood, whole villages and townes;
> Yes, they have eate up many wealthy men,
> Besides widowes and orphane children;
> Besides our statutes and our Iron Lawes,
> Which they have swallowed down into their mawes:—
> Till now I thought the proverb did but jest,
> Which said a blacke sheepe was a biting beast.'[11]

William Harrison in 1577-87 has much to say of the tyranny and greed of landlords, and of the effects to which it had given rise. His complaints are largely, however, of the enclosure and emparcation of commons, rather than the enclosure of open fields. He speaks very bitterly, though, of the engrossing of farms and tenancies—a very usual concomitant of enclosure— and of the depopulation of the countryside which resulted from this. According to him, the countryside fell naturally into two divisions, the (champaign) champion (open-field area), and the woodland (enclosed). A typical open-field village might have as many as three or four hundred houses, and up to two thousand communicants, a typical enclosed one only forty or fifty houses, and not above two or three hundred communicants:

> 'whereof the greatest part nevertheless are very poor folks often-
> times without all manner of occupying, sith the ground of the

[11] *Chrestoleros*, 1598, Bk. IV.

parish is gotten up into a few men's hands . . . (whereby the) rest are compelled either to be hired servants unto the other, or else to beg their bread in misery from door to door.'[12]

Probably his statements are grossly exaggerated, but there is a measure of truth behind them. It was no doubt in deference to opinions of this kind that in general the Queen continued the agrarian policy of her predecessors. She was, however, less successful than they, and it appears that the enclosure movement continued throughout her reign, though possibly with diminished force. About this time too, there began to be heard the economic argument for enclosure, as opposed to the social argument against it.

Agricultural Improvement

Fitzherbert in the 1520's had argued for enclosure, with certain restrictions to protect the interests of the poorer tenants. Thomas Tusser, whose works are a mine of information on farming technique in Elizabethan times, was as wholeheartedly in favour of enclosure as was another great agricultural writer, Arthur Young, in the eighteenth century:

> 'The champion robbeth by night,
>   And prowleth and filcheth by day:
> Himselfe and his beast out of sight,
>   Both spoileth and maketh away
> Not onely thy grasse but thy corne,
>   Both after, and er it be shorne.'
> . . .
> For commons these commoners crie,
>   Enclosing they may not abide:
> Yet some be not able to bie
>   A cow with hir calfe by hir side.
> Nor laie not to live by their wurke,
>   But theevishlie loiter and lurke.'[13]

[12] There is a convenient and inexpensive version of Harrison's book in *Elizabethan England*, 1888, L. W.'s edition of W. J. Furnival's reprint of 1876.

[13] Tusser, Thomas, *A Hundredth good pointes of husbandrie* 1557, from 1573 onwards *Five hundredth pointes*. . . . The standard modern text is one set forth by the English Dialect Society in 1878. There is a very attractive facsimile modern reprint of the original work, 1571, with a good deal of ancillary matter, ed. Marshall, Miss D., 1931. The verses given are from *c*. 52, 'A Comparison between Champion Countrie and Severall' sts. 13, 17, 1878 edn., pp. 143–4.

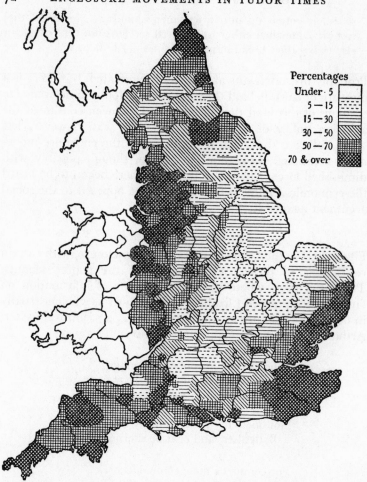

Percentages
Under 5
5 — 15
15 — 30
30 — 50
50 — 70
70 & over

7. Estimated percentage of land in the various English counties
without common or open field *c.* 1600; *see p. 199*

There is abundant evidence that the landed classes acted on
Tusser's advice to enclose, and that a great many enclosures
were carried on in the great Queen's time with as little regard
for the rights and interests of the peasantry as had been shown
in the worst of the previous periods. Tawney says: 'The
descendant of the illiterate, bloody-minded baron who is
muzzled by Henry VII becomes a courteous gentleman who
rhapsodises in verse at the Court of Gloriana. But all that the
peasants know is that his land-agents are harsher.'[14]

[14] Tawney, *op. cit.*, p. 193.

It may have been partly in response to the riot of the peasants in Oxfordshire in 1596, against 'the gentlemen who took the commons', certainly it was largely due to the rapid growth of enclosure, that the depopulation act of 1563, which expired in 1593, was replaced by two others in 1597. As Bishop Joseph Hall puts it in 1598–9:

> 'Would it not vexe thee where thy syres did keepe,
> To see the dunged foldes of drag-tailed sheepe,
> And ruined house where holy things wer said
> Whose free-stone wals the thatched roofe upbraid, . . .'[15]

The Government had adopted special measures for the maintenance of tillage (and therefore population) on the Scottish border, and on many occasions during the Queen's reign the courts had intervened to check particularly harsh or unconscionable acts of enclosure. A proposal in 1601 to repeal the depopulation acts was crushed through the opposition, *inter alia*, of no less a person than her Secretary, Robert Cecil, who believed that 'Whosoever doth not maintain the plough destroys this Kingdom',[16] and that of Francis Bacon, who said, alluding to former statutes, 'The inconvenience being then scarce out of the shell is now full ripened.'

[15] Joseph Hall, the (self-styled) 'first English satirist', attacks in his sermons 'the oppressing gentleman, that tyrannizes over his cottagers, encroaches upon his neighbour's inheritance, encloses common, depopulates villages, screws his tenants to death' (Sermon XIII, *Works*, V, p. 195). The quotation is from his *Virgidemiae*, 1598, 1599, ed. Davenport, A., Liverpool, 1949, Sat. V, I. ll. 115–19 (cf. Sat. V, III, ll. 34–80).

[16] D'Ewes, Sir S., *Journals* . . . , edn. 1682, p. 674.

CHAPTER 7

ENCLOSURE IN THE SEVENTEENTH
CENTURY

WITH THE SEVENTEENTH century, the arguments for enclosure on economic grounds became more frequent. In 1602 the county historian of Cornwall says 'they fal everywhere from commons to inclosures[1] and similar statements are made by the historians of at least half a dozen other counties throughout the century. There were still many writers who opposed the movement. One in 1604 speaks of enclosure as 'a mighty Thorne sprung up of late . . . not only to impoverish your Majesty's subjects but quite to roote them out'. The old prophecy is being fulfilled, 'Horne and Thorne shall make England forlorne'. In 1604 again, Sir Edward Montagu, one of the knights of the shire for the county of Northampton, conveyed to Parliament the grievances of the countryside. He himself was strongly impressed with the inconveniences of open-field husbandry, but popular feeling was so strong that he could do no less than present this request to the 'consideration of your wisdom'.[2]

No redress was given, and in 1607 the countryside was in armed revolt again throughout Northamptonshire, Warwickshire and Leicestershire, while there were stirrings of revolt in Derbyshire and Gloucestershire:

'Wheresoever the rioters came they were generally relieved by the neer inhabitants, who sent them not only many cartes laden with victual, but also good store of spades and shovells for speedy performance of their present enterprize' [the levelling of hedges and the filling up of ditches].

The rioters took the name of Levellers (of which a good deal was to be heard later), and their manifesto makes it clear that

[1] Carew, R., *Survey of Cornwall*, 1602. Compare the rather similar Aubrey, *Wiltshire*; Dugdale, *Warwickshire*; Morton, *Northamptonshire*; Nichols, *Leicestershire*; Plot, *Oxfordshire*; Thoroton, *Nottinghamshire*, etc.

[2] Gay, *op. cit.*, p. 212, fns. 2, 3. *House of Commons Journal* 1. 151, 23 Mar. 1604 and *Bull. Inst. Hist. R.* IV, 12, Feb. 1927, p. 126. The quotation is given by Gay, p. 214, from Edmund Howes's additions to the 1615 edn. of Stow's *Annales*, p. 289. The Montagus of Boughton were among the more enlightened and humane cavalier families, though I do not know that Sir Edward showed further concern about enclosure.

the agrarian grievance was almost the sole cause of the unrest. The course and progress of the insurrection is dealt with in outline elsewhere. One of its results was the issue of the usual not very effective commission of inquiry (the returns to which, however, form a mine of information as to agrarian development in the Midlands at the time).

Another was the preparation of a memorandum for the Council concerning 'the cause in question before the Lords touching depopulation'.[3] The author professes to sum up the arguments for and against enclosure, and summarizes heavily in its favour. On military, social and economic grounds he can find little to say for the old system, and he asserts that enclosure need not necessarily cause depopulation which, he grants, 'admitteth noe defence'. Such enclosure as has already taken place could be 'redressed' either by the passing of new laws, or by the authority of the Council. A general survey of the champion counties of the country should be made, and each place should be bound to maintain a due proportion of its land in tillage, so:

'The poore man shalbe satisfied in his ende; Habitation; and the gentleman not hindred in his desier; Improvement.'

The gentleman certainly was not unduly hindered. Pamphlets of 1612 and 1636 make it clear that the process was continuing.[4] In 1632 when Philip Massinger painted (? from Sir Giles Mompesson) his portrait of Sir Giles Overreach, he did not draw wholly on imagination for the picture of the landlord justly called:

'Extortioner, tyrant, cormorant or intruder
On my poor neighbour's right or grand incloser
Of what was common to my private uses; . . .[5]

Enclosure and Agricultural and Moral Improvement

Many of the numerous and vocal agricultural propagandists of the time wholeheartedly urged enclosure. Some, however,

[3] This is printed as App. B to Archdeacon Cunningham's book above cited, II, ii.
[4] Cited with several others by Miss Leonard, *op. cit.*, p. 143.
[5] Massinger, P., *A New Way to pay Old Debts*, (1633), Act I, Sc. 1, ll. 143–6.

argued that in it steps must be taken for protecting the interests of the poor, for example Arthur Standish, writing in *The Commons' Complaint*, 1611, who hoped that enclosure need not necessarily involve conversion and depopulation. Gabriel Plattes, whose *Discovery of Infinite Treasure* appeared in 1639, anticipated the eighteenth-century argument that the poor actually benefited by enclosure, but even Plattes suggested that in every enclosure a cow common should be set aside for the poor. This was indeed fairly generally done in County Durham, where much enclosure took place about this time.

Conservatives arguing altogether against the change as it was carried on and as it was likely to be, were Robert Powell, whose pamphlet *Depopulation Arraigned* appeared in 1636, and a certain John Moore, a Leicestershire puritan parson who wrote against enclosure in 1612, and whose more famous son was the principal anti-enclosure propagandist of the middle of the century.[6] We discuss elsewhere the Government's rather feeble efforts to do something in response to all this agitation, and the unpleasant trail of finance which besmeared its agrarian policy. In 1649 Walter Blith, in his *English Improver*, stated very emphatically the case for enclosure. 'The open field farmers,' he says, 'are in dire poverty, and would be better off in Bridewell.'

During the Interregnum the controversy went on. Samuel Hartlib's *Legacie*, 1651, contains *inter alia* a letter by Robert Child, which puts the question 'Whether Commons do not rather make poore, by causing idleness than maintaine them: and such poore who are trained up rather for the Gallowes or beggary than for the Commonwealth's service'. To be quite fair one must admit that there seems sometimes to have been real substance in this argument. An examination of the Quarter Sessions records of Warwickshire for instances of rates-in-aid shows that in 1635–71 there were nineteen Warwickshire parishes which received or petitioned for a grant from neighbouring parishes, because of their exceptionally heavy burden in maintaining the poor. Seven of these were boroughs and

---

[6] Since, like everyone else who has written on this aspect of the subject since 1912, when R. H. Tawney's book appeared, I owe very much to Tawney, I venture to point out a trifling error in it. Tawney, p. 376, confuses this John with his more famous son and namesake, whose work is dealt with below. (There is another little error on p. 348 where his reference to Coke's *Institutes*, edn. 1644, taken from Miss Leonard, should be to Bk. III, p. 205.)

market towns, three others were suburbs of Coventry. Of the
rest one claimed relief because it was contributing to Ather-
stone, and another petitioned because of special circumstances
—plague. Of the remaining seven, four: Sambourne, Studley,
Tanworth, and Stretton-on-Dunsmore, certainly had extensive
wastes or heaths. The long history of the attempts to enclose
Sambourne Heath makes it clear that, while the Heath was
certainly a source of profit to the poor, the proportion of poor
in the village was still very high. It is not difficult to believe
that the opportunity of gaining squatting rights was an attraction to some of them.

Other writers, particularly some of the puritans, anticipated
the eighteenth-century discovery which Tawney unkindly but
not unjustly summarizes as this: that the poor are of two classes,
the industrious poor who are content to work for their betters,
and the idle poor who prefer to work for themselves. On the
other hand, a certain Henry Halhead in 1650 published
Inclosure Thrown Open, and in 1653 John Moore, son of the
John already mentioned, attacked enclosure in his *Crying Sin
of England in not Caring for the Poor*. He was answered by another
Leicestershire cleric, Joseph Lee, and these two carried out a
wordy warfare on the subject in pamphlets, and apparently in
sermons, which must have much enlivened the pulpits of
Leicestershire in the mid-seventeenth century.[7] However, the
Government had other matters to consider besides the agrarian
problem, and throughout the Commonwealth, apart from
rather spasmodic efforts by some of the Major-Generals, little
attention was given to it. In any case direct action of the
Diggers, among the extreme 'left' parties of the time, perhaps

---

[7] The Moore-Lee pamphlets are:

Moore, J., *The Crying Sin of England* . . . 1653. 'Pseudonismus' [apparently
    not Lee], *Considerations concerning Common Fields and Inclosures*, 1654.
Moore, J., *A Reply to a Pamphlet entitled Considerations* . . . 1656.
Lee, J., *Vindication of a Regulated Inclosure*, 1656.
'Pseudonismus', *A Vindication of the Considerations* . . . or a *Rejoynder to that
    Reply* . . . 1656.
Moore, J., *A Scripture Word against Inclosure*, 1656.

John Moore died in 1657. He duly appears in *D.N.B.* but Lee does not.
He was rector of Catthorpe, Leics., and the controversy arose from his
activity in enclosure there. Moore's second work was thought to be lost,
and is so described in Gonner, *op. cit.*, p. 160. There is, however, a copy in the
Bodleian (Godwyn Pamphlets 1118). For the Diggers see below, pp. 148–50.

tended, on the whole, to dissuade the state from taking measures to deal with a grievance which still existed, and which could have been redressed.

After the Restoration of 1660 there was little fear that the state would upset an influential class by interfering with the economic activities of its members. From about this time onwards writers also in general no longer argue the pros and cons of enclosure, or for that matter of engrossing, or of converting the peasant proprietor into a wage-earning labourer.

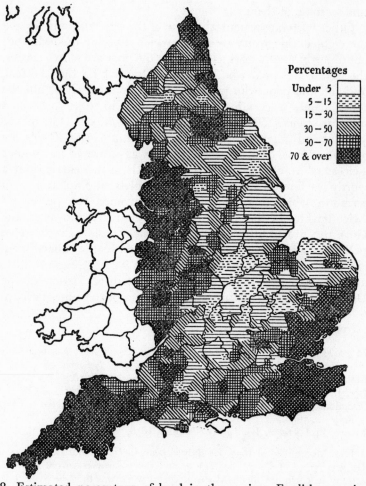

Percentages
Under 5
5 — 15
15 — 30
30 — 50
50 — 70
70 & over

8. Estimated percentage of land in the various English counties without common or open field *c.* 1700; *see p. 199*

All three alike are in general taken for granted. Church and state no longer fine or anathematize enclosers; the poor are apparently less vocal and much more amenable than previously (probably the Poor Law of 1662 has done something to show them their true place in a properly organized society!). The agrarian revolution which has been continuing in spasms for a couple of centuries or more now goes forward in great waves, engulfing in its progress the open-field system, the self-governing village, and often the peasant proprietors, the 'ancient and godly yeomanry of England'.

CHAPTER 8

GEORGIAN ENCLOSURE

FOR OUR PURPOSE we may consider the 'Georgian' era as beginning not in 1714 when the Elector became King. The operative date is rather, perhaps, 1660, when the impoverished squires returned from the Continent (having first-hand experience of continental farming methods) or perhaps better still 1688/9, when their sons established the parliamentary monarchy. This, in the very nature of things, was not at all disposed to any action which would affect adversely the economic interests of the dominant landed classes. There was now no thought of the power of the state being used to arrest the current of agrarian change. Very soon the enclosure movement went on by leaps and bounds. The motives behind it were, however, by no means all of them those of naked self-interest.

Agricultural progress

The experimental scientific study of agriculture had now begun. Change and improvement were in the air. The open-field system placed a substantial obstacle in the way of either experiment or improvement. Roots were now generally introduced as a field crop, and attention was drawn to the valuable results to be obtained by a thorough drainage of the subsoil. Turnips had been known, though probably only as a garden vegetable, in Shakespeare's day. Now swedes also were introduced. It was discovered that by folding sheep on them, and eating them on the land, the soil could be much enriched. So, clearly, it was desirable to grow roots as a field crop. It was difficult, however, to grow roots on open ground;[1] they were a crop that ripened

[1] It was not impossible, for in many open-field villages the unit of cultivation was the furlong rather than the field. An Act of 1773, below p. 194, made it legally possible to create a fourth field, given the consent of a three-quarter majority of the proprietors in number and value. There is abundant evidence firstly, that even before the passing of the Act, progressive village communities had agreed on the making of a fourth field and had, in fact been able to create such a field, and secondly, that the powers given by the Act were used much more widely than most writers on agrarian history have supposed.

only after the corn harvest had been gathered. From time immemorial, in an open field, one's neighbours' cattle had then been turned loose to graze over the stubbles; they would make short work of the roots. Similarly in the early seventeenth century it had been found possible to effect a great improvement in drainage methods. Formerly, drainage had been carried out by ploughing in ridge and furrow, and by carrying the water away in open 'hags', but by placing the drains underground, the subsoil would be kept at once much drier and a great deal warmer. Much sour, waterlogged land could be made productive, pasture improved, and the yield of arable land increased; but how could one introduce subsoil drains if one's estate lay in narrow selions, scattered all over the parish, and interspersed with similar selions belonging to scores of other proprietors—it would be quite impossible to secure any control of the outfalls. Both these problems were solved if enclosure was adopted.

Common rights would be commuted, and the land of each proprietor would be gathered in two or three complete blocks, which he might improve to his heart's content, without any interference from his more conservatively minded neighbours. From the 1660's onwards, then, the current of propaganda in favour of enclosure becomes stronger and stronger. In 1663 Samuel Fortrey argues that only by enclosure can land be used for that purpose for which it is naturally best fitted.[2] In 1677 Andrew Yarranton, who has already burst into verse in praise of clover (which of course could not easily fit in with a three-field system), shows how, given the new agriculture, we could 'outdo the Dutch without fighting, pay debts without money and set at work all the Poor of England'.[3]

John Worlidge's book, Leonard Meager's, Richard Blome's

[2] Fortrey, S., *England's Interest and Improvement*, 1663.
[3] Yarranton, A., *The Great Improvement of Lands by Clover*, Worcester, 1663.

> . . . give me the goose's quill
> That's fed with clover, and I'll try my skill
> But three-leaved grass soon yield a three-fold profit
> Three volumes may be writ in praises of it.

England's Improvement by Sea and Land, 1677–81.

Yarranton was an old Parliamentarian soldier who had been imprisoned in 1662 as suspected of implication in a Presbyterian plot. His biographer gives him the rather dubious distinction of being 'the founder of English political economy'.

and Timothy Nourse's all appeared 1667–1700.[4] Almost without exception, these and other agricultural writers of the day either take for granted the desirability of enclosure, or strongly recommend it. The most readable of them is John Houghton, who amid a wide variety of other interests, ranging from the inauguration of registry offices to the retailing of chocolate, published 1681–3 and 1692–1703 a periodical journal dealing with all kinds of political and economic subjects. In his *Collection of Letters for the Improvement of Husbandry and Trade* Houghton has much to say of the reclamation of commons and the enclosure of open fields. Typical references are: 'I cannot but admire that people should be so backward to *inclose*, which would be more worth to us than the mines of *Potosi* to the King of Spain', and even 'Given a general inclosure I would be content not to be drunk for ten years'.[5]

John Ogilby

The gentry were not slow to profit by the profusion of good advice which was showered upon them by the agricultural experts. John Ogilby compiled a great roadbook, *Britannia*, in 1675.[6] He marks enclosed roads / / open roads ╎ ╎ and he

[4] Worlidge, J., *Systema Agriculturae*, 1669. Meager, L., *The Mystery of Husbandry*, 1697 (with, as one of its many subtitles, 'the great Advantage of Inclosures'). Blome, R., *The Gentleman's Recreation*, 1686. (Blome is a compiler rather than an original writer; his *Britannia* is quite famous in another connexion, and his editions of Guillim's *Heraldrie*, 1660 and 1679, are still valued.) Nourse, T., *Campania Fœlix*, or a Discourse of the Benefits and Improvements of Husbandry, 1700. (Nourse is another interesting man, an Oxonian high-churchman who eventually joined the Roman communion.)

For further details of all the agricultural writers above mentioned, as of others before or after this time, there are two or three critical bibliographies readily available: McDonald, D., *Agricultural Writers*, 1200–1800; the Ministry of Agriculture *Library Catalogue* 24/117, 1930; the Rothamsted Library *Catalogue*, 2nd edn. 1940; and Fussell, G. E., *The Old English Farming Books*, 'Fitzherbert to Tull', 1523–1739; 1947, 'Tull to the Board of Agriculture' 1731–93, 1950.

[5] Houghton, like Yarranton, enjoys a rather questionable celebrity, for he was also, if not quite the inventor, the great pioneer of modern newspaper advertising. His *Collection of Letters for the Improvement of Husbandry and Trade* appeared 1681–3, and a second series 1692–1703. The second series was reissued 1727 in three volumes by Richard Bradley, the Cambridge professor of botany whose career came to a somewhat ignominious end.

[6] John Ogilby was Cosmographer to Charles II. He published in 1675 *Britannia or an Illustration of the Kingdom of England. . . .* This was often reprinted by later topographers, with alterations and modernizations

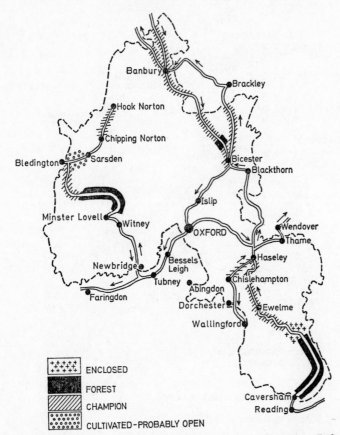

ENCLOSED

FOREST

CHAMPION

CULTIVATED-PROBABLY OPEN

9. Open and enclosed land in Oxfordshire *c.* 1540 (based on Leland);
see p. 199

gives a great many strip maps showing all the major highways
of England. On the reasonable assumption that in general
enclosed roads traversed land generally enclosed, unfenced
roads went over commons, wastes, heaths and open fields, it is
possible to trace from his book fairly accurately how far enclosure had gone by 1675. Comparison of Ogilby's maps with
those based on the notes of John Leland, who had ridden
through the country in Henry VIII's time, makes it clear how

which were not always improvements. A facsimile reprint in colour (p.p.)
was issued by a commercial concern (not of publishers) in 1939, and distributed as a gift to their main customers in the motor trade. It is sometimes
possible to borrow, buy or even beg a copy from a leading local garage. A
map of the whole country, based on Ogilby, is appended to Gonner *op. cit.*

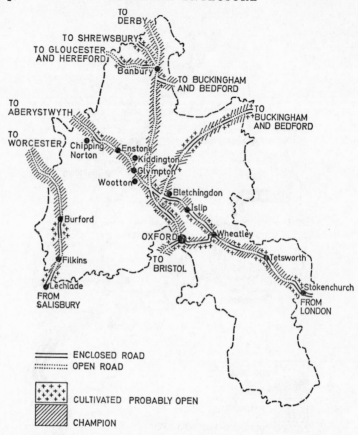

10. Open and enclosed roads in Oxfordshire *c.* 1675 (based on Ogilby); *see p. 200*

largely enclosure had taken place, though also what extensive areas still remained open.[7] Ogilby may sometimes be checked from the notes of Celia Fiennes, a lady of Newton Toney, Wilts., who also went through the countryside in the last years of the century, and who left detailed notes on the agrarian state of much of the country she passed through.[8]

The controversy on the rights and wrongs of enclosure broke out again a little after the middle of the eighteenth century,

[7] A map based on Leland's notes is to be found in Slater (App. 2 below). A better one could be made by anyone who would work through the revised version of Leland's text ed. Toulmin Smith, Miss L., 1907–10.

[8] Ed. Morris, C., *The Journeys of Celia Fiennes* [*c.* 1685–1703], 1947.

perhaps under the influence of a series of high corn prices in the 1760's, and it lasted throughout the 1770's and 1780's. Nearly all the controversialists admitted the economic gain. The most that the anti-enclosure party could suggest was that this was more than outweighed by the social loss. The adverse social consequences of enclosure are much stressed in an interesting pamphlet by David Davies, the rector of Cookham, Berks., *The Case of the Labourers in Husbandry*, 1795.[9] According to Davies:

> 'for a dubious economic benefit, an amazing number of people have been reduced from a comfortable state of partial independence to the precarious condition of mere hirelings, who when out of work immediately come on the parish.'

Of the twenty-odd pamphlets which appeared about this time,[10] among the most interesting is the *Remarks on Inclosure* 'by a Country Farmer', 1786. The author takes the view that enclosure is a swindle, pushed by the gentry and the farmers at the expense of the cottagers and labourers. It is often carried out upon solemnly sworn testimony which is outrageously false, it always means consolidation, perhaps twenty tenancies being consolidated into four, and it therefore means depopulation. Because of enclosure many villages that formerly contained five hundred souls have been reduced to eighty or even forty.

A very different point of view is taken by John Howlett, rector of Great Dunmow and of Great Baddow, Essex, but although he writes as an advocate of enclosure, he admits the charge of depopulation. He instances indeed Wistow and Foston, Leics., which are worse examples of depopulation than

[9] Davies, D., *The Case of the Labourers in Husbandry stated and considered*, 1795. Davies was rector of Cookham, according to *D.N.B.* also of Barkham, Berks. It is particularly interesting to have this testimony at just this time from Berkshire, a heavily pauperized county. The unfortunate Speenhamland System was (invented in Buckinghamshire Jan. 1795 and) developed in Berkshire May 1795. Cholesbury, Bucks., where perhaps its worst results were manifested a generation later, is quite near. In fact all the three villages named lie close together, and none of them is very far from Aylesbury and Newbury, where the magistrates made their well-intentioned but truly disastrous decision. Of Speenhamland and Poor Law matters generally there is a short account in my *Parish Chest*, Cambridge, 1946 and edns., pp. 187–239.

[10] There is a convenient table of these in Ernle, *op. cit.*, p. 303.

anything quoted by the opposition writers. These villages have been reduced respectively from thirty-four or thirty-five habitations to three homes and one respectively. Nevertheless, Howlett argues that in general enclosure is justifiable, and indeed necessary.[12] Henry Homer, rector of Birdingbury, Warws., wrote a pamphlet in 1766, advising enclosurers how to set about their undertaking.[13] He sums up (on the whole very fairly) the cases for and against enclosure, but concludes that in most instances the arguments in favour have an over-whelming preponderance. He offers some very reasonable and fair suggestions as to the measures which are to be taken for ascertaining every one's proportion of open land, and for securing to him a proper proportion of enclosed lands. Homer's work is very valuable to all who wish to obtain a 'close up' view of enclosure at work in the eighteenth century.

After the 1780's little more is heard of the case for open-field agriculture and the maintenance of commons. In general, the writers of the period take it for granted that enclosure has come and come to stay. Occasional political theorists criticize the measures which have to be adopted for achieving the change, and suggest rather late in the day the steps which ought to have been taken in order to secure that it should be carried out with a maximum of efficiency, and a minimum of hardship. But that change had to come, almost all are agreed. Arthur Young and William Marshall, the two great agricultural theorists of the latter part of the eighteenth century, are very much at one on this point, however much they differ upon others.[14] Young's work, in particular, teems with denunciations of the 'Goths and Vandals' of open-field farmers, and with suggestions for the statutory measures which should be adopted for liquidating them at the earliest possible moment.

[12] Howlett, J., *Enquiry into the Influence . . . of Enclosures*, 1786; *Enclosures a Cause of Improved Agriculture*, 1787.

[13] This is Henry Homer the elder, 1719–91. He often appears as an enclosure commissioner in the MS. enclosure awards of various counties. His pamphlet is '*An Essay upon the Method of Ascertaining the Shares of Proprietors upon . . . Inclosure . . .* 1766.

[14] Full accounts of the works of both Marshall and Young appear in the bibliographies cited. Between them they wrote enough works on agriculture to fill a hand-cart. Marshall planned the Board of Agriculture (below) and was not pleased when Young became its Secretary. One result of this was his very convenient digest and summary of all the County Reports (below, App. 1, p. 177), which appeared in six volumes as *Review of the Reports*, York, 1808–17, and which serves as a convenient guide to the series.

When the Board of Agriculture was established by William Pitt in 1793, almost its first undertaking was to commission the preparation of a series of reports on the agriculture of the various counties in England. In general these exist in two forms, the quarto drafts circulated by the Board in 1793 and 1794, and the octavo revised versions published from 1796 to 1817.[15] The reader who is concerned with the agriculture of any particular county, as it was a century and a half ago, may be referred with confidence for some very interesting reading to the two or more *General Views . . .* of the shire concerned. However much the writers differ upon other points, almost as one man they recommend more and cheaper enclosure as the remedy for a host of rural ills. The ninety-odd volumes are almost monotonous in their reiteration of the point that agricultural improvement has come through enclosure, and that more enclosure must take place before any substantial further progress is to be looked for. Tithing in kind is the only other mediaeval survival comparable with the existence of open fields and commons in the hindrances which it offers to improvement. Young, like many other theorists of the time, considered that both these evils should be dealt with simultaneously, the open fields and commons being enclosed, and the tithes commuted at the same time for allotments of land or for corn rents.

Some Statistics

Actually many millions of acres were enclosed (and much of them made tithe-free) about this time. The best available statistics suggest that altogether from *c.* 1700 to the 1890's some six and a half million acres were enclosed, the amounts as estimated by Slater being as shown in the table on page 88.[16]

Slater's statistics are certainly an understatement. They take no account whatever of the land enclosed under the General Acts of 1836 and 1840, and only partial account of that enclosed under the General Acts of 1845 *et seq.* Neither they nor my revised figures make any allowance whatever for land enclosed by private agreement. Different authorities estimate this as at various periods anything from '3 to 5 p.c.' to 'a half to five-sevenths' of the amount enclosed by parliamentary means, i.e.

[15] See App. 1 below.

[16] These are Slater's figures *op. cit.*, pp. 140-7, as summarized by Johnson (see below, App. 2).

(not very satisfactorily) anything from another 300,000 acres to another four or five million![17] It is quite certain at least that there were enclosed in England in some 5,400 individual enclosures during the eighteenth and nineteenth centuries, under nearly 4,200 acts and under the various General enclosure acts, more than seven million acres. About a third of them were common

PERIOD	COMMON FIELD AND SOME WASTE		WASTE ONLY		TOTAL	
	Acts	*Acres* (1,000s)	*Acts*	*Acres* (1,000s)	*Acts*	*Acres* (1,000s)
1700–60	152	238	56	75	208	313
1761–1801	1,479	2,429	521	752	2,000	3,181
1802–44	1,075	1,610	808	939	1,883	2,549
1845 and after	164 (awards)	187	508 (awards)	335	672 (awards)	522
TOTAL	2,870	4,464	1,893	2,101	4,763	6,565

My revised figures are (*circa*):

| | 3,200 | 4,700 | 2,200 | 2,300 | 5,400 | 7,000 |

and waste. Seven million acres is rather less than the gross area of eight English counties—the four largest, the West and North Ridings of Yorkshire, Lincolnshire and Devonshire; and the four smallest, Bedfordshire, Huntingdonshire, Middlesex and Rutland. This gives some idea of the extent of the movement, and the effect it must have had on the rural population.

The Deserted Village

What they thought of it is difficult to say. The peasant was rarely brilliant in either the oral or the literary expression of his

[17] These wildly divergent guesses are made, respectively by Gonner, p. 52 and Slater, pp. 191–2. A great deal more work on the subject is needed before any reasoned estimate may be offered, and I cannot commit myself further than in stating my general agreement with Gonner, cited elsewhere (p. 53). He notes here that in the earlier period of enclosure the change was normally by agreement, not act (in fact there were no enclosures by *ad hoc* act until 1530—the Thames marshes, etc., above, p. 50, fn. 4), or, as some scholars would prefer to reckon, until 1 Jac. 1 *Public* c. 30 (1603). Certainly enclosure by agreement was less common in later times, when the process of working by act-and-award had been worked out, but there are well-recorded instances as late as the nineteenth century, and even a few rather dubious ones in the twentieth.

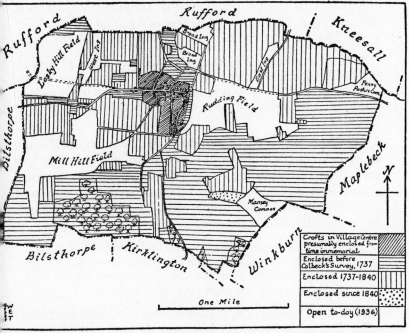

11. Piecemeal enclosure of Eakring, Notts. *ante* 1737—*post* 1840;
see p. 200

thoughts and emotions. Such contemporary writings as are
available are usually the work of members of a very different
class in society, who have tried to project themselves into the
peasant mind. The very neat epigram of 1821 on the common
and the goose is well known:

> The fault is great in man or woman
> Who steals a goose from off a common,
> But what can plead that man's excuse,
> Who steals a common from a goose.[18]

Rather more elegant verses on the same subject are not
lacking, and of these the best are to be found in *The Deserted
Village*.[19] Critics have often claimed that this village existed

[18] This seems to have first appeared in print in *The Tickler* (Magazine),
1 Feb. 1821.

[19] Goldsmith, O., *The Deserted Village*, 1770. *Dedication* and ll. 307–10.
There are, of course, in the works of John Clare several very touching
references to enclosures which had come within his own experience in
Northamptonshire: see, for example, 'The Fallen Elm', 'Remembrances',
'Enclosure'.

only in Goldsmith's imagination—that the village in its days of
prosperity is an English one, in its time of decay an Irish one, and
so on. The poet anticipates these arguments in his *Dedication*:

> 'I sincerely believe all I have written. I have taken all possible
> pains in my country excursions, for these four or five years past,
> to be certain of what I allege, and all my views and inquiries have
> led me to believe those miseries real, which I here attempt to
> display.'

A careful reading of Goldsmith shows that he refers, specifically
or by inference, to all the ill-effects which for centuries had
been alleged to result from enclosure: depopulation, extensive
tillage, land engrossing, imparcation, as well as to enclosure
itself, both that of open arable fields and that of commons.
As for the dispossessed peasant:

> 'If to some common's fenceless limits stray'd
> He drives his flock to pick the scanty blade,
> Those fenceless fields the sons of wealth divide,
> And even the bare-worn common is denied.'

With some justification, a Swiss scholar said in the land of his
exile: 'You tell me you have improved the land, but what have
you done with the labourers?'[20] As to this last, it seems clear that
the dispossession of the small landed proprietor—before or after
enclosure—was usual. The degradation of the labourer after the
loss of his common 'rights' was very usual. The actual depopulation of the countryside following eighteenth century enclosure
was more exceptional, though there are examples of it. It is,
however, concerning this last that another more usual criticism
of enclosure was offered, then and now. It was not without
reason that a landowner, whom no less an authority than Karl
Marx styled an exceptionally tender-hearted one, contem-
plated the desolation he had made. 'It is a melancholy thing
to stand alone in one's country', said Lord Leicester, when
complimented on the completion of Holkham. 'I look around,
and not a house is to be seen but mine. I am the giant of Giant
Castle, and have eaten up all my neighbours.'[21]

[20] Sismondi, J. C. L. S. de, 1773–1842. He had come to England in
1793 expecting to see the labourers settled on the reclaimed commons, but
found them in fact in the workhouses. Garnier, R., *Annals of the British
Peasantry*, 1895.

[21] *Das Kapital*, 'Everyman' trans. by E. and C. Paul, ed. G. D. H. Cole,
1930, II, 767.

CHAPTER 9

THE PROCESS OF PARLIAMENTARY
ENCLOSURE: (A)

Parliamentary Proceedings, with an appended Note on Enclosure Acts

I HAVE DELIBERATELY made this chapter and its immediate
successor much more detailed than the other ones in the
book, and I have concluded each, pages 103–6 and 115–20,
with some practical suggestions on where prints of acts and
manuscript copies of awards may be found. This is in the hope
that the interested reader will accept only provisionally the
generalizations of all works on the subject, as set forth in
Appendix II (most of all, perhaps, mine), and may feel inclined to investigate the matter for himself in his own parish or
neighbourhood, and from his own local records in print and
manuscript. For this is a branch of history lending itself very
well to original work by the enlightened amateur, and until
the results of a great many more detailed local investigations
are available, the necessarily more eclectic studies of the
national historian must often rest upon a very insecure foundation.

Clearly it is not without reason that historians have criticized
very strongly the enclosures by private act in the eighteenth
and nineteenth centuries.[1] Numerous well-known works are full
of strictures on the movement, the aims of its promoters, the
means by which they contrived to put these aims in practice,
and the agrarian revolution generally, alike in its causes and in
its consequences. One historian is certain that the Parliamentary proceedings were a mere mockery. 'Parliament was all for
them [the wealthier landowners]. Did not their own man-
datories, their friends and relatives sit in the House? The heads
of the ancient nobility in the House of Lords, as also the many
country squires in the House of Commons, were the representatives of the great landed interests.'[2] Another pair of eloquent and
learned writers go into more detail, and give instances supporting their view that the parliamentary proceedings were a mere
formality, gone through mechanically as a preliminary to the

[1] E.g. Hasbach, see below App. 2, Eng. Trans. 1908, pp. 61–63.

[2] Mantoux, P., *La Revolution Industrielle*, Eng. Trans. 1928, new edn. 1961,
166–7.

members confiscating the meagre properties of Lazarus in order to extend the broad estates of Dives.[3]

They follow this with instances of unjust clauses in enclosure acts, which they say could never have passed through a House fairly constituted or a truly representative committee, and they contrast the treatment meted out in committee to counter-petitions submitted by influential persons, with that afforded to similar counter-petitions submitted by the poor and friendless. The indictment is a heavy one, and the instances quoted, for example, by the Hammonds, and stated at length in their Appendix, show that in some instances it is justified.[4] It is no part of my purpose here to enter into the controversy, in which there is a good deal to be said on both sides. It is, however, proper to direct the reader's attention to the main unexplored (printed) source of information upon some of the many interesting and important points on which discussion has arisen. Given this, if he is interested in the parliamentary enclosure of any particular parish, or in the movement generally in any specific county or other area, he will be able to look into the matter to some extent for himself, and to come to a conclusion based on first-hand knowledge of a principal source of information on the subject.[5]

On many of the main points at issue such an invaluable source of factual material is the *House of Commons Journals*, a print of which is of course to be found in any reputable major library. The sheer bulk of these—for the period 1760–1810 alone they run to forty-eight substantial folio volumes—means that a systematic and detailed exploration of them would be a very onerous undertaking. It is, however, quite possible to use them for individual inquiries as to specific villages or larger geographical areas of England, or of course for the whole country during a limited time-span. Before, however, one can even venture to abstract data from the *Journals*, it is necessary to understand something of Commons' procedure. Without this the inquirer may very well spend much time examining the *Journals* records of stages which normally afford very little information to the student, at the expense of neglecting those

[3] The Hammonds, see below App. 2, compare below p. 101, fn. 8.

[4] *Op cit.*, App. A, pp. 333–97.

[5] Much of the text below is based on my *Nottinghamshire Parliamentary Enclosures*, above noted, Preface, fn. 2. There is another treatment of this aspect of the matter in *Econ. Journ.* LIV, 14, Apr. 1944, pp. 75–94.

for which the *Journals'* records are often full of valuable information, useful alike to the sociologist, the historian, and the economist. Add to this the fact that the technicalities of Commons procedure are a study in themselves, and one in which the outsider is very likely to be misled. Clearly some account of the manner in which the House dealt with enclosure petitions and bills must precede any attempt to interpret the records of the proceedings at various stages.

House of Commons Procedure—The Journal

Let us consider then the information to be obtained from the Commons' *Journal*, in the order of the stages in the proceedings, as they are chronicled in that invaluable record.

The Petition

The Petition to the House is recorded thus:

(Date) The Petition of . . . (often *the Petition* of the Lord of the Manor, and the *Humble Petition* of the Incumbent and the other proprietors) *the Persons whose Names are thereunto subscribed being Owners and Proprietors of Lands, Messuages, Tenements and Persons interested in the Open Arable Fields, Meadows, Pastures, Commons, and Waste Grounds within the Parish (Manor, Lordship, Liberty) of . . . in the County of . . . was presented to the House and read. Shewing that the Petitioners are possessed of certain Lands . . .* (as above) *and that the said* (Lands etc. . . . .) *are intermixed and dispersed in small parcels and in their present situation are incapable of any considerable improvement, but if the same* (Lands etc. . . .), *were divided, inclosed, and allotted it would be very much to the advantage of the said Petitioners and of the Public, but as such* (Division etc. . . .) *cannot be effected without an Act of Parliament therefore praying that Leave may be granted to bring in a Bill for the Purpose of* (dividing etc. . . .) *the said* (Lands etc. . . .) *under such regulations as to the House shall seem requisite.*

Ordered that Leave be granted to bring in a Bill pursuant to the Prayer of the said Petition, and that . . . and . . . (generally two local Members) *do prepare and bring in the same.*

The earlier petitions are, as a rule, markedly more detailed than are the later ones. Almost invariably they give fairly full particulars both of the petitioner(s) and of the lands in respect of which the petition is submitted. As a rule the petition is drafted with the support of the lord of the manor, generally with that of the incumbent, often with that of the impropriator when there is one, and with that also of the other principal

proprietors. After about 1800, for some reason which does not
appear, the carefully graded list of lord of the manor, patron,
rector or impropriator, vicar, esquires, gentlemen, yeomen, and
other freeholders, becomes the much less informative 'several
proprietors', 'the owners of lands, tythes and common rights',
'the landowners and persons interested', 'several freeholders
and others', etc. It does not seem that this is due to any change
in the standing orders of the House, since there is no record of
this to be found, and since also detailed petitions sometimes
occur in the later part of the period, just as, more rarely, those
with little detail are found in the earlier one. Instances of
enclosures carried out on the petition of one or two petitioners
only are very exceptional. From what one knows of the
eighteenth century, it is not surprising that on the rare occasions
when a petition is submitted without the support of the lord of
the manor, it is very unusual for it to come to anything.

Very often the petition asks for powers other than those
relating to enclosure, and occasionally other powers are sought
in an amending or supplementary petition. Of these the most
usual are those having reference to tithe commutation.[6]
Throughout the Midlands, tithes are very generally commuted
at enclosure. In general, the counties where tithe commutation
under enclosure acts is most usual are those where the average
area affected by each act is fairly considerable, and where the
land to be enclosed consists mainly of open-field arable. Very
often acts contain specific powers as to the exchange of old
enclosures in order to round off each proprietor's estate.
Because of the omission to include a clause of this sort, an act
for a Derbyshire parish in 1812 has to be followed by another
separate act passed later in the same session. A great many acts
for Lincolnshire, Somerset, Norfolk, etc., contain drainage
provisions.

As noted above, many early acts confirm existing agreements.
Some acts of this type themselves make the allotments. Others
appoint commissioners to do this in the usual way, and to
embody their decisions in an award. Often these acts relate to
parishes where the greater part of the land is held by but one or
two proprietors, and where, therefore, a measure of agreement

[6] There are in Gonner, pp. 315–17, not very satisfactory lists of the
counties where tithe commutation was or was not usually carried out at the
same time as enclosure. In very general terms one may say that in the
Midlands it was, elsewhere it was not.

as to enclosure is fairly easily obtainable. (Probably in most such parishes the enclosure has already been carried out by agreement only, without an act of any kind.) Sometimes these agreements have been executed quite shortly before the act was passed, elsewhere the act may follow a century or more after the agreement. Clearly here the agreement has long ago been put in operation, but doubt has lately arisen concerning its validity. As we have noted above, the early enclosures of Leicestershire give several good illustrations of agreements and acts of this sort. Unless the student of any particular enclosure clearly understands whether or not the act is one of this type, he may very well spend much time and energy in trying to run to earth an enclosure award which cannot be found—because it does not exist!

Bill Ordered

Generally the bill is ordered as soon as the petition has been presented and read. Occasionally, however, when there is known to be strong local opposition, or when the standing orders of the House have not been complied with, the petition is referred to a committee, and the bill is not ordered unless and until the committee has made a satisfactory report. The members ordered to 'prepare and bring in the same', like those reporting the bill at a later stage, are usually the county members, or those for some neighbouring constituency. There is no rule against their being personally interested in the lands intended to be enclosed. There are indeed a fair number of petitioners who also 'bring in the bill pursuant to the prayer' of their own petitions. To modern eyes it is rather surprising to find such instances as the bills for Basford, Notts., 1774, where the Earl of Lincoln helps to prepare the bill brought in to the petition of the Most Noble Henry Duke of Newcastle (the Earl of Lincoln's father), or Worksop, Notts., 1782, prepared and brought in by the Earl of Surrey, when the principal petitioners have been Charles, Duke of Norfolk, and the Rev. Philip Howard, presumably a relative. The eighteenth century sees nothing unfair or even unseemly in such an arrangement, however strange it may appear to modern eyes. The acts are almost always private acts, and the members promoting them are usually friends or relatives of the petitioners, just as in the other main classes of private act, those for divorce, estate settlement, barring entails, etc.

Bill presented and read

The record of the presentation and first reading of the bill rarely contains much of interest. It is usually in some such words as:

(Date) *Mr. . . . presented on behalf of the Committee the Bill for . . . (Dividing etc.) The same was read a First Time. Ordered that it be read a Second Time.*

When a petition against the bill has been submitted to the House it is usual to refer it to the Committee on the Bill, generally with the instruction that both petitioners and counter-petitioners be allowed to state their cases by counsel.

Bill committed

The next record is that of the committal of the bill:

(Date) *The Bill for* (Dividing etc. . . .) *was read a Second Time. Ordered that it be referred to* (a Committee generally consisting of members for the County and for neighbouring Counties) *who shall meet for the First Time in . . . on . . .*

It is against this aspect of eighteenth-century Parliamentary proceedings upon enclosure bills that the strongest modern criticism has been levelled.[7] Various authorities say that even if a Parliamentary committee composed largely of substantial landed proprietors could ever be wholly disinterested on questions affecting land, the system was open to abuses. 'Enclosure bills were passed through the House without sufficient enquiry.' 'No member of Parliament not directly interested would take any notice of the Bill in its passage through the House.' 'After the second reading a committee, selected by the promoters of the Bill, was nominated to deal with it . . . petitions might be received against the Bill, but unless the opposition included some large landowner, little notice was taken of them.'[8]

[7] E.g. by Hasbach, p. 62, the Hammonds, pp. 45–46.
[8] Thus in 1781, and again in 1784, 'someone' had the audacity to petition for the enclosure of East Leake, Notts., without the concurrence of Sir Thomas Parkyns, Squire, and sole owner of the next parish, Bunny, and having also substantial interests in Leake. The petition, of course, came to nothing. Another petition, 8 Feb. 1798, had Sir Thomas's support, and the enclosure was completed before 10th June 1799 (Sir Thomas's brother-in-law being one of the commissioners).

VII Exchange of selions in 1760 as a preliminary to enclosure
at Tideswell, Derbys., enclosed 1807–21; *see p. 208*

To Lieutenant Colonel The Right Honorable Lord Churchill or other the Officers commanding the 1st Regiment of Oxfordshire Yeomanry Cavalry.

It having been proved on Oath before us the — — undersigned Justices of the Peace for the County of Oxford that riots and disturbances have lately taken place at Otmoor in this County and in the neighbourhood thereof and that there is good and sufficient reason to apprehend that persons will riotously and — tumultuously assemble together at or in the neighbourhood of Otmoor on Monday the Twenty sixth instant or at some time thereabout These are to require you the Officer commanding the 1st Regiment of Oxon Yeomanry Cavalry to cause a sufficient body of private soldiers of your Regiment with the requisite number of Officers and non Commissioned Officers the whole not being less in number than One hundred men forthwith to assemble and proceed to Islip in this County or to some other adjacent Town or place there to remain subject to the order and direction of the Civil Power and to be aiding in the suppression of any riot and tumult which may happen. Given under our hands this 24th day of September 1831

H. H. Ashhurst
J. W. Henley
Chas Peers
J. Bertie

and that the Civil Power now at the disposal of the Magistrates is incompetent to the Preservation of the Peace —

VIII Popular opposition to enclosure of Otmoor, Oxon., 1831 (enclosure discussed and in operation 1788–1829); *see p. 209*

It is sometimes asserted that the system of 'opening the committees'—i.e. carrying a resolution that 'all who attend shall have voices'—clearly means that if the county members are hostile to a particular scheme, the promoters call for an open committee, which, of course, they pack with their friends. Alternatively, if the county members support the scheme, but some powerful personage holds that his interests or those of his friends have not been sufficiently considered in the division of the spoil, he will call for 'all to have voices', and so compel the promoters to satisfy his claims. Some colour is lent to this argument by the speeches of Henry Aglionby and the Earl of

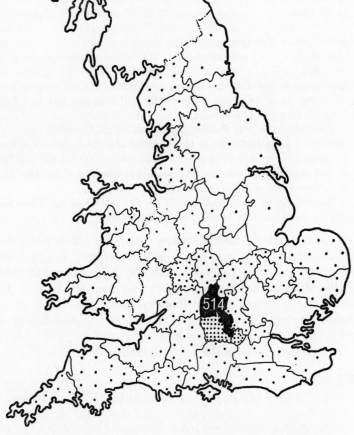

12. Constituencies of M.P.s concerned with Oxfordshire Parliamentary enclosures 1696–1853; *see p. 201*

Lincoln, in 1844 and 1845 respectively. According to these (the committees) 'were attended only by Honourable Members who were interested in the bill in their being Lords of the Manor, and the rights of the poor had frequently been taken away . . .', and 'in nineteen cases out of twenty Committees of this House sitting on private Bills neglected the rights of the poor'.[9]

Petition against Bill

Very occasionally one finds a petition against the bill:

(Date) *A petition of . . . and . . . on behalf of Themselves and Others, being Owners and Proprietors of Messuages and Cottages, and of Lands etc. and Common Right over and upon them within the* (parish etc. . . .) *in the County of . . . was presented to the House and read. Setting forth That the Petitioners are Owners and Proprietors etc. . . . and taking Notice that a Bill is now depending for* (dividing etc. . . .) *the said* (Lands etc. . . .) *and alleging that the Petitioners conceive that If the said Bill shall pass into Law, the Same will be greatly injurious and detrimental to their Estates, and desiring that the Petitioners may be heard by themselves, or their Counsel against the said Bill, and have such Relief as to the House shall seem meet.*

Ordered that the said Petition be forwarded to the Committee (etc. . . .) *and that it be an Instruction to the Committee that the Petitioners be heard by themselves, or their Counsel upon their Petition against the said Bill, if they shall think fit. Ordered that Counsel be admitted at the same Time in Favour of the said Bill against the said Petition.*

Sometimes it was: *Ordered that the Petition lie on the Table until Report Stage, and then be considered by the House.*

In the relatively rare instances when the bill is petitioned against, the counter-petition is usually referred to the Committee on the Bill, generally with the instruction that both parties shall be heard personally or by counsel. In very few cases do the dissentient smallholders avail themselves of the House's permission to indulge in the expensive luxury of briefing counsel to state their case.

The Report Stage of the bill is thus recorded:

Bill reported

(Date) *Mr. . . . reported from the Committee to whom the Bill for* (dividing etc. . . . Lands etc. . . .) *and the Petition of . . . and . . . on Behalf of Themselves and Others . . . against the said Bill have been*

[9] Dr. and Mrs. Hammond quoting Hansard, 5 June 1844, 1 May 1845.

referred That the Committee have examined the Allegations of the said Bill and found them to be correct, and that the Provisions of the Standing Orders of the House have been complied with, and that the Proprietors concerned have given their Consent to the Satisfaction of the Committee (except Proprietors whose Property in the Lands intended to be inclosed is assessed to the Land Tax at l . . . s . . . d . . . per Annum, who being applied to refused to sign the Bill, and also except the Proprietors of Lands who declared themselves neuter, and also except the persons who could not be met with, or on being applied to returned no answer) . . . and that the Whole of Property intended to be inclosed is assessed to the Land Tax at l . . . s . . . d . . . per Annum, and that no person appeared before the Committee to oppose the Bill (or very rarely that . . . and . . . Petitioners against the said Bill have been heard by their Counsel, or occasionally, have declined being heard by their Counsel), and that the Committee have been through the Bill and made certain Amendments thereto, which they have directed him to report to the House, and he read the Report in his place, and afterwards delivered the Bill with the Amendments in at the Clerk's Table, when the Amendments were once read throughout, and then a second Time one by one, and upon the Question severally put thereon were agreed to by the House.

Ordered that the Bill with the Amendments be ingrossed.

(Occasionally) A Clause was offered to be added to the Bill by way of Ryder to permit . . . And the said Clause was twice read, and upon the Question put thereon was agreed to by the House to stand part of the Bill.

Very usually the bill is reported without amendment, or with amendments which (? because of their relatively small importance) are not recorded in the *Journals*. When the committee has made its report, unless the entire body of proprietors is unanimously in favour (or at any rate not sufficiently opposed to it to decline to sign the bill) the inquirer is certain to find interesting data in the *Journals'* records of this stage of the proceedings. The committee has to state whether or not the House's standing orders have been complied with, and if not why not. Occasionally, for good reason given, the committee report that although the orders have not been complied with, the promoters should be dispensed from the consequences of their neglect.

Much more interesting and more commonly found are the data arising from another part of the committee's functions. This is the duty either of stating that there is no opposition, or if there is any of assessing its amount. The committee is concerned, of course, with the *value* of the opposition, not its numerical strength. As the Hammonds put it, 'The suffrages were not counted but weighed'.[10] No *quantum* of consent is ever imposed, either by statute or standing order. There is, however, a general understanding that a three-quarters or four-fifths majority of the proprietors in value is necessary if the enclosure is to proceed. Probably a fair proportion of the instances in which the bill reaches committee stage but is never reported, are due to the discovery by the promoters that this three-fourths or four-fifths majority cannot be obtained; just as possibly most of the much commoner instances of a petition being read and a bill ordered, but the bill never reaching the first reading, are due to the applicants discovering in good time that this proportion of consents cannot be arrived at, and therefore dropping the proceedings at this earlier stage before any further expense has been involved.

Part of the committee's duty is to report that the proprietors concerned 'have given their consent to the same to the satisfaction of the committee'. As to the units in which the proprietors' estates shall be reckoned there is apparently no rule, and not even any generally accepted understanding. The proportion of consents is given in acres, yardlands, oxgangs, common rights, toftsteads, messuages and cottages having right of common, sheep-gates, horse commons, cow commons, beast-gates, and all imaginable combinations of these units; in total rack rental value of land having common right, in rateable value, and in quarterly or annual assessment to the land tax. It has been suggested that on occasion the committee chose which of these units would show the larger majority in favour of the enclosure proposals. However, it would not be easy to parallel one often-quoted example of a bill being reported with a rather narrow majority in favour of the scheme, then re-committed and again reported, when the quantum of consent, *expressed in different units*, shows an enhanced majority in its favour.[11]

One is not surprised to find that the preponderance of opinion in favour of enclosure is almost invariably much stronger when expressed in acres, oxgangs, ploughlands, land-tax assessment, etc., than when expressed (in respect of the same enclosure) in toftsteads, or common-right cottages: i.e. that the *property* of the parish may be strongly in favour of the enclosure

[10] *Op. cit.*, p. 49.

[11] p. 51. This was in the enclosure of Histon and Impington, Cambs., 1801–6.

when the *population*, especially the smaller proprietors, are not. Often the weight of opinion in favour of enclosure is 10, 20, or even 40, 50, 100 or 200 to one, as expressed in property units of various kinds.

It is in the records of Report Stage that one finds, especially in the earlier reports up to 1780 or thereabouts, interesting little personal notes explaining why some proprietors decline to sign the bill:

'She was an old woman, and the inclosure would be of little service in her lifetime (but her sons are both for it)', 'he had not the naming of a commissioner and surveyor,' 'had always been against inclosures but assents to the bill, and desires he may name a commissioner, which he did, and the rest of the proprietors consented to his nomination', 'thought the inclosure would be of no service to them, and had rather it remained uninclosed', 'refused to sign the bill, although many of them made no material objection thereto', or 'said they would neither meddle nor make'.

Almost always the committee report that they have made several amendments to the bill. Amendments made by the House at report stage seem to have been comparatively rare, and such as are recorded (most are not) are clearly of minor importance. Generally the reporting of the bill is followed by the order that it be engrossed. Occasionally, if many amendments are necessary or if there is much influential local opposition, the bill is re-committed, and the order that it be engrossed comes after it has been reported the second time.

Bill passed: King's Consent signified

Sometimes the next stage is that of having the King's consent signified. This stage in the proceedings has, of course, no connexion with the royal assent to the bill. It occurs only when the Crown is interested in the lands to be enclosed, generally as landowner, patron, or impropriator. As a rule at the third reading the bill is passed:

(Date) *The Bill for* Dividing etc. . . . *was read a Third Time, and it was resolved that the said bill do pass (with certain Amendments viz. . . . and that the Title be* 'An Act for dividing' etc. . . .

The records of this stage also rarely seem to contain any information of great interest. Here and there, the *Journals* record that amendments to the bill are made at this stage. Particulars of these are not usually given, and when they are, they seem generally of little importance.

Bill agreed to by the Lords

Agreement to the Bill by the Lords is thus recorded:

(Date) *The Lords have agreed to the Bill entitled* An Act for Dividing etc. . . . . (occasionally *with some Amendments, to which Amendments their Lordships desire the Concurrence of this House*).

With few exceptions, the Lords either pass enclosure bills without question, or introduce amendments which are utterly unimportant. As one would expect, their Lordships show their traditional concern for the interests of the church. In one place they stipulate that the vicar's allotment shall be worth at least £30 per *annum*, that his allotment shall be fenced, like that of the impropriator, at the general charge of the other proprietors. Elsewhere they add a clause to the effect that the enclosure shall not affect the duty of parishioners to pay Easter Offerings, and that proprietors who are affected by the enclosure only insofar as their tithes are commuted for a corn rent shall pay only a fair proportion of the commissioners' costs. The Lords, however, amend an act of 1819 very thoroughly indeed. They provide that the vicar's allotment shall not be exchanged without the consent of the patron and the Archbishop of York, and, finding that throughout the bill a devisee who is also a re-married dowager duchess has been referred to by her former courtesy rank, rather than her true legal description, so that the 'Right Honourable' lady has been repeatedly characterized as 'Most Noble', they wade methodically through the bill, correcting this deplorable error upon each of the occasions on which it is found. If the Lords have made any amendments, the bill is next returned to the Commons for their concurrence. The records of this stage in the proceedings seem rarely to contain any data of value to the historian, for the amendments are almost invariably accepted by the lower House.

Royal Assent expressed

This too seems to have been always forthcoming, as a mere matter of form. Since an enclosure act is the result of a petition by the subject, the royal assent is expressed in the ancient formula, *Soit faite come il est desiré.*

The House was acquainted that . . . His Majesty has assented to . . .
An Act for Dividing, Allotting and Inclosing the Open Arable Fields
Common Meadows, Common Pastures, Commons and Waste Lands
within the Parish of . . . in the County of . . .

The Lords' *Journals* rarely contain any matter of great interest relating to enclosure bills. These hardly ever originate in the Lords, and the few amendments which the Lords introduce can be turned up, as a rule, by reference to the appropriate volume of the Commons *Journal*, where they are recorded with the Commons' approval of the Lords' amendments.

A Further Note on Enclosure Acts

This may be taken as concluding the present chapter on the process of parliamentary enclosure, as completing the very general survey of the subject in Chapter 4 and as a necessary preliminary to the understanding of the note on enclosure awards on pp. 115–20, in connexion with which it should be read.

The prints of enclosure bills and acts with which the inquirer is likely to come in contact are normally stitched paper foolscap folios, i.e. of dimensions $13\frac{1}{2}$ inches by $8\frac{1}{2}$ inches or so, before any trimming they may have undergone. Earlier ones rarely bear an imprint, later ones often that of Luke Hansard, the King's printer. Until 1798 they were printed in very small numbers, often by local printers, for the use of members of parliament and commissioners.[12] In 1798–1801 it was ordered that the King's printer should print not less than 306 copies of each local and personal act. It is to be noted that the odd copies of enclosure 'acts' which turn up from time to time in the hands of the second-hand booksellers, and which are found in considerable numbers in many local reference libraries, although their text begins 'An Act for Dividing and Inclosing . . .' etc. are actually very often copies of enclosure bills. Not that the point matters very much for, as noted above, the bills were rarely subjected to any substantial amendment in their passage through either House. Often the Bill carries on its final page

[12] It has been officially stated by a government department that a few enclosure bills were never printed at all. In fact there were orders of the House in 1705 and 1706 that all private bills (on the distinction between public and private acts see below) should be printed before their first reading. So the statement, though not inaccurate, is misleading, for there were before 1705, by the most generous computation, only ten enclosure acts, and only three of these fall into the category of 'private' acts.

the name of the local attorney who acted as clerk to the commissioners, sometimes also that of the London parliamentary agents who in fact 'solicited' it.

Fortunately we need not concern ourselves here a great deal with the technical distinctions among acts and bills in various categories.[13] A public act concerns the national community generally; one in the private or 'local and personal' class is, of course, more limited in its scope. Throughout most of the eighteenth century (A) enclosure acts were not public (a) but private (b), hence they are listed, but not printed, in the annual volumes of statutes, etc.[14] They were numbered, like the statutes, in arabic figures but with a separate series numeration. In and after 1798 'B' the statutes were arranged in three series, (a) public general, (b) public local and personal, and (c) private, and in 1803 'C' there was another rearrangement, (a) public general, (b) local and personal acts printed (in the *Statutes*), (c) local and personal acts not so printed.[15] The practical information which is to be drawn from these technicalities (without some reference to which it is difficult to set it out) is that acts in category A(b) but are to be found in a complete series nowhere except on the statute roll. Prints of those in B(c) and C(c) were sent to every clerk of the peace in the country, so are normally available in or near the county record office. All from 1727–1812 are listed under their respective sessions in Bramwell's *Analytical Table*, . . . Vol. 1, 1813, all from 1801 onwards are (not listed but) indexed under XV classified heads in H.M.S.O. *Index of Acts Local and Personal*, 1801–1947 (1949).

[13] The reader having occasion to go further into the very confusing business of the classification and printing of private acts will find guides to the whole subject by Mr. R. W. Perceval in [the Hansard Society's] *Parliamentary Affairs*, III, 4, 1950, by Mr. M. Bond in House of Lords Record Office *Memorandum* 16, 1957 (obtainable gratuitously on application to the Clerk of the Records) in *Archives* III. 20, 1958, and in the *Amateur Historian*, 4, 6, 1959/60.

[14] Also in the *Statutes at Large*, and in the various non-official collections made by Dutton, by Ruffhead and by Tomlins, etc., which are sometimes more easy of reference by the inquirer than are the official texts. It is to be noted that in the capitulation these collections sometimes differ from one another, and from the *Statutes at Large*, which is the first printed official text.

[15] It is often convenient to anticipate the later practice, which began in 1869, that is to cite all public general acts by arabic numerals, all public local ones by roman numerals, and all other (local or personal or private) acts by arabic numerals italicized.

It is interesting to find quite often in local libraries bound volumes of enclosure acts, widely scattered in their topographical reference, and having a date-range of perhaps thirty or forty years. Their origin is explained when one notices that the one thing the acts in any volume have in common is that the name of the same commissioner, or clerk, or surveyor, with a diversity of other names variously associated with his, appears in each act. Clearly the man concerned has been businesslike enough to keep a file copy of every act for every enclosure in which he has been concerned, and to have the prints bound together for his reference, and for eventual retention in his library.

There are excellent, though not quite complete, collections of private, etc., acts of all kinds in the House of Lords and House of Commons Libraries; in the House of Lords Record Office, in the Bodleian Library, the Cambridge University Library, the British Museum and, oddly enough, in the Salt Library attached to the County Record Office at Stafford. Most county record offices have, or are building up, complete sets of prints of the bills/acts for enclosure in the respective county areas. There is no adequate national index of enclosure acts, much less of enclosure awards. My *Domesday of English Enclosure Awards* (in progress) is intended to supply the one, and in some sort to obviate the need for the other. Until this is published, the inquirer failing to trace, by use of the hints above given, either an act or an award of which he is in search, will usually do well to ignore the other local parochial, urban or civic local authorities, and address his inquiries to the county archivist at the local county or shire hall. He may or may not have the records desired, but he is likelier than anyone else to know whether or not they exist, and if so where originals or copies may most usefully be sought.

The clauses of an individual act rarely call for much notice —the point is that it was unusual for any act to differ much, save in detail, from its fellows. Variants occur mainly in such matters as the fraction of the common which is to be allotted to the lord of the manor in lieu of his rights in its soil, and that of the other open land which, when tithe is commuted at enclosure, is to go to the tithe owner—often one-seventh of the open land, and the equivalent of one-tenth of the old enclosures. Occasionally there are specific clauses safeguarding the interests of individual proprietors, very exceptionally clauses for the benefit of the smaller or poorer proprietors generally. Usually, however, the toilsome task of reading through a whole series of acts results mainly in the reflexion that a great deal of time and money have been spent to little purpose in producing them. If the General Act of 1801, or better still that of 1836, had been passed a century earlier than it was, the admittedly necessary work of enclosure could have been carried out more economically, more expeditiously and certainly more equitably. Even so, if one is studying an individual enclosure it is obviously well to begin with a careful scrutiny of the act concerned. The notes above will usually enable the inquirer to obtain access to a copy of this for any area with which he is specially concerned. In the next chapter we consider how the act was implemented by the commissioners, and their decisions duly embodied in an enclosure award.

CHAPTER 10

THE PROCESS OF PARLIAMENTARY
ENCLOSURE: (B)

*Enclosure Commissioners and their Work, with an appended Note on
Enclosure Awards*

THE ORDINANCES OF an English enclosure act were
normally put into effect by an *ad hoc* body of commissioners,
usually with a clerk and a surveyor as their subordinates. It is
logical then to follow our study of the parliamentary proceedings leading to the passing of the act, the Members who took
part in this, and so on, with some account of the enclosure
commissioners who implemented the act, and in due course
incorporated their decisions in a formally executed and legally
binding award.[1] Not that every act necessarily appointed
commissioners, or implied the execution of an award. As noted
above, on occasion the act might ratify a pre-existing enclosure
agreement, or on even more rare occasions, it might itself
make the allotments in detail. The usual procedure was,
however, for the act to appoint commissioners (in fact nominated by the promoters of the bill). These were often three in
number, but occasionally more than a dozen. When there was
a high degree of unanimity among the landed interests affected
sometimes, for the sake of convenience, economy and dispatch,
a single commissioner was appointed.

The Development of the Enclosure Commission
There are interesting analogies and contrasts between Chancery
procedure in enclosure, and its practice in inquiring into and
adjudicating upon other matters of local concern. Thus, after
the Charities Act of 1601, Chancery had power by Pious Uses
Commission to inquire into alleged maladministration of local
charities, and to take measures for redress of grievances set
forth. In each case the court empowered local commissioners

[1] The first such commission I have noted is one under 37 Hen. VIII *c.* 2,
1545, for, *inter alia*, partitioning Hounslow Heath among the various interests having rights in it. It is arguable whether or not this, rather than the act
for Radipole, Dorset, 1603, should be taken as the first known enclosure act.
If so, the period of parliamentary enclosure by commission and award
becomes 1545–1914, not, as generally held, 1603–1914. For the awards
generally see above, pp. 52–4, and below, pp. 115–20.

to look into the matter, to take evidence on oath, and if they thought fit, eventually to issue a decree ensuring that justice was done.[2] It might be added that in each case the resulting documents are much less known to students than they should be. Pious Uses decrees are the most neglected archives of the history of charities; seventeenth-century enclosure decrees have been worked at much less than any of the other records of enclosure.

For obvious reasons it was desirable that commissions of a semi-judicial nature should be made up of an odd number of members. As indicated, in enclosure commissions this became customarily three, a number which fitted in very conveniently with the customary eighteenth-century grouping of the landed interests affected (a) the lord of the manor, (b) the impropriator (if there was one, failing this the clerical rector) and the vicar of the parish, both concerned as tithe-owners, the rector or vicar also as holder of the glebe, and (c) the comprehensive 'other interests', the remaining freeholders great and small.

'Professional' Commissioners

This accounts for the fact which cannot but strike the attention of anyone who reads through a fair number of printed enclosure bills or acts, or who even cursorily examines a number of MS. awards—that the name of the same commissioner occurs time after time, not only in acts dealing with his own locality, but in those for parishes in perhaps half a dozen widely-separated counties. Names like those of Jonas Bettison of Holme Pierrepoint, Notts., John Chamberl(a)in of Cropredy, Oxon., and William Fillingham of Flawborough, Notts., become very familiar to him. No one has essayed the frightening task of tabulating and identifying all the commissioners named in some 4,200 acts, or (what is not quite the same thing) those subscribing some 4,200 awards. Students inquiring in detail into the history of enclosure in specific (county or other)

[2] In Chancery's activities, both as to enclosure and on pious uses the procedure was through a commission of (largely local) persons, who it was hoped might be at once expert and impartial. In each case large nominal commissions tended to be replaced by smaller executive ones, the House took over a jurisdiction which had originally been that of the court, and in each case again it ultimately handed over much of this to salaried 'civil service' commissioners of its own appointment. The last major changes were in 1845 for enclosure, as described below pp. 135, 139, 141; for charities in 1853 and 1960.

localities have, however, done something in this, and there is an absolute concurrence of their testimony.[3] Sometimes, clearly, a commissioner was making what could be a very lucrative business of his enclosure activities. An outstanding example is George Maxwell of Fletton, Hunts., who (*teste* Beresford) was concerned in at least a hundred enclosures, 1773–1800.[4] Dozens of these were taking place simultaneously; hence perhaps (Russell suggests) the unreasonable delay which often elapsed between the passing of the act and the execution of the award.

Commissioners as Representatives of 'Interests'

On looking further at the names of the commissioners as they become familiar, one notices also another interesting fact— also one which has been little dwelt on by historians of the movement. When, as often, there are three names in a whole series of acts, the same name crops up over and over again in the same position, (*a*), (*b*), or (*c*). The act rarely states specifically that an individual commissioner is the nominee of a definite interest; it often says, however, what amounts to much the same thing—that if he 'dies, becomes incapacitated or refuses to act' he shall be replaced by a nominee of (*a*) the lord of the manor, (*b*) the appropriator and/or other tithe owner(s), etc. or (*c*) the remaining proprietors.[5] So clearly he has been chosen to represent a particular point of view. Thus in Oxfordshire, Thomas Hopcraft appears in five different commissions, always as representing manorial interests; the Rev. John Horseman is shown nine times, always acting on behalf of rector, appropriator or vicar. John Chamberl(a)in sat on sixteen commissions, 1789–1803, and on twelve of them represented 'other proprietors'. The point appears to be of some little importance. An enclosure commissioner combined the delicate functions of advocate and judge. An official report in 1808 says 'his prospect of future employment in this profitable capacity depends upon

---

[3] The counties for which such analyses exist include *Lincolnshire—Lindsey* (Russell, also Swales), *Nottinghamshire* and *Oxfordshire* (myself), *Staffordshire*, *Warwickshire* and *Worcestershire* (Beresford), *Warwickshire* (Martin).

[4] Maxwell is, of course, an extreme instance. Again according to Beresford, in 400 enclosures in Staffordshire, Warwickshire and Worcestershire 1720–1845, 328 individual commissioners were concerned. 194 acted on 1 occasion only, 22 on 3 occasions, 13 on 5, and so on, up to 1 on 15, 1 on 17, 1 on 20, 1 on 22, and 1 on 29 occasions.

[5] For some reason which is not apparent, this feature of enclosure acts is specially marked *c.* 1780–*c.* 1810.

his character for integrity and justice'.[6] Some well-known authorities have implied (rather than stated) that it was much likelier to depend upon the satisfaction he gave to the interests which (ultimately) had appointed him, since similar interests alone could offer him the prospect of further handsomely paid employment.

Some Contemporary References to Commissioners

Enclosure commissioners have not enjoyed a very good 'press'. There are a few casual references to commissioners and to surveyors, and to commissioner-surveyors, and these are rarely flattering. Arthur Young, while still an enthusiastic advocate of wholesale enclosure, has several adverse mentions of enclosure commissioners. The fact that the criticisms are from Young gives them all the more point, and is doubtless the reason why they are so often reproduced in the textbooks. He speaks of the commissioners as 'hacknied sons of business', and 'having neither integrity, abilities, or attention', and yet 'having the property of the proprietors, and especially the poor ones, entirely at their mercy' since they are 'vested with a despotic power known in no other branch of business in this free country'. Young is not a very consistent writer in this, as in other matters, and his strictures may be set against his very favourable and detailed account of the activities of another well-known commissioner, William Elmhirst of West Ashby, Lincs. Elmhirst stated—and Young implicitly endorsed his claim—that in numerous enclosures (sometimes as many as nine at once) in which he had been concerned, he had always considered first public interests, then those of the smallest proprietors, 'since there can be no *partiality* in defending *those* who cannot defend or help themselves'.[7]

The Commissioners Personally

It it extraordinarily difficult to generalize on how far the commissioners were chosen as specially qualified in character and ability for the delicate and highly skilled task they were to undertake. As to their specialized knowledge, here as elsewhere clearly an evolutionary process was taking place throughout

[6] Board of Agriculture, *General Report on . . . Inclosures*, 1808, p. 119.

[7] Young's opinions are cited (with incorrect references) in such standard works as Curtler and the Hammonds. They will be found set forth in some detail in his *Northern Tour* 1770, pp. 252–64. The other reference is to (Young's) *General View . . . of Lincolnshire*, 8vo edn. 1799, pp. 84–86.

the eighteenth century. At first, as with the Pious Uses commissioners above referred to, or with turnpike commissioners, the nominees might include a dozen or more local notabilities, landowners and often magistrates, with two or three professional men, who presumably did the work. As Beresford says, an early commission often resembles a county grand jury. Later, as the rage for enclosure gathered momentum, the work—originally recognized as honorary, or paid for with a quite nominal fee—became professionalized, and the 'gentlemen' or 'esquires' (the words still meant something in the eighteenth century!) with an occasional 'yeoman' or (tenant) 'farmer' are superseded by a smaller executive commission, made up in the main of land stewards, or attorneys or land surveyors. There are still in English country towns flourishing firms of solicitors, estate agents, land surveyors, etc., which seem first to have been established because of the ready market for their activities created by the enclosure movement. Beneficed clergy are quite often found as commissioners. There were then as there are now a fair number of country clergy ready to supplement their modest incomes by any honest means. It is fair to point out that then, much more than now, the country parson had usually a practical knowledge of agriculture, for he often farmed his glebe and collected his tithes in kind.

The Payment of Commissioners

Here again it is hard to generalize save to make it clear that as a rule, even allowing for the fall in the value of money, later commissioners were generally paid much more handsomely than earlier ones. Not all early acts contain provisions as to the precise sum each commissioner should be paid for each day's work. When it is possible to distinguish commissioners' payments from other expenses, as set down in the accounts or in the balance sheet sometimes attached to the award, it is not easy to disentangle these from sometimes quite reasonable, sometimes patently extortionate, charges of other kinds. It might or might not be laid down in the act that a commissioner coming from afar should be allowed a couple more days' fee (at full or at half rate) for travelling, with of course reasonable incidental expenses, and with bills for meals and accommodation overnight in a reputable local inn. When the act specifies the daily fee, this commonly ranges from as little as half a guinea a day in the early eighteenth century to as much as five or six guineas in the nineteenth. Sometimes expenses were fixed according to predetermined (and widely varying) scales, sometimes they were apparently at the commissioners' discretion.

It is evident that these sometimes interpreted the act with no undue harshness to themselves and to one another. It is abundantly clear that the proprietors, especially the smaller proprietors, were often fiercely angry about this, and some of their allegations—whether or not well founded—have passed *via* folklore into the literature of the subject. This is understandable enough: enclosure had been wished on or forced on the small proprietors. Had the commissioners served *gratis*, many of the peasantry would have felt their work dear at the price. The greater interests also seem sometimes to have been apprehensive on this point: a body of (Yorkshire) proprietors enjoins 'that the greatest economy in expenses are [*sic*] to be observed', a body of enclosure promoters will stipulate for a lump sum all-in payment to be laid down in the act, or for the commissioners to be paid on a sliding scale, the longer they take about the business the lower the daily fee. Even so, the actual work of enclosure might be a very profitable business for those taking part in it regularly. The most glaring example seems to be Mr. Russell's John Burcham, of Coningsby, Lincs. He is known to have acted in at least sixty-nine enclosures, 1801–40, literally dozens of them carried on simultaneously; he died in 1841 leaving a fortune of £600,000! Russell is not unduly cynical when he says that, although he does not allege that the whole of Burcham's fortune came from enclosure, 'it would certainly be surprising if, after being a commissioner in at least sixty-nine enclosures, John Burcham had *not* died a rich man'.

The Commissioners' Procedure

There was in the period with which we are specially concerned, no statutory control whatever over the commissioners' procedure.[8] So again, generalization is difficult, though it may be

---

[8] It was not until the years 1774–1801 that the House of Commons adopted a series of standing orders relating to enclosure bills. These almost all concerned proceedings in the House, not the activities of the commissioners. In 1774 they included provision that the commissioners should keep account of the very considerable expenditure they were undertaking, this in due time of course to be levied *pro rata* on all the proprietors of the lands, etc., affected. The standing orders are summarized with accuracy (as well as some acerbity) in the Hammonds' book elsewhere referred to, Chap. 4.

noted that my brief outline below is written after examination of a fair number of MS. minute books. The facts set forth may or may not be typical of the procedure adopted by the (ninety-four per cent. of) commissions for which no minute books are available—it might, of course, be argued that the mere existence of these books shows that the commissioners concerned were more businesslike than their fellows, and that the missing books are absent, not as being the subject of either careless or deliberate destruction, but because they have never existed.

The first step in the process[9] was normally for the commissioners to advertise in a local newspaper that they had been appointed, and proposed to undertake their duties. They gave public notice that their first meeting would be at a (named) local inn on a fixed date about a fortnight or a month ahead, and a similar announcement was affixed to the door of the parish church. At this first meeting the commissioners duly qualified by taking the necessary oath (the act contained special authorization for them to administer this to one another, and to their surveyor, etc.) and they also usually appointed a clerk and a surveyor. Then, quite often, they took a preliminary view of the lands to be affected, dined together and perhaps then met again to receive the claims in writing of all persons alleging interest in or over the lands. Quite usually, then, having arranged that the claims should be published in summary in the local newspaper, or affixed to the church door, or perhaps left in fair copy at one or two of the local inns or at their clerk's (the local attorney's) office, they adjourned for a month or two. Meanwhile the proprietors were invited to object to any ill-founded claims, compensation for which might diminish the area of land available for their own allotments. The next meetings might be wholly devoted to hearing and deciding on claims and counter-claims. And so the process continued, perhaps for only a few months, perhaps for several years.

The Commissioners at Work

Meanwhile the general course of agriculture in all the open lands was being carried out under directions laid down by the commissioners.[10] The surveyor was proceeding with his 'true

[9] There is an excellent account of the whole business in Curtler's book, elsewhere cited, second part of Chap. XIV, pp. 156–7.

[10] Quite usually the commissioners had been empowered also, in order to ease their very complicated work, to determine—if necessary with

and exact plan and admeasurement' of the lands as they now stood, on which he was to set out, as decision after decision was arrived at, the new allotments which the commissioners judged proper as a fair equivalent[11] ('in full and perfect satisfaction', as the phrase went) of pre-existing open lands and common rights. These plans, in due course, were to be verified by him on oath. He was to set down also the provisions made for highways, bridle roads, footpaths, any arrangements as to land drainage and a carefully worked out apportionment of the obligation of making, and future maintenance, of the boundary hedges and fences.[12] The clerk was, one hopes, recording most scrupulously the commissioners' numerous arbitral decisions. It was usual for them to be concerned only with the situation as it was at the time of the act, and as it was to be in future. They were debarred from considering matters of title, though any such arising could be dealt with at quarter sessions or elsewhere. Usually, encroachments on the common, etc., were to be recognized and compensated for if they were of twenty-one years' standing or more; those of shorter standing were to be ignored, and the land treated as allottable. The clerk had already worked out roughly the ratio in which the land was to be apportioned. This was the basis of the rate which the commissioners normally levied from time to time to meet, firstly, the costs already undertaken in parliament, etc., then their own expenses as they were incurred, the accounts being finally balanced and adjusted after the execution of the award.

compensation—all leases having less than 21 years to run. Copyhold open lands were, of course, compensated for by the allotment of enclosures to be held as copyholds (i.e. ultimately as allotted in law to the lord, not to his tenant). Tenancy at will was no business of the commissioners; this was a matter entirely between landlord and tenant.

[11] Less of course his apportioned share of the allotment to the lord of the manor of one-sixteenth or so of the common, his proportion of the tithe owners' one-seventh, or thereabouts, of the gross open area, and possibly with a further deduction on account of his share of fencing tithe (sometimes also glebe) allotments, and any further deduction to which he had become liable on not paying promptly his share of the commissioners' working expenses, as they were levied from time to time.

[12] This point has been little dwelt on by the historians. Fencing charges and obligations were in proportion not to the area of land, but to the length of boundary. It may be proved by elementary mathematics that a one-acre close of any particular shape has a tenth of the length of boundary of a hundred-acre close of the same shape. The gross cost for the smaller area is one-tenth of that for the larger one—but the cost *per acre* is tenfold.

Any payments still outstanding were, of course, to be collected before the allottees were admitted to clear possession of their holdings.[13] These costs, clearly, must often have been very hard on a peasant 'subsistence' farmer, with little monetary capital and quite unable either to sell or to mortgage land at a fair price in what was locally a 'buyer's market'.

It now remained to wind up the whole business in due legal form. The substantial parchment documentary 'award' had been engrossed by the clerk, and at the commissioners' final meeting it was solemnly executed—'signed, sealed and delivered'. After proclamation at matins in the parish church next Sunday, it was (normally) handed to the incumbent and churchwardens, 'to be laid up in the parish church of X for ever'. And there it may still be, though legally the secular parish meeting or parish council, established in 1894, has succeeded to nearly all the civil functions formerly exercised by these ecclesiastical authorities. Meanwhile (or perhaps considerably later, when next the clerk had business in the county town) a duplicate of the award was entered with the clerk of the peace for the county—this copy normally not sealed—and this was endorsed by the clerk of the peace as accepted by him for custody among the 'rolls and records of the county'. Again, there it still is, usually and very properly in the county muniment room or record office; and there, members of the public are entitled to see it, and, if they wish, to make extracts from or abstracts of it.

A Further Note on Enclosure Awards

This may be taken as concluding this present chapter on the commissioners and their work, as completing the very general survey of the subject in Chapter 4, and as referring back in particular to the note on enclosure acts on pp. 103–6, in connexion with which it should be read.

An enclosure award is a lengthy legal document, usually,

[13] The exception is the tithe-owner(s) (above, pp. 87, 94, below, p. 151). Tithe was sometimes commuted at enclosure for land or corn rent (see Glossary), sometimes not. There was no settled policy in this, it depended entirely on the terms of the individual act. When tithe was commuted at enclosure for land in lieu, it was usual for the act to order the allotment of one-seventh of the open titheable land. Presumably this was on the ground that the tithe had been theoretically a tenth of the gross product, making no allowance for the expense of cultivation. For the same reason, tithe-owners, great and small, were normally exempted from bearing as such any share in the costs of enclosure.

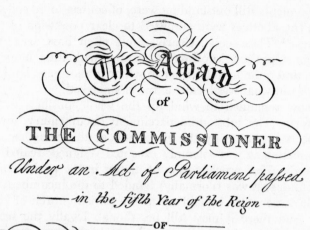

The Award

(of

THE COMMISSIONER

Under an Act of Parliament passed
— in the fifth Year of the Reign —

— OF —

His Majesty King George the Fourth

for INCLOSING LANDS in

the

Parish of Long Crendon,

in the

County of Buckingham

Commenced in 1824.
Completed in 1827.

Thomas James Tatham, of Bedford Place, London, Commissioner[s].
Richard Raine, of Doughty Street, London, ——— Surveyor
John Rose, of Essex Street, Strand, London. ——— Solicitor
John Hollier, of Thame, Oxfordshire, ———————— } Clerks alternately.
Henry Francis Mavor, of Woodstock, Oxfordshire }

13. A typical Enclosure Award, Long Crendon, Bucks. 1827 (enclosed
1824–7); see p. 201

in early times, in roll form, and containing often thirty or forty skins of parchment, each perhaps about three feet by two. After about 1800 some commissioners preferred to make the award, clearly for convenience of future reference, in book form. An award of this kind is often a substantial calf-bound volume, the skins of parchment being folded in the middle to give folios about two feet by one foot six inches. An award usually—by no means invariably—refers to an appended large-scale plan, with a schedule of reference numbers. The plan illustrates the positions, and usually indicates the areas, perhaps also the tenures, of the allotments made, and clarifies also the decisions the commissioners have come to on highways, land drains, responsibility for fencing, etc.[14] Perhaps half the enrolled copies of the awards contains also copies of the plans, without which the awards are, of course, much less illuminating. The commissioners had been ordered to enrol the award, not the award-and-plan, and, perhaps for economy's sake, had interpreted their instruction rather narrowly.

Original Awards

An award usually begins with the customary . . . *Greeting* . . . and *Whereas* . . . , and first recites at great (and what seems to the layman quite unnecessary) length the act under which it is executed. After two or three skins it seems to begin to come to the point, with its *Now Therefore* . . . , but in fact it next begins to recite the proceedings of the commissioners from the beginning, when they took their qualification oaths, to the end, when they executed, signed and sealed the award (as above). Then come, in great detail, their numerous decisions and arbitraments, firstly as to any lands allotted for highways or other public uses, then on those allotted to the individual proprietors from the lord of the manor downwards. Finally comes the dating clause, with the record of signing and sealing. When the original award and the enrolled copy are now, as often, in the county record office, it is sometimes possible to distinguish between them because the commissioners and their clerk have duly subscribed and sealed the original, but not always the enrolled copy.

The idea of leaving the original in the custody of the incumbent and churchwardens was, of course, so that it might

14 See above, p. 114, fn. 12.

ever be available for reference by the parishioners. As indicated above it is, in fact, sometimes in the church, sometimes in the personal custody of the incumbent, legally in the custody of the (secular) parish council or parish meeting, sometimes (especially where the county archivist has been particularly active in collecting parish records) in the county record office, or again, occasionally with the squire at the manor house, or in his estate office, or with his solicitors. (Not all estate office copies have been improperly removed from the parish chest. Often, of course, the major landowner would have an office copy made at his private expense for his personal use. Some of these copies also have now found their way, with other family and estate archives, by the goodwill of public-spirited landowners to permanent deposit in the county record office.) In a few of the remoter parts of Yorkshire (and presumably also elsewhere in places where the manorial organization survived in some degree of completeness), the act ordered the commissioners to deposit the original award or to make the enrolment not with the parochial or county authorities, but with those of the manor.

Enrolled Copies

As indicated above, enclosure awards normally exist at least in duplicate, the original parish copy (whether or not it still is physically in the parish) and the enrolment (whether this last is in effect a 'duplicate' copy, or is a mere transcript). This is the copy which is now, and always has been (normally) with the county records.[15] From time immemorial it had been the

---

[15] The only noteworthy exception is in the enrolled awards belonging to places formerly within that curious little quasi-county, the Ainsty of York. Not all the 'county' records passed, as presumably they should have done, to the 'town clerk and clerk of the peace for the City and County of the City of York' when the Ainsty was liquidated in 1836. It is by way of exception also that a few (521 awards altogether) were enrolled in the national courts, the Chancery, the King's Bench and the Common Pleas and in the records of the Duchy of Lancaster. These have long been in the Public Record Office. Again by way of further exception, in Middlesex, in the Isle of Ely, etc., and in the three Ridings of Yorkshire, enrolment was often in the local statutory Registry of Deeds, and in Co. Durham that of a few awards in the records of the Halmote Court. A few enrolments in most counties were made on the court rolls of local manors. It seems clear that some commissioners, despite the instructions of their act, saved time, trouble and money by enrolling the award nowhere. In such instances the (parish) original award may be unique—if it is not to be found, the student has no further resort.

custom that documents of importance might, on payment of a suitable fee, he *in*rolled (the lawyers prefer *in*rolled, and for that matter, *in*closure) on the dorse of the (Chancery) Close Rolls, or the (King's Bench) Plea Rolls, the (Common Pleas) Recovery Rolls, and so on. This enrolment was of course a valuable safeguard of their contents in the event of the loss of the originals. Legislation of 1536 had ordered, for a different purpose, the enrolment of deeds of 'bargain and sale', but gave those concerned the option of enrolling at Westminster or in the county town. Henceforward, numerous documents were enrolled with the various clerks of the peace, and these came later to include many hundreds of enclosure awards.

In the early days of parliamentary enclosure, the clerk of the peace customarily enrolled the award on any spare folios of parchment or paper he might have available. Later he was often businesslike enough to begin a special series of (usually paper folio) enrolment books. Later still, quite often the enrolment consisted simply of the deposit by the clerk to the commissioners of a duplicate copy of the (roll or book) award, neatly engrossed, and, presumably, made for this purpose at the same time as the original. The clerk of the peace collected his fee, and endorsed his copy (or both) as 'inrolled by me this day among the records of the County of Barset. Smith,[16] Clericus Pacis'. This is the official copy, physically, of course, in the care of the county archivist, but legally still in that of his chief officer, the clerk of the peace, who is also normally clerk of the county council. It may be useful to repeat here that the 230-odd awards under the Act of 1836 and its extension in 1840, almost always exist in duplicate. One copy was made for the parish, one for the county.

The 950-odd awards under the Act of 1845 and its successors are in triplicate, the parish copy (though this may well by now have found its way to the county record office), the county copy, and the Board (now the Ministry) of Agriculture copy, which is now in the Public Record Office. Under this act the salaried assistant commissioners carried out the work of enclosure, the salaried valuer under their direction drew up and signed the award, they signed and sealed it, and it was transmitted in triplicate to the (national) Commissioners in

[16] The clerk of the peace had, and still has, an odd privilege. He may sign himself officially with his surname only, as though he were a peer of the realm, having his surname as title.

London for confirmation. These also signed and sealed all three copies, and it then became legally binding on all parties. For an enclosure under the later acts there is, then, no practical distinction among the three identical copies of the award.

CHAPTER 11

ENCLOSURE AND THE STATE: (A)
IN TUDOR AND EARLY STUART TIMES

IT IS CLEAR that enclosure introduced many economic and social changes to the countryside. It is of interest to note how governments from time to time viewed these changes, and what action they took to stimulate or to check the current of agrarian change. Leaving out of account the Statutes of Merton and Westminster II, briefly dealt with already, we may follow in outline the story of the central government in its dealings with a change which affected the life of the countryside, and the prosperity, or the very existence, of the peasantry. As it happens, changes in policy in this respect synchronize closely with changes of dynasty, and it will be convenient to discuss the matter under four heads, the Government and the Enclosure Movement:

(i) In the Tudor period, say 1480–1600   } Chap. 11
(ii) In the early Stuart period 1600–1660 }
(iii) In the post-Restoration, Georgian
      and Victorian periods 1660–c. 1880) } Chap. 12
(iv) In recent years   c. 1880–1965 } Chap. 13

Governmental Motives

In its legislative and administrative measures the central government was swayed by a bewildering complex of motives—military, social, political, financial, economic and philanthropic. These exercised different degrees of influence at different periods. From the military point of view, enclosure was in general unwelcome in early times. It was alleged on the one hand, that a hedged and fenced countryside was more defensible than an open one. On the other hand, a more weighty consideration was that the yeomanry or landed peasantry—freeholders, copyholders, leaseholders and to a less extent tenants-at-will—were, apart from the navy, the backbone of national defence. In an invasion, a depopulated countryside could offer little resistance to a foreign aggressor. Moreover, men fought all the better for having a stake in the country they were defending. This motive weighed heavily in the sixteenth century, to a less extent in the seventeenth and the eighteenth. At the time of the Napoleonic

Wars it counted for very little, since in any case by this time it was generally held that enclosure would not necessarily or even usually involve depopulation.

The Tudor Governments

From the social and political points of view too the Tudor governments disliked such enclosures as led or threatened to lead to depopulation. Several of the Tudor rulers, certainly Henry VIII and the Lord Protector Somerset, had a quite genuine desire to be fair to the small proprietor, who was usually, with good reason, bitterly opposed to enclosure. All had a lively apprehension of the danger of dynastic or religious rebellion, and all were unwilling that malcontents should be presented with the opportunities afforded by the existence of a dispossessed and starving peasantry. Even before Henry VIII's time anti-enclosure measures had been placed on the statute book, and throughout Tudor times there was a long stream of statutes, proclamations and commissions, all designed to check a process felt to be utterly destructive of the common weal. Thus in 1517 there was the commission already referred to. Thirty-two years later a main count in the indictment against Somerset, under which at last he lost his head, was that he had been so slack in suppressing Kett's Rebellion in 1549 as to give the rebellious peasantry an idea that he was in sympathy with their feelings on the agrarian grievances which had led to the disturbance.

The first landmarks in the story of enclosure in Tudor times are the Depopulation Act of 1489 'agaynst pullying doun of Tounes', a proclamation of 1515 against engrossing of farms, and certain inquiries by the justices, etc., made the same year.[1] A temporary act of early 1516 was virtually made permanent later in the year, and the next year was the commission of 1517, addressed to the nobles and gentry of all save the four most northerly counties of England, with other anti-enclosure commissions in 1518 and 1519. In 1519 Wolsey, as Chancellor, ordered that those claiming the royal pardon for enclosure should destroy the hedges and ditches made since 1488. A proclamation of 1526 made a similar order. There was an act for restraining sheep farming in 1534, and two further depopulation acts in 1536. At the same time proceedings were taken in the Chancery and the Court of Exchequer against enclosers,

[1] References to all the acts mentioned are given below, Table of Statutes.

sometimes those of lofty station. Evidently the acts and proclamations were little observed, and in 1548 the Protector
Somerset issued yet another proclamation. A movement in the
reverse direction was made in 1550, when as part of the policy
of the nobility and gentry who had triumphed over him, the
Statutes of Merton and Westminster II[2] were confirmed and
re-enacted, and measures were taken to check hedge and fence-
breaking. However, only two years later another depopulation
act was passed, in 1552.

There was still another in Philip and Mary's time, 1555, and
one five years after Elizabeth I's accession, in 1563. This repealed
as ineffectual the three latest depopulation acts, of 1536, 1552,
1555 but re-enacted the earlier one of 1489. It was repealed in
part in 1593. Most of these acts endeavoured to re-establish the
status quo, to forbid under penalty of forfeiture the conversion of
arable to pasture, and to compel the rebuilding of decayed
houses, with the reconversion to arable of pasture which had
lately been put down to grass. Probably the multiplicity of acts
is an indication of their ineffectiveness. The reason was that the
administration alike of acts and commissions was largely in the
hands of the landed classes profiting by agrarian change.
In 1589 was passed Elizabeth's famous act prohibiting the
erection of any cottage without four acres of arable land [? and
of course, proportionate pasture rights]. This remained in
force, theoretically at any rate, until 1775. The difficulty with
which the government was faced is well illustrated by two acts of
1593, which passed through Parliament together, and which in
fact stand next to one another on the statute book, but which
adopt markedly contrasting points of view towards enclosures
of different kinds.[3] The first of them, as noted above, repeals
much of the 1563 act, that part forbidding the conversion of
arable to pasture. The second of them anticipates legislation
of the nineteenth century. It orders that no persons shall enclose
commons within three miles of the City of London, 'to the
hindrance of the training or mustering of soldiers, or of walking
for recreation, comfort and health of Her Majesty's people,
or of the laudable exercise of shooting . . .' etc.

The last Depopulation and Tillage Acts

The more complacent attitude towards enclosure evidenced by
the first of the 1593 acts did not last very long. In 1597 were

[2] Above, p. 25, *Bull. Inst. Hist. R.*, 1927, p. 26.   [3] 35 Eliz. *cc.* 6, 7.

passed two acts, again neighbours on the statute book, the first for the re-erection (though with some qualifications) of houses of husbandry which had been decayed. At the same time the government clearly recognized that if it merely tried by legislation to maintain or to restore the *status quo*, its efforts would be in vain. So the same act specifically authorizes lords of manors, or tenants with their lord's consent, to exchange intermixed open-field holdings in order to facilitate improved husbandry. The preamble of the second act sets out that since 1593 [and the partial repeal of the tillage acts then] 'there have growen many more Depopulacions by turning Tillage into Pasture', and the first act orders that decayed houses were to be re-erected, and lands reconverted to tillage under a penalty of 20s. per acre per annum. The second act relates to twenty-three counties only, generally those of the Midlands, with one or two southern counties, and Pembrokeshire in South Wales.[4] These were the last of the depopulation and tillage acts, and they escaped the general repeal of such acts in 1624, and remained in force (in theory) until 1863.

The Policy of the Early Stuart Governments

Probably in Stuart times baser motives weighed more heavily with the governmental authorities. The Stuart policies, especially that of Charles I, were as Tawney says, 'smeared with the trail of finance'.[5] Enclosure, at any rate enclosure leading to depopulation, was an offence against the common law.[6] Commissions inquired into it, and in many cases the statesmen and divines who composed these were inspired by the loftiest motives. The general action of the government,

[4] 39 Eliz. *cc.* 1, 2. It is not always noted that the two Elizabethan Poor Laws of 1597 and 1601 were each parts of whole codes of social legislation, 29 Eliz. I, *cc.* 1–6, 21, 43 Eliz. I *cc.* 2–4. It would not be hard to argue that the first steps towards the Welfare State in England were taken 1597–1601.

[5] *Op. cit.*, p. 391.

[6] Coke (Chief Justice of the King's Bench, 1613–16), was very emphatic on this, *Institutes* III, 1644 edn., p. 205. Ellesmere, his great rival (Lord Chancellor 1603–16), was more favourably disposed to enclosure, and himself authorized some enclosures by Chancery Decree. The point is of interest, since it may well have been Ellesmere's attitude which emboldened his kinsmen, Arthur Mainwaring, to embark on the enclosure of Welcombe, near Stratford, in 1614. In the story of this, Shakespeare plays a (very minor) part. Tothill, W., *Transactions of the Court of Chancery* etc., 1649, edn. 1827, p. 109, and Ingleby, G. M., *Shakespeare and the Welcombe Inclosure*, 1885. I owe this reference to Mr. Philip Styles.

however, was to use the Privy Council and the courts, especially the prerogative courts, the Court of Requests and the Star Chamber, the Councils of Wales and the North, as means of extortion. The offenders were 'compounded with', i.e. huge fines were levied so that the culprits might continue their malpractices.[7]

In 1601 a proposal to repeal the depopulation acts was crushed upon the ground that the majority of the militia levies were ploughmen.[8] In 1603 the Council of the North were ordered to check the 'wrongful taking in of commons' and the consequent 'decay of houses of husbandry . . .'. From about 1607 to 1636, the Government pursued an active anti-enclosure policy.[9] In 1607 the agrarian changes in the Midlands had produced an armed revolt of the peasantry, beginning in Northamptonshire, where there had been stirrings of unrest at any rate since 1604. The counties mainly affected were Northamptonshire, Bedfordshire, Buckinghamshire, Huntingdonshire, Leicestershire, the three divisions of Lincolnshire, and Warwickshire. The leader was a certain John Reynolds, nicknamed Captain Pouch, 'because of a great leather pouch which he wore by his side, in which purse he affirmed to his company there was sufficient matter to defend them against all commers, but afterwards when he was apprehended, his Pouch was searched, and therein was only a peece of greene cheese'. John was soon dealt with after a skirmish at Newton, where a body of mounted gentlemen with their servants dispersed a body of a thousand rebels, killing some forty or fifty of the poorly-armed rustics. Some of his followers were hanged and quartered. Promises of redress made by various proclamations were fulfilled only to the extent of the appointment of still another royal commission to inquire into agrarian grievances in the counties named. After it had made its return, however, it was discovered that on legal technicalities the commission was invalid, and little action seems to have been taken upon its laboriously compiled returns. The local gentry were soon busily at work again in enclosing their own land and that of others, though in 1620 Sir Edward Coke, the greatest of English judges, who had already shown himself a keen opponent of

---

[7] There is a tabular statement of the proceeds in Gonner, p. 167.

[8] See D'Ewes, *op. cit.*, p. 674, for Cecil's speech on this.

[9] The activity was mainly 1607–18 and 1636, the first spasm being due presumably to the Midland riots, the second to a period of high corn prices.

enclosure, declared depopulation to be against the laws of the realm, asserting that the encloser who kept a shepherd and his dog in the place of a flourishing village community was hateful to God and man.

A reaction set in when in 1619 there were good harvests, and the Privy Council was concerned to relieve farmers and landlords who were suffering through the low price of corn. This is why commissions were appointed to grant pardons for breaches of the depopulation acts, and why in 1624 all save the two acts of 1597 were repealed. The county justices still, however, attempted to check the change, and in this received more or less spasmodic pressure from the Council. In the 1630's corn prices rose again, and in 1630 the justices of five Midland counties were ordered to remove all enclosures made in the last two years. In 1632, 1635, and 1636 more commissions were appointed, and the justices of assize were instructed to enforce the tillage acts. In 1633 they were cited before the Board to give an account of their proceedings. From 1635–8 enclosure compositions were levied in thirteen counties, some six hundred persons in all being fined, and the total fines levied amounting to almost £50,000. Enclosers were being prosecuted in the Star Chamber as late as 1639. However, the Star Chamber was to vanish in 1641, and the Stuart administrative policy disappeared with the engines by which it had been—somewhat ineffectively and spasmodically—put in force.

If the reign in its social and agrarian policy may be judged solely from the number of anti-enclosure commissions set up, then undoubtedly King Charles I is the one English monarch of outstanding importance as an agrarian reformer. How far his policy was due to genuine disinterested love of the poor, and how far it followed from the more sordid motive of a desire to extort fines from offenders, it is difficult to say. But even the most unsympathetic critic must allow a good deal of honest benevolence to his minister Laud, Archbishop of Canterbury, and some measure of it to his master. On the whole it is perhaps not too much to say that for a short time after the commissions issued in 1632, 1635, and 1636, Star Chamber dealt fairly effectively with offenders. The lack of ultimate success of this last governmental attempt to stem the tide of enclosure was due, no doubt, partly to the mixture of motives on the part of its proponents. Still more its failure is to be attributed to the fact that again the local administrators, upon whom the Crown depended to implement its policy, were of the very [landed] class which included the worst offenders. A (practising) poacher does not make a very good gamekeeper!

The Commonwealth

During the Commonwealth there was little legal or administrative attempt to check enclosure of open fields. It is not clear how far this was taking place, though there was great activity in the enclosure and drainage of commonable waste. Some of the Major-Generals, especially Edward Whalley, held strong views upon agrarian matters, and attempted to use their very extensive powers to carry their ideals into operation. Petitions were prepared and presented, a committee of the Council of State was appointed and numerous pamphlets were written.

In 1653 the mayor and aldermen of Leicester complained of local enclosures and sent a petition to London, very sensibly choosing their neighbour, John Moore, as its bearer.[10] Apparently it was because of this that the same year the Committee for the Poor were ordered 'to consider of the business where Enclosures have been made'. The question arose again in 1656 when Whalley, the Major-General in charge of the Midlands, set on foot local inquiries, and took fairly drastic action in response to petitions adopted by the grand juries in his area. He hoped that as a result of his action 'God will not be provoked, the poor not wronged, depopulation prevented, and the State not dampnified'. The same year he brought in a Bill 'touching the dividing of commons', but it failed through the opposition of William Lenthall, the Master of the Rolls, and indeed was not even given a second reading. This was the last bill to regulate enclosure. Ten years later, in 1666, another bill was read in the Lords, to confirm all enclosures made by court decree in the preceding sixty years. It also was un-unsuccessful, but the fact that it was introduced is indicative of a great change in the general attitude towards enclosure displayed by those in authority.

[10] See above, pp. 76, 77, below, p. 150.

CHAPTER 12

ENCLOSURE AND THE STATE: (B)
AFTER THE RESTORATION

IT HAS ALREADY been suggested that when the squires and clergy came back to their manor houses and parsonages in the 1660's, there was no chance that the Government would antagonize them by showing excessive concern for the interests of the poor. A new flood of propaganda in favour of agricultural progress was reinforced by a marked change of feeling on social questions, so that, for example, in relation to the Poor Law, Charles II's advisers showed no undue sympathy with the under-dog.[1] There were no more depopulation commissions, and no more state prosecutions of enclosers. Perhaps the financial distress of the gentry, due to their wartime expenditure and the enormous fines levied on them and 'compositions' made with them, may have been one of the strongest incentives towards economic change. John Houghton, in 1682, includes amongst the principal benefits following from 'His Majesty's most happy Restoration' the disparking of parks and the enclosure of commons.[2] Moreover, the theorists of the day were honestly convinced that the level of rents formed an index of national prosperity, and that therefore enclosure, which indubitably tended towards the raising of rents, could not but benefit the public. Such a conservative as Roger North who speaks of conversion of arable to pasture as 'the destruction of mankind' or John Aubrey telling of the 'world of labouring people' maintained by 'a Church Ale at Whitsuntide' where 'since the Reformation and Inclosures these parts have swarmed with poore people', were but voices crying in the wilderness.[3]

Eighteenth Century Governments: the Commons 'Standing Orders'
For more than a century after the abortive bills of 1656 and 1666 referred to above, the government authority, as such, took not the least notice of the agrarian revolution then in

---

[1] The abominable 'settlement' laws date from 14 Car. II c. 12 (1662).
[2] Above, p. 82, fn. 5.
[3] North, R., *Lives of the Norths*, 1744, p. 50. The reference is Miss Leonard's. Aubrey, J., *Natural History of Wiltshire*, 1685, p. 104. Aubrey is speaking of the period c. 1550.

AN

ACT

FOR

Dividing and inclosing the open Fields, Meadows, Common Pasture and Waste Grounds, and also the Marsh and Fenny Grounds, in the Manor and Parish of Yaxley, in the County of Huntingdon.

 𝕎𝔼ℝ𝔼𝔸𝕊 there are several Open Arable Fields, Open Preamble. Meadows, Common Pasture, Waste Grounds, and Marsh and Fenny Grounds, in the Manor and Parish of *Yaxley,* in the County of *Huntingdon*:

And whereas the Right Honourable *John* Lord *Carysfort,* in the Kingdom of *Ireland,* is Lord of the said Manor, and also Impropriator of the Rectory, and great and small Tythes of the said Parish of *Yaxley,* and is possessed of, or intitled to, by far the greatest Part of the Lands within the said Manor and Parish:

A   And

IX A typical Enclosure Act; Yaxley, Hunts., enclosed 1767–73; *see p. 211*

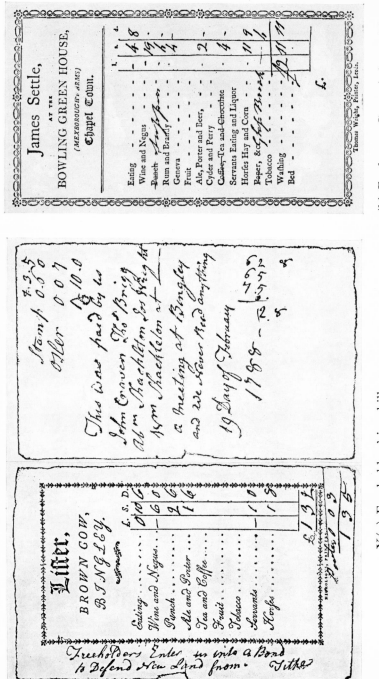

X(a) Freeholders' inn bill, Riddlesden in Bingley, Yorks. 1788, enclosed 1788–90; see p. 211

(b) Enclosure Commissioners' inn bill, Chapel Allerton, Yorks. W., enclosed 1802–12; see p. 211

progress. Lords and Commons passed, generally after very cursory consideration, such enclosure bills as were presented to them. Concerning these bills and the proceedings upon them I give some details elsewhere. During this period, while numerous individual enclosures were sanctioned and these involving vast acreages of land, until 1774 there were formulated no general principles of any kind concerning the terms and conditions on which enclosure should be carried out. In this year were drawn up the first standing orders of the House dealing with enclosure bills.[4] These gave some security against gross abuses which had sprung up. The fact that they were necessary is some indication of how improper, by any standard, must have been some enclosure carried on according to the practices forbidden. They prevent, for example, enclosure bills being promoted entirely over the heads and without the knowledge of some of the proprietors concerned. They enjoin promoters to publish a notice on the church door of the parish. They introduce some control over unreasonable extortion by the commissioners. They order that the draft bill presented to the House shall contain the commissioners' names, and details of the compensation proposed to be allotted to the lord of the manor and to the tithe owner.

The standing orders were revised in 1775, 1781, 1799, 1800 and 1801. In general, the new provisions introduced in the later series were further attempts to secure equity and fair dealing in the work of enclosure. The Orders of 1801, for example, contain a clause to the effect that the lord of any manor, or his steward or bailiff, may not serve as commissioners in any enclosure in which manorial interests are involved.[5]

The General Enclosure Acts

No general act concerning enclosure appeared until 1801, although there were, of course, innumerable private acts dealing with the enclosure of specific areas, and one or two general acts dealing with the reclamation of waste for afforestation. A

[4] There are of course several editions; My copy is of *Standing Orders of the House of Commons* . . . 1685–1838 . . . 1838.

[5] I am informed by Mr. R. C. Russell, below p. 181, that in Lincolnshire this clause was frequently evaded. I have noted no such evasion in the *post-*1801 enclosures of Nottinghamshire and Oxfordshire, the only two counties in which I can claim to have worked through every one of the [35/38] acts and [51/53] awards.

general bill had been introduced as long ago as 1621, and in February 1641, while the Commons were busy with the impeachment of Strafford, there was another bill in the Long Parliament 'for confirming inclosures'. The reason for this demand was of course that enclosure by ordinary parliamentary process was necessarily a complicated business. It was outrageously expensive, hence the early demand for a general act which would render proceedings simpler and cheaper. This was reiterated very frequently, at any rate from the time of John Worlidge's *Systema Agriculturæ*, 1669. It appears in the works of Daniel Defoe, John Houghton and Sir William Petty. Eventually the first general enclosure act was passed in 1801; there was another important general act in 1836; still another general act went successfully through both Houses in 1845. The circumstances attending the 1801 Act deserve some notice.

The General Act of 1801

Consideration of agrarian matters was forced upon the Government again in the difficult years of the 1790's. Bad harvests, wars and famine prices made it necessary that more land should be brought under the plough, and that land already in tillage should increase its productivity. The Board of Agriculture was established in 1793 as a semi-private concern, but with a substantial government grant in aid of its expenses. Arthur Young, the most eminent agricultural writer of the day, was appointed Secretary to it. From him, both before and after this appointment, there was an endless stream of propaganda in favour of agricultural improvement, especially of such as could be put in operation only through enclosure. Young pointed out that the methods of enclosure then in vogue necessarily discouraged a movement which should receive every possible assistance, and it was through his efforts that eventually the General Enclosure Act of 1801 was passed.[6] His original hope was for such a general act as would permit enclosure to take place without specific reference to Parliament upon every occasion, and the unnecessary expense, delay and inconvenience which this occasioned.

---

[6] References to this and to the other acts mentioned are given below, Table of Statutes. There is a convenient abstract of 1836, with prints of all the acts 1801–36 in Pratt, J. T., *Law for facilitating the Enclosure of Open and Arable Fields*, 1837.

About 1795, the agricultural crisis made it imperative that there should be designed a better method of enclosure than that in vogue, which Young stigmatized as a 'composition of public folly and private knavery'. Sir John Sinclair, the President of the Board, supported his Secretary's prose in verse:

'Let us cut off those legal bars
Which crush the culture of our fruitful isle,
Were they removed, unbounded wealth would flow
Our wastes would then with varied produce smile
And England soon a second Eden prove.'

Scotland had had two General Enclosure Acts since 1695,[7] and in 1795, 1796, 1797 and 1800 attempts had been made to pass the long-desired bill for England. All these had failed, however, mainly because of clerical opposition to tithe commutation proposals which were very unwisely inserted in the bills. The promoters of the 1801 Act were warned by their previous experience. They carried the bill successfully through both Houses; it met some at any rate of their needs, and part of the act remained in force as late as 1899. It was a 'model clauses' act, setting out the clauses normally included in enclosure bills, and found acceptable to Parliament. It did not, therefore, obviate the necessity of a separate act for each enclosure, but it simplified and cheapened the passage of individual bills so that they duly became enclosure acts. Despite its limited

[7] Not one, as I think all other English historians say: Sir John was delighted to point out the fact. He possessed, however, to perhaps rather more than the normal degree, a characteristic not unknown among his compatriots today. For he found it a pleasant duty towards his English neighbours to explain to them, usually at length and with some point and accuracy, as well as great assurance, exactly wherein lay their main ignorances, negligences and shortcomings generally. It is, of course, a *trait* which tends to earn for his fellows, as it did for him, rather an earnest and grateful hearing than any unbridled affection.

It is fair, however, especially for an Englishman, to note that Sir John was right (as he usually was)! Not only had the Scots possessed since 1695 two general acts, fairly comparable, *mutatis mutandis*, with the kind of thing Sir John had in mind (while the 1801 act, as noted below, was a mere Clauses act only—it was not until 1831 and 1840 that reasonably businesslike acts were passed). It may be worth mentioning also that the 1801 English act is in 44 sections, and has four appendices. The two Scottish acts of 1695 are each contained in a single-column paragraph of between thirty and forty lines.

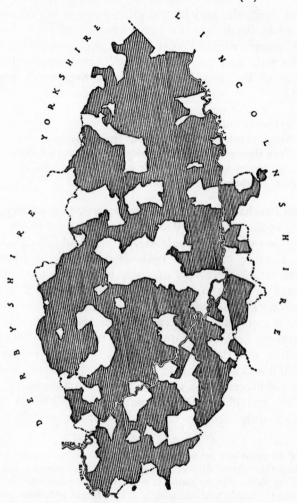

14. Parishes subjected to Parliamentary enclosure
in Nottinghamshire 1743–1868; see p. 202

nature, it marks a definite epoch in the story of enclosure
legislation in England. References to it are incorporated in
almost all 'private' enclosure acts after 1801. Another general
bill of 1805 passed the Commons, but (very much to its
credit!) the House of Lords rejected it. Later attempts were
made, but none of these met with any great success until 1836,
though various other general measures of minor importance
had been passed in 1821, 1831 and 1834.

The General Act of 1836

The 1836 Act is of some importance. It permits enclosure by consent of two-thirds of the interests affected, without the necessity of any special application to Parliament. The owners could appoint their commissioners as though the enclosure had been specifically authorized by act. If seven-eighths of the interests in value were agreed, the owners could enclose for themselves—no commissioners were necessary. In some parts of the country very extensive areas of land were enclosed by the

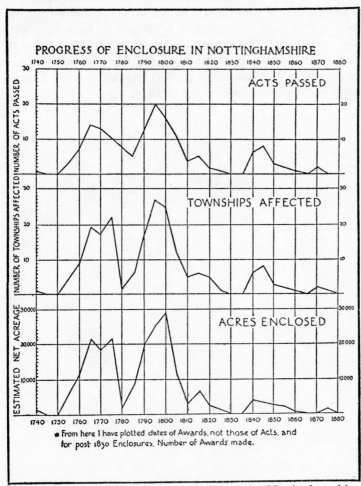

PROGRESS OF ENCLOSURE IN NOTTINGHAMSHIRE

ACTS PASSED

TOWNSHIPS AFFECTED

ACRES ENCLOSED

* From here I have plotted dates of Awards, not those of Acts, and for post 1830 Enclosures, Number of Awards made.

15. Progress of Parliamentary enclosure in Nottinghamshire 1743–1880; see p. 202

cheap and equitable methods provided under this act. Such enclosures have received little attention from historians, no doubt largely because the awards, unlike nearly all others, were never enrolled nationally, only locally. Some care for public interests is shown by the clause in the 1836 Act prohibiting its application to open fields within ten miles of the centre of London, and within varying distances, according to a sliding scale referring to the size of the town concerned, from the centres of other large towns. This is reminiscent of the Elizabethan act of 1593, and it anticipates the later legislation for the protection of commons. The act in its original form covers open arable fields only, but it is alleged to have been often improperly applied to common pastures, manorial wastes, etc. Vast areas of waste, in Wales especially, are [?wrongly] said to have been enclosed under it. It was extended to cover Lammas lands, etc. by an amending act of 1840.

CHAPTER 13

ENCLOSURE AND THE STATE: (C)
IN RECENT YEARS

The General Act of 1845

THE LAST GREAT general enclosure act was passed in 1845. The enclosure question had been agitated since 1842, and a select committee, under the chairmanship of Lord Worsley, who had already introduced a bill upon the subject, had reported on it in 1844. By this time, it was evident that a good deal of enclosure had taken place in such a way as to dispossess small proprietors, and that often, for example in the matter of village greens, it had been conducted with total disregard for the general interests of the neighbourhood concerned. On the report of the committee, a better scheme was worked out in the 1845 Act, which passed through the House after much opposition. A (standing) Enclosure Commission was appointed. This was to work through assistant commissioners and (valuers) surveyors.

(a) They were to carry out local inquiries in each case of proposed enclosure and:
(b) If enclosure were sanctioned by the House on the Commission's recommendation, they were to be responsible for the actual work of enclosure and allotment.

The times were peculiarly favourable to such an act. The waste lands had been freed by the Tithe Act of 1839 from liability for increased tithe upon enclosure. The rapid improvement of drainage, with the introduction of artificial manures, gave a prospect that the reclaimed land would be brought into proper cultivation at a moderate cost. Further economies could be achieved by the use of the elaborate surveys which had lately been made for the purpose of tithe commutation.[1] For some years Radical politicians had been opposing in the House all enclosure bills which made insufficient provision for the exercise and recreation of dwellers in the district and clauses on this point were included in the bill. Public interests were secured by the insertion of a sliding scale, similar to that of the 1836 Act, but framed upon more generous lines. A permissive clause allowed the persons interested, if they thought fit, to authorize the commissioners to make

[1] Under 6 & 7 Wm. IV c. 21 (1836).

allotments for public purposes, roads, drains, charities, etc., and another empowered them to allot land for the benefit of the labouring poor, and made special mention of recreation grounds.

In one important matter, the act did not meet the wishes of the committee. Every enclosure of waste, etc., had to be submitted to Parliament for approval, but for seven years, until the act was substantially amended in 1852, enclosures of open fields, etc., had not. In such cases the Commission could issue its provisional order instructing the Assistant Commissioner to proceed in the matter and make his award after proper notification to the parties concerned and to the public, but without any further statutory authority. In other cases the Commission must include the proposed enclosure in its annual report to Parliament, and the enclosure could not be completed until its inclusion in the schedule of an annual general act, sanctioning all enclosures approved by the House on the Commission's recommendation during the session. In 1852, under an amending act, it was provided that *all* future enclosures should need the specific sanction of the legislature.

Evidently it was thought that the Commission, publicly appointed (though indirectly so) and publicly controlled, could be trusted to carry on its duties with discretion. For a quarter of a century it worked with very little supervision, and when the matter was inquired into in 1869, during Gladstone's first Government, the famous Reform Administration, the House was astounded to find how much enclosure had taken place, and upon what terms. The Commissioners had conceived it as their duty to authorize enclosure wherever possible—in no case giving the open lands the benefit of any doubt, and had in fact sanctioned an average of thirty-nine enclosures annually with a total, 1845–69, of 946 enclosures and 618,000 acres. Actually they were dealing rather more drastically with what few open lands remained than their predecessors, the commissioners under private acts, had done in the first half of the century.[2]

The last Anti-Enclosure Movement

In 1864 the fact that the Commissioners had ventured to lay hands on Epsom Common, with a proposal by Earl Spencer

[2] These are the figures as given in the House. I am aware that they do not tally with those set out above, p. 88, or my own, below p. 184. A very useful though somewhat 'coloured' account of the whole business is found in Lord Eversley's *English Commons and Forests*, 1894.

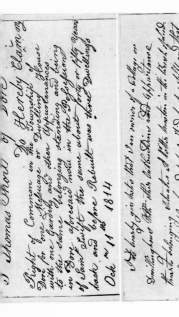

XI(a). The Commissioners' notes of claims submitted at Ulley, Yorks. W., enclosed 1798–1800; see p. 212

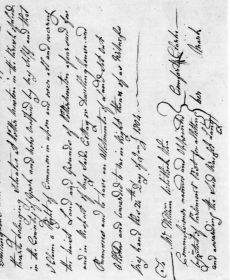

(b) Original claim submitted at Dore, Derbys. 1814, enclosed 1809–22. Original claim submitted at Potter Newton, Yorks. W. 1800, enclosed 1803–6; see pp. 212–13

XII Ejection of a farm worker [in A.D. 1962!] from a tied cottage at Stawell, Som., enclosed 1791–5; see p. 213

to enclose part of Wimbledon Common, aroused a good deal of concern, and very marked and vocal opposition. The public mind was already somewhat exercised upon the subject because of the extensive encroachments which had been made upon such other metropolitan commons as those of Wandsworth, Barnes and Tooting, largely by railway companies in search of ground for their lines into London. Henry Doulton, the Member for Lambeth, moved in the House for a committee to inquire into the question. A great deal of evidence was heard, and several schemes of enclosure, regulation and preservation were proposed, on behalf of manorial lords, commoners and public bodies. The Metropolitan Board of Works submitted a grandiose scheme for acquiring the whole of the manorial and common rights at a total cost of £6 million, the money to be raised by the sale of outlying portions of the London commons for building purposes. The Committee eventually reported by a two to one majority in favour of a rival scheme. This was for repealing the Statute of Merton, forbidding all future enclosures in the Metropolitan area under the Act of 1845 and trusting to the activities of the commoners and other public-spirited local residents to keep the local manorial lords in check. These last took prompt action to enclose at once, wherever they thought they had chance of success, and consequently in 1865 the Commons Society was formed, with Charles Shaw Lefèvre, Viscount Eversley, as Chairman.[3]

The Commons Society

This entered at once upon a whole series of anti-enclosure activities, most of them markedly successful. The next year W. F. Cowper Temple, as First Commissioner of Works, piloted through the Commons a measure which had been drafted by the Society, the Metropolitan Commons Act of 1866. By this, provision was made for the regulation of metropolitan commons. The (Inclosure) Enclosure Commissioners (then in the Board of Agriculture) were empowered, on the application of interested persons, to authorize a scheme for the

[3] This is now the Commons, Open Spaces and Footpaths Preservation Society, Suite 4, 166/70 Shaftesbury Avenue, London, W.C.2. Any public-spirited reader who learns of an attempt to close a footpath or encroach on a common should at once inform the Society of it. Like most societies dealing with the public good, it badly needs money. Its annual subscription for individuals is a guinea; Life Membership costs fifteen guineas.

management of a metropolitan common by a board of conservators. This board was to be elected by the ratepayers, the scheme being submitted to Parliament in precisely the same fashion as a provisional order for enclosure. This could be approved without the consent of the lord of the manor, though if he was not an assenting party, his existing rights were to be covered by a saving clause. Since this act, most metropolitan commons have been fairly secure.

Open Fields are not to be expected of course in the metropolitan area, and they survive only occasionally, and in a more or less vestigial form, elsewhere. Commons, however, existed and still exist, both in rural areas and attached to some large towns.[4] The blind statesman Henry Fawcett turned his attention to these, especially to the rural commons. Annual bills for enclosing were brought forward each year, and a few of these were being passed quite automatically, with no discussion whatever. Fawcett discovered that in the annual bill for 1869, of 6,916 acres of land scheduled for enclosure, a total of nine acres was to be allotted for public purposes, three acres for recreation, and six for field gardens (i.e. 'allotments'). Of 320,000 acres of common enclosed since 1845, for which the poor were to have been compensated under the allotment system, only some 2,000 (!) acres had been allotted for the benefit of the labourers and the cottagers.

Fawcett attacked the Bill at every stage, and contrived to secure the reference of the matter to a select committee, the operation of the Bill meanwhile being suspended. At length, the committee reported, much impressed by evidence on the marked deterioration of the labourer's condition which had followed the enclosure of the commons. They stated that the Act [of 1845] needed many amendments, and that the provisions for allotments and recreation grounds made in awards under it were most inadequate. Local inquiries had certainly been held in accordance with its terms, but the sittings had been at times which made it impossible for them to be attended by the labourers, so that these could not be present and state

---

[4] Above, p. 39. There is an interesting table of them in Hoskins and Stamp (above, *loc. cit.*, fn. 7). A few urban commons of outstanding interest are those of Beverley, 1184a., Bristol, 87a., Cambridge 226a., Coventry 39a., Doncaster 165a., Durham 11a., Hereford 200a., Huntingdon 241a. (with Godmanchester another 330a.), Ipswich 169a., Newcastle on Tyne 1037a., Norwich 190a., Oxford 436+a., Southampton 240a., Stafford 111a., York 513a. See also p. 182 below.

their views. It was the view of the Committee that no further
enclosures should be sanctioned until the 1845 Act had been
thoroughly overhauled, and the regulations for the Commissioners' conduct radically amended. In fact the Bill passed,
after the excision of references to two particularly ill-judged
enclosures of commons, but there were no further authoriza-
tions of enclosure by annual general act until 1878. Meanwhile,
in 1871 Shaw Lefèvre introduced a bill to carry out the recom-
mendations of the 1869 Committee, and indeed in several
respects going beyond them. After approval by still another
select committee, the Bill was dropped, because of the pressure
of other business. In 1872 it was introduced again in the Lords,
but a provision as to allotments for public purposes was
bitterly opposed by the Marquis of Salisbury and others, and
eventually the rejection was moved by the Duke of Northumberland and carried against the Government by 65 to 53.

The Commons Act of 1876

Meanwhile the Commissioners continued to recommend
enclosure schemes, but none of these was confirmed by Parliament, and by 1876 schemes for dealing with thirty-eight
commons were awaiting attention. By reason of the recom-
mendations of the 1869 Committee, the terms of many of these
were much more generous than had been originally proposed.
It was still felt, however, that many of these enclosures ought not
to be sanctioned at all, since no public good, as distinct from
private profit, would result from them. The Conservative Home
Secretary, Richard Cross, introduced a bill in which for the
first time this touchstone of public benefit was to be applied to
all projected enclosures, and the government undertook that
after the passing of this into law all proposed enclosures should
be brought to the notice of the House. The Bill was not so
generous to the smaller interests as the abortive measure of
1871 had been, but on Cross's assurance, and after the inclusion
of certain amendments, the champions of the Commons Society
withdrew their opposition. The thirty-eight schemes scheduled
in the Bill were withdrawn from it, and referred afresh to the
Commissioners for decision on the principles newly laid down.
This time only eighteen of them were recommended. After the
passing of the Act—the Commons Act of 1876—a standing
committee of the House was set up to scrutinize all enclosure
proposals, and on this the Commons Society has always had

representation. From 1878–93 only 24 commons were enclosed under 'normal' enclosure procedure, with a total area of 26,500 acres, of which about 800 acres were allotted for public purposes. Only one of them was *post* 1886. From 1893 to the present day all save one of the awards made under the 1893 Act (the exception is that for Skipwith Open Fields and Commons, Yorks, E.R.), were for regulation only. At Skipwith the open fields were enclosed, but the commons regulated, in 1901–4.[5]

Enclosure at the Present Day

The best indication of the present official attitude towards the matter is to be gained by reference to the documents furnished lately by the Ministry of Agriculture[6] to any person inquiring as to the possibility of enclosing any specified common. The *Instruction with respect to schemes for the Regulation and Management of Commons* (under the act of 1899) gave full details as to the then power of local authorities to make schemes for the regulation of commons in their areas, subject to the Ministry's approval. The *Information regarding applications for the Regulation or Inclosure of Commons* gave particulars of the formalities to be observed in applying for either regulation or enclosure under the acts of 1845–99, and noted in capital letters:

'INCLOSURE IN SEVERALTY, AS OPPOSED TO REGU-LATION, WILL NOT BE SANCTIONED UNLESS IT CAN BE PROVED, TO THE SATISFACTION OF THE MIN-ISTER AND OF PARLIAMENT THAT INCLOSURE WILL

---

[5] It is true, of course, that commons are still enclosed in whole or in part by act of Parliament, usually a local authority's 'General Powers' Act. It is extremely difficult to make any estimate of the extent to which this process has gone on in the last seventy years or so, for very often the enclosure is effected under one or two sections of an act containing perhaps seventy or eighty and dealing with a wide variety of matters. Thus in 1963 the Bath Corporation obtained powers to enclose a small common, and while this is in the press a G.L.C. (General powers) Bill, passing through the House of Commons, has suffered in Committee the deletion of a clause authorizing the enclosure for a camping and caravan ground of a little land in Hainault Forest, though an unopposed Metropolitan Water Board bill now (April, 1967) in progress allows the Board to acquire a small part of Epping Forest and to extinguish common rights there.

[6] Form 702 L.G. It is to be noted, however, that the Ministry itself has enclosed several thousand acres of improvable common under the provisions of the Agriculture Act of 1947 (for which see below, Table of Statutes).

BE OF BENEFIT TO THE NEIGHBOURHOOD AS WELL
AS TO PRIVATE INTERESTS, AND TO THOSE WHO ARE
LEGALLY INTERESTED IN THE COMMON. THE EX-
PRESSION "BENEFIT OF THE NEIGHBOURHOOD"
INCLUDES THE HEALTH, COMFORT, AND CONVEN-
IENCE OF THE INHABITANTS OF ANY CITIES, TOWN,
VILLAGES, OR POPULOUS PLACES IN OR NEAR ANY
PARISH IN WHICH THE COMMONS OR ANY PART
THEREOF IS SITUATED'.

The Present-day Legal Position: Some Speculations

The Law of Property Act of 1925 and the Commons Registration Act of 1965 are the most recent major enactments regarding commons. The first-named refers to all metropolitan
commons, all manorial wastes, all commons situated within
boroughs or urban districts, and all further commons to which
the Act shall afterwards be applied. Subject to provisions for
protecting the common itself, securing it from misuse, and
maintaining the lord of the manor's interest in the minerals,
it gives the public generally a right of access for air and exercise
to all the lands covered by the Act.

The 1965 Act provides for the registration, 1967–70, by the
major local authorities, of all commons in their territorial
areas, with an extended period for objections to proposed
registrations, 1968–72. The Ministry specifically offers technical
assistance to both common-right claimants and to objectors,
and this whether persons taking action have or have not any
legal interest in the land concerned. Plainly the intention is
that, from 1972 the (rather more than a million acres of)
commons in England, shall be precisely recorded, and their
status as common be most carefully safeguarded throughout the
foreseeable future. They are regarded, by the Act and by the
Ministry, primarily as a public amenity, but the registration is
to be with due attention to all existing proved legal rights, either
in the soil, or of user over the surface. The Statute of Merton,
passed as long ago as 1235—in fact amended in part in 1893–4,
when it was hedged round with such restrictions that it could
not be used anti-socially—was finally repealed in 1953. The
reader may care to speculate upon what might have happened
had the early anti-enclosure movements met with the same
success as the later ones, so that the check had been applied
before so much mischief had been done. Had the political

careers of Wolsey and Somerset, and possibly that of Laud, not met with sudden terminations, English social history might have been a very different story. Enclosure no doubt would have come, but on very different terms and by very different methods from those actually adopted. England might conceivably have been still a country of peasant proprietors—no dispossessed yeomanry might have brought its virile blood and its acute class-consciousness into the urban aggregations of the Industrial Revolution. The Industrial Revolution itself might have begun or developed elsewhere than in England. Possibly there would have been no Commonwealth, and it is just conceivable that there might have been still a benevolently despotic monarchy. Agrarian matters have affected social, political and industrial affairs in no little degree, and England would assuredly have been a very different place could she have developed as a granary rather than as a workshop.

CHAPTER 14

ENCLOSURE AND THE CHURCH

THE FIRST ENGLISH writer to castigate enclosers was a cleric, John Rous, the Warwickshire chantry priest.[1] Before the end of the fifteenth century he expounded the Church's view in this way: The depopulator was so hateful to God and man that at the end of his misspent life he (?) should be forbidden Christian burial. He had taken land from his fellow-Christians in life; he should not share land with them after death.

The clergy of the Reformation period in general took the same point of view, whatever were their opinions upon the religious issues of the time. Some of the heads of the Religious Houses were no doubt among the worst of the bad landlords of the time. More, as we have noted above, goes out of his way to castigate among these, 'certain Abbottes, holy men no doubt'.[2] These, however, seem to have been quite exceptional. Amongst the Romeward-looking sections of the clergy, Thomas Starkey and Thomas Lupset[3] led the literary protests against enclosure, and their arguments were reinforced by those of clerics who disagreed with them upon almost every subject under the sun, save this one, notably by Henry Brinkelow[4] and Robert Crowley. Lever said: 'the greatest griefe that hath been sente the people in thys realme hath bene the inclosing of comons',[5] but considered it wisest for individuals to leave to the authorities the redressing of it. Becon chastized 'the greedy caterpillars of the common weale'. He said:

'The cause of all this wretchedness and beggary in the common weal are the greedy gentlemen, which are sheepmongers and

[1] *Op. cit., supra*, p. 63, fn. 1; 'Cavit etiam jus canonicum quod depopulator agrorum non gaudebit immunitate ecclesie . . . Consonum multis videtur quod qui se villarum destructione abstrahunt a vivis, cum eisdem localiter non communicent in sepulturis'.

[2] *Utopia*, edn. cited above, p. 39.

[3] *Dialogue between (Reginald) Pole and (Thomas) Lupset* (temp. Hen. VIII), E.E.T.S., N.S. XII, 1871.

[4] *Complaynt of Roderyck Mors* (c. 1542), E.E.T.S., N.S. XXII, 1874.

[5] *Op. cit., infra*, p. 156, fn. 6.

graziers. While they study for their own private commodity, the common weal is like to decay . . . So they may be enriched they care not who be impoverished. They are right brothers of Cain, which had rather slay his brother Abel, than that he should have any part with him of worldly possessions.'[6]

Crowley openly showed his sympathy with the rebels who rose under Kett to redress their agrarian grievances, and para-phrased some very pointed Old Testament denunciations of those who oppress the poor:

> 'You thoughte that I woulde not requyre,
>   The bloode of all suche at your hande,
> But be you sure, eternall fyre,
>   Is ready for eche hell fyre brande.
> Both for the housynge and the lande
>   That you have taken from the pore
> Ye shall in hell dwell evermore.'[7]

Latimer and the Commonwealth Party

But of all the clerical characters of the time perhaps the most attractive is Bishop Hugh Latimer. As a yeoman's son he was thoroughly 'class-conscious':

> 'For if ye bring it to pass that the yeomanry be not able to put their sons to school . . . and . . . to marry their daughters to the avoiding of whoredom; I say, ye pluck salvation from the people. . . . For by yeomen's sons the faith of Christ is and hath been maintained chiefly. Is this realm taught by rich men's sons? No, No, read the chronicles.'[8]

Latimer's sermons are full of references to the agrarian question. Taking one of the least hackneyed:

> 'Furthermore, if the king's honour, as some men say, standeth in the great multitude of people; then these graziers, enclosers, and rentrearers are great hinderers of the king's honour. For whereas have been a great many householders and inhabitants, there is now but a shepherd and his dog. . . . My lords and masters I say also that all such proceedings which are against the king's honour . . . do plainly intend to make the yeomanry slavery, and the clergy shavery.'

[6] *Works* 1564, 'The Jewel of Joy (1553), Parker Soc. reprint 1844.
[7] *Thirty-one Epigrams*, etc. (1550–1), E.E.T.S., N.S. XV, 1872.
[8] *Op. cit.*, *supra*, p. 69, fn. 10, 'First Sermon before King Edward VI'.

Latimer and his fellows of the 'Commonwealth' party seem to have cultivated with some success the difficult art of making friends with authority without the sacrifice of principle. Even though they succeeded neither in reforming the House of Lords nor in checking the agrarian revolution, it is interesting to find in the English Church, nearly four centuries ago, a definite party of Christian Radicals, with clearly marked social aims, and with enough influence to include at least one bishop among their number and to affect the action of Thomas Cranmer and of the Protector himself. It is perhaps not too fanciful to see a trace of their influence to this day in the Prayer-Book Commination Service. Both the Edwardian Prayer-Books, like the present-day (1662) Book, have their curse, after those on idolaters, and on children who curse father and mother, and long before those on mere adulterers, fornicators, slanderers and drunkards: 'Cursed is he that removeth awaye the marke of hys neighbour's lande.'

The 17th Century Clergy

In the early part of the seventeenth century both Church and State (the latter then of course very largely under clerical influence) held the traditional point of view that enclosure was an offence to God and man. In 1604, for example, the Rev. Francis Trigge, the rector of Welbourn, Lincs., in the *Humble Petition of Two Sisters* (the Church and the Commonwealth) pointed out how diligently the statutes for whipping the poor were being executed by the same magistrates who quite ignored the tillage acts passed at the same time to protect the poor.[9] In this, and in his *Godly and Dutiful Sermon preached at Grantham,* Trigge castigated the greed of the new landlords. We have noted already that it is uncertain how far the numerous measures of agrarian reform adopted by Charles I and his Council were really due to disinterested care for the poor: but Laud, at any rate, seems to have been quite sincere. In one of his sermons he gives as his view of society and its obligations:

'If any be so addicted to his private, that he neglect the common, state, he is void of the sense of piety, and wisheth peace and

[9] *Humble Petition . . .* 1604, *Godly and Dutiful Sermon . . .* 1592. I have not seen either of these, and I quote from Scrutton, *op. cit.,* p. 96. The quotation on the title page is from the *Humble Petition . . .*

happiness to himself in vain. For whoever he be, he must live in the body of the Commonwealth, and in the body of the Church.'[10]

Wentworth, later Earl of Strafford, too, was as 'thorough' in putting into practice his social and economic theories.[11] When even (Sir) Cornelius Vermuyden, a Court favourite, fell foul of the commoners of Hatfield Chase, Wentworth ranged himself definitely upon the side of the peasantry.

On one occasion Laud told indignant freeholders to 'plead law' (as distinct from justice) 'in inferior courts. They should not plead it before him.' In 1636, in a private letter to the Warden of All Souls College, he declined resolutely to 'oblige the college' in a matter of enclosure, 'partly because I am a great hater of depopulation in any kind, as being one of the greatest mischiefs in this kingdom, and of very ill example from a college, or college tenant'. In 1630 the King himself had ventured upon a rather dubious enclosure in order to make a park between Richmond and Hampton Court, largely upon his own waste, but in some part of which neighbouring parishes had common right. He intended to acquire the remaining land and was so set upon the scheme as to 'begin walling the land not less ten or twelve miles about'.

The chief opponents of the scheme were Francis Cottington, Baron Cottington, Chancellor of the Exchequer, and Laud. Cottington grudged the expense, but even after he had yielded to royal importunity, perhaps according to Hyde, Earl of Clarendon, mainly to annoy Laud, the latter remained firm, and 'grew into much passion telling him that such men as he would ruin the King', and finally drew upon himself a royal reprimand for his vehemence. Laud paid for his principles. In 1641 the Grand Remonstrance attacked him bitterly as having 'drawn many millions out of the subjects' purses without any considerable profit to His Majesty' for, as Clarendon says:

'the Revenue of too Many of the Court consisted principally in Enclosures . . . which he still opposed passionately, except they were founded upon Law; and then if it would bring Profit to the

[10] Laud, W., *Works*, 1847, I, pp. 28–29, *H.L.J.* VI, 468B, 'Articles against Laud'. Since 1438 the Archbishop has had, *ex officio*, special responsibilities in respect of All Souls.
[11] Tawney, R. H., *Religion and the Rise of Capitalism*, 1926, quoting Reid, Miss R. R., *The King's Council in the North*, pp. 412–3.

King, how old and obsolete soever the Law was he thought he
might justly advise the Prosecution . . . which was likewise cast
upon his account.'[12]

In 1642 Thomas Fuller's *Holy State* stigmatizes enclosure as a

'Canker in the Commonwealth . . . Woeful experience shows how
it unhouses thousands of people, till desperate need thrusts them
on the gallows.'

As late as 1648 this traditional view was upheld by Sir John
Cooke, an Anglican, and at one time a member of one of
Charles's governments.

The Agrarian Problem and the Puritans

It is perhaps allowable here to admit the not-very-adequate
dictionary definition of Puritans as 'the more extreme Protest-
ants, whether within or self-excluded from the established
Church'. If we do this, and accept further the traditional
division of the group into (relatively moderate) Presbyterians,
and (more extreme) Independents-and-Others, we shall find it
difficult indeed to speak in general terms of the 'puritan
attitude' towards the agrarian problem, or indeed towards
almost anything else. There might be a good deal of difference
between the social teaching of the Presbyterians and the fierce
individualism of some at any rate of the Independents. For
that matter there might be even more between the inferences
which seem to follow from Presbyterian postulates, and the
actual practice of Presbyterian landlords, who had inherited
estates, or who (formerly merchants) contrived to acquire
them at bargain prices, by using the wonderful opportunities
offered to smart business men by the land changes of the
Interregnum. So far as Richard Baxter was concerned, 'new
presbyter' was very emphatically 'old priest writ large'.
Baxter was of yeoman stock, and in his *Christian Directory*
under 'Cases of Oppression, especially of tenants', he has a
good deal to say of engrossing and of rack-renting. 'An oppressor is an Anti-Christ and an Anti-God, . . . not only the
agent of the Devil, but his image,' he says. Ordinary landlords
must not let their land at market rates, must not enclose it
without considering the effect upon their tenants, and must not

---

[12] Clarendon, *History of the Rebellion.* I quote the Oxford edn. of 1725, I,
p. 98. The Cooke reference below, from *Unum Necessarium*, I owe to Dr.
Margaret James's book, pp. 273–5.

evict them without compensation. But even Baxter approved 'enclosure done in moderation by a pious man'.[13]

Walter Blith, the leading agricultural theorist and enclosure propagandist of the day, had been a captain in Cromwell's army.[14] He is one of the first writers to anticipate a favourite eighteenth-century argument that not only are commons and common fields economically unsound; they are also a source of moral evil, in that they encourage the poor in all manner of idleness and mischief. These would be better morally, as well as better off economically, if deprived of their dangerous independence. As to depopulation and the other problems attending enclosure, Blith rather naïvely confesses 'How these things should be mended is beyond my sphere'. He is however so excited by the thought of the coming Golden Age that mere prose is inadequate to express his feelings, and he bursts forth into verse:

> 'Though this a Paradox may seem to you,
> Experience and Reason proves it true.'

The cottagers whose commons were to disappear, and whose morals were to be improved, were by no means so enraptured by either prospect, and there were members of other social classes who shared their apprehension. Some went so far as to suggest that if the commons must be ploughed, there was no need for the ploughing to be done by the hired labourers of the lord of the manor and the wealthier proprietors—it would be still more profitable to the public if the poor undertook the work for their own benefit, upon co-operative lines. Not only the commons but also the private parks of the wealthy, which had in many instances once upon a time been commons, should be put into cultivation.

The Diggers[15]

On 16 April 1649 the Council of State was informed that William Everard, a cashiered army officer 'who termeth himself a prophett', together with one or two hundred kindred

---

[13] Baxter, R., *Christian Directory*, 1678. Selections from this, ed. Mrs. Jeanette Tawney, appear in *Chapters from Richard Baxter's Christian Directory*, 1925.

[14] Blith, W., *The English Improver*, 1649, *The English Improver Improved*, 1652.

[15] There are, of course, numerous works on the Levellers and the Diggers, especially those published of late by historians of the 'Left'. A good

spirits, had begun to dig up the (commonable) land on St. George's Hill in Weybridge, Surrey, and to sow it with carrots, parsnips and beans. While the Council was wondering what action to take, Gerrard Winstanley and Everard, the leaders, appeared in person before them, hat on head, with a detailed Christian-Socialist-agrarian programme. The Surrey enthusiasts were left undisturbed until the autumn of 1649, and when at last they were forcibly dispossessed their missionaries went out on tour through, at any rate, Middlesex, Bedfordshire, Berkshire, Buckinghamshire, Hertfordshire, Huntingdonshire and Northamptonshire. In 1653 they appeared in Staffordshire, and in 1654 in Northumberland. Of their war song, probably one stanza will suffice:

'With spades and hoes and plowes stand up now!
With spades and hoes and plowes stand up now!
Your freedom to uphold, seeing Cavaliers are so bold
To kill you if they could, and rights from you withold,
Stand up now, Diggers all!'

In fact, there was no need for the central government to take against the Diggers any such violent measures of repression as were thought appropriate in dealing with the allied—indeed, overlapping—political radical party, the Levellers. Property interests rather than mere political equalitarianism were at stake here, and it would be—it was—quite safe to leave these locally to look after themselves, they knowing that if necessary they had the forces of law and order on their side.

The Digger movement is, then, one of the interesting might-have-beens of English social and economic history, and it had no practical result. (Except, perhaps, that it scared landholders great and small into closing their ranks against proposals for land reform of almost any kind, which might ultimately lead to social revolution, far more frightening than mere political

introductory one is the classical Berens, L. H., *The Digger Movement*, 1906. A much more modern and very readable short work covering both Levellers generally and Diggers is Petegorsky, D. W., *Left-Wing Democracy in the English Civil War*, 1940. H. N. Brailsford's posthumous book *The Levellers and the English Revolution*, ed. Hill, C., 1961, is a most stimulating and yet a very scholarly and balanced work. It contains, Chap. XXXIV, 656–70, 'The True Levellers', what seems to me much the best short account of the Diggers. For more detailed bibliographical information see Petegorsky, Brailsford and [several of the books of] Christopher Hill.

change.) Perhaps at this distance of time one may admire some features of the Digger propaganda particularly the neat way in which they harnessed a bit of imaginary history concerning 'Charles, our Norman oppressor' to the service of their ideal (so, like Tom Paine, a century and a half later, turning against their opponents the same feudal theory of land-holding which the lawyers had for generations been using against popular claims). There is matter for admiration too in the fashion in which they demonstrated that large-scale cultivation was not necessarily incompatible with agrarian reform, by anticipating in some measure the modern growth of producers' co-operation.

After the suppression of the Diggers the controversy went merrily on. Perhaps the two most interesting men among the champions of the opposing sides were the two Leicestershire ministers of the (Commonwealth) Church already mentioned, John Moore of Knaptoft, and Joseph Lee (of Catthorpe and) Cotesbach. Moore painted a dismal picture of the evicted cottagers wandering drearily from town to town begging, 'Can you help me to a farm or a little land to employ my team?', and to the authors of such poverty and misery he said: 'Thou must look whether thou has right in the Court of Conscience, as well as in the Court of Law.'[16] Lee, on the other hand, insisted upon the economic argument, and anticipated the eighteenth-century discovery of the providential arrangement by which the good of all is best secured by allowing each individual to follow the prompting of enlightened self-interest. He and his supporters put a very awkward question when they queried why communism in land should be held as natural and proper by the same persons who objected to communism in all other property (including, for example, wives).

It is clear then that at any rate some of the Puritans had inherited, even if in a somewhat diluted form, the social traditions of the mediaeval Church, and that others built up a social conscience of their own in that total reconstruction of all ideas which accompanied their efforts after a new heaven and a new earth. How far their teaching proved sterile, and how far it has been a genuine influence upon later thought it is difficult to say. The Quakers, as one might have expected, maintained their ideals to some extent even in the dark days of the eighteenth century. In 1767 their celebrated pamphleteer, John

---

[16] Above, p. 77, fn. 7. The quotation is from *The Crying Sin* . . . 1653.

Hustler, attacked as the cause of rural depopulation, large farms, the corn bounty, and the enclosure movement.[17] As late as 1792, Catherine Phillips in *Considerations on the High Price of Grain* adduced as the causes of rural poverty the prevalence of large farms, the waste of food in making starch, and tea drinking (leading to the conversion of arable land to cow pasture in order to produce milk and butter). She suggested as remedies an increase of small farms, and the division of commons (if they must be enclosed) equitably among all concerned, with special care for the interests of the poor.[18]

The post-Restoration Clergy

Before the Restoration of 1660 the clergy generally had been always in the van of the opposition to enclosure. Now it is hardly too much to say that they concentrated rather on securing for themselves as large as possible a share of the proceeds.[19] Most of the enclosure propagandists from the middle of the seventeenth century onwards took care to include the commutation of tithe at a generous valuation among the advantages to accrue from the adoption of their schemes. In fact it was largely clerical suspicion of the tithe-commuting activities of the first Board of Agriculture which led to its untimely demise in 1819. Perhaps the clergy shared the apprehension of their old antagonist Cobbett that 'as a General Enclosure Bill will pauperize the countryside, so a general commutation will lead to the disestablishment of the church and the abolition of the monarchy'. It is because of this close connexion between enclosure and tithe commutation that one has difficulty in estimating how largely such clerical opposition as there was to enclosure is to be ascribed to disinterested love of the poor, how much to an apprehension that conversion of arable to pasture, following enclosure, or tithe commutation on insufficiently generous terms, might lead to the impoverishment of benefices. Certainly it is not unduly cynical to suspect that sometimes, when the opponent was a rector, not a vicar, he

[17] A Manufacturer [Hustler J.] *The Occasion of the Dearness of Provisions* . . . 1767.

[18] *Considerations* . . . especially pp. 19–21, 'if the voice of humanity was prevalent in our senates . . . would it not dictate the securing to the poor of their little habitations . . . even further to leave . . . parts of commons . . . free for cottages'.

[19] This statement should be considered against the background of the facts introduced by Hill, C., *Economic Problems of the Church*, 1956.

might well fear that enclosure-and-conversion might have dis-astrous effects on his great tithe (see Glossary s.v. *tithe*).

I hope that the loftier motive was the one affecting such a noteworthy cleric as William Territt, rector of Bainton, Yorks, E.R. In 1748 he put himself at the head of his parishioners in objecting to some enclosures which the lord of the manor was making, broke down the fences with his own hands (and landed himself at York Assizes for his pains. The reader may be glad to know that, after a five-hour trial the lord was non-suited, and the rector won!)[20] Certainly John Jones, rector of Boln-hurst, Beds., 1749–67, entered in his parish register this wish concerning any enclosure of his parish (actually carried through in 1778):

> 'If ever a general inclosing of This Parish should be agreed upon, I would willingly hope that the restoring and confirming the benefit of the Commons to the poor Cottagers will be remembered and made at least One of the Conditions of such Agreement. There are many Reasons against the general inclosing of Parishes as being detrimental to the Public, in many cases injurious to private persons: on which considerations some intelligent and conscientious Clergymen will never consent to the making of such inclosures, tho' they have considerable advantages offered them.[21]

David Davies, rector of Cookham, Berks, wrote the best defence of the labourer in his invaluable pamphlet of 1795, *The Case of the Labourers in Husbandry*.[22] In it he protests very forcefully against the separation of the labourers from the land, and prophesies, with some accuracy, the evils which he thinks will result from it.

Some Eighteenth-century Clergy

But there were clergy innumerable on the other side. Even the bishops took a hand. The county palatine of Durham, where the bishop was all-powerful, was largely enclosed soon after the Restoration, and by 1726 it was said 'nine parts in ten are already enclosed'. Bishop Richard Watson, of Llandaff, was a keen planter and encloser, and contrived to reconcile a

---

[20] Ollard, L., *History of Bainton* . . . 1934, p. 42.

[21] Bolnhurst Parish Register (communicated by Mr. F. G. Emmison, Essex County Archivist).

[22] See above, p. 85.

So, God bless King George, And defend us from Evil
And send all Enroathers oppinions to th Devil
Let him flea y Sharp Squire? who worrys poor
like ours too oft wealthy, And live with on those
Derry down

If Gentlemen venture Damnation at last
Let all honest Fellows be modest & Chast
Let us kiss our Wives, And let Wenthes alone
And every man be content with his own
Derry down

XIII Popular reaction to the enclosure of commons,
(a) in Charnwood Forest, Leics. 1753,
formally enclosed 1808–29; see p. 214

Wm. Mason, Thomas Brook, Edmund Chilley, and Ann Rush, were indicted for wilfully and maliciously damaging a fence the property of Charles Green. made under the Lopham Inclosure Act, which offence is made felony by Act of Parliament. The prisoner Mason addressed the Court, as champion of the rights of the poor, whose property he said the commons were. The Judge stated distinctly to the prisoners and to the Jury, that the poor had no such right as was asserted by the prisoner Mason.— In the present case it appeared that 200 acres of land had been allotted for the use of the poor.— Mason was sentenced to 12, and the others to 3 months' imprisonment.

(b) in North and South Lopham, Norfolk, 1815,
enclosed 1812–15; see p. 214

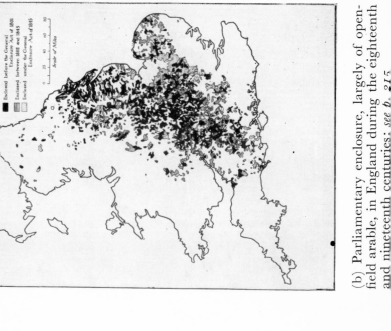

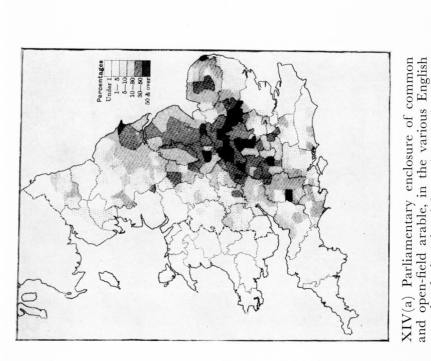

XIV(a) Parliamentary enclosure of common and open-field arable, in the various English counties during the eighteenth and nineteenth

Percentages
Under 1
1 — 5
5 — 10
10 — 30
30 — 50
50 & over

(b) Parliamentary enclosure, largely of open-field arable, in England during the eighteenth and nineteenth centuries: *see p. 215*

Enclosed before the General Enclosure Act of 1801
Enclosed between 1802 and 1845
Enclosed under the General Enclosure Act of 1845

Scale of Miles
0   20   40   60   80

residence in Westmorland (where he spent his time largely in agricultural pursuits) with the performance of the duties of his Welsh see, 'so honourably providing for his family'. He wrote the preface and part of the text in the *Agricultural Report* on his county, and half a dozen other clergy were among the Board's surveyors who all spoke, almost with unanimity, in favour of general, immediate, and universal enclosure. Perhaps the most reliable evidence of clerical concern for the poor in the eighteenth and early nineteenth centuries is to be found in the fact that in a few (perhaps one per cent) of 4,200 'private' enclosure acts, provisions were inserted for safeguarding the interests of the cottagers. This was, as a rule, at the instigation of the incumbent of the parish, though, very exceptionally by the goodwill of the lord of the manor.[23] It seems clear then that in this, as in many other matters, the Church has spoken, if not in a different voice, with a very different accent, at different times. It is perhaps not unfair to suggest that while the Tudor Church, almost to a man, claimed what it regarded as justice for the poor, the most, as a rule, that could be offered by the Georgian Church was an occasional suggestion of 'charity'.

[23] See Slater, *op. cit.*, pp. 126–8, for a few instances. I can say from personal examination of very many acts and MS. awards that Slater rather overstates than underestimates the extent of seigniorial consideration for the poor in this respect.

CHAPTER 15

ENCLOSURE AND THE LANDLORD AND FARMER

FROM WHAT HAS been said above it will be manifest that at all times enclosure has been in general imposed from above rather than demanded by the rural populace. This is not of course to deny that some individual peasants from mediaeval times to relatively modern days have been businesslike enough to see the economic gain of enclosure, and often where possible to carry out such enclosure of their own land, while firmly opposing any tendency on the part of others to do likewise.[1]

Enclosure and Rent

According to almost all writers, the enclosing landlord's interest in the matter was largely one of financial return. Whether he was a courtier of Henry VIII's time, who enclosed open fields for use as sheep pastures, or a Georgian squire who reclaimed the waste in order to put it under the plough, he was primarily concerned with securing from the land in its new form a much higher monetary yield than it could ever afford in its open state. In the latter part of the seventeenth century and throughout the eighteenth, when contemporary economists were genuinely convinced that the amount of rent paid was a fair index of national prosperity, this does not mean that every encloser was necessarily governed in his actions by the basest of motives.[2] From the landlord's point of view it did not signify a great deal whether extra profit was to come from an increased corn yield per acre with much the same rate of expense, or from a valuable crop of wool raised with low labour costs (rather than an equally valuable crop of corn with high labour costs). In either case there would be a greater surplus of product over the expenses of production, and some share of this, at any rate, he might confidently hope would find its way into his pocket.

---

[1] There is a good illustration of peasant enterprise in this at Little Gringley, Notts. before 1547/8, in a document analysed in an article of mine in *Trans.* (Notts.) *Thoroton Soc.* XLIII, 1939, pp. 33–48, and reproduced above facing p. 44 as Plate IIIb.

[2] Lord Ernle, *op. cit.*, p. 213, traces this idea back to Locke, quoting Locke, *Works*, edn. 1823, V, p. 69.

Rise of Rent on Enclosure

One of the earliest enclosure propagandists, Sir Anthony Fitzherbert, who wrote in 1523, has a very interesting chapter advising the lord who intends to enclose how to set about the business.[3] This chapter is very significantly entitled: 'How to make a lordship that is worth XX marks a year worth XX li a year'. Fitzherbert's estimate (an increase of fifty per cent— see Glossary s.v. *mark*) is a very reasonable one, and it seems certain that landlords could often make a much more handsome profit than this. To some extent indeed they were compelled either to increase their incomes or to face insolvency. Such fixed revenues as they had were payable in a currency several times debased, and their standard of living was in danger. They met the situation in two main ways. Estates let at fixed rents, but at fines uncertain, had as much as possible of the peasant's unearned increment skimmed off in the form of vastly increased fines. Better than this, from the landlord's point of view, would be to destroy altogether the old rustic society, with its complex network of mutual rights and obligations, and let the land at what it was worth, i.e. at a rack rental. Enclosure would help this process in two ways, by breaking up the old community and driving its members elsewhere to seek a livelihood, and by enabling the new tenants who took over the enlarged and consolidated farms to make a modest profit, although paying a vastly increased rent.

Rack Renting

The Tudor pamphleteers again and again denounce this practice of rack renting. A writer of 1549 puts the landlord's point of view:

'In all my life time I looke not that the thirde part of my lands shall come to my dispocition, that I may enhaunce the rent of the same; but it shalbe in men's holdinges either by lease or by copie graunted before my time. . . . We cannot rayse all our wares as you maye yours.'[4]

However, few landlords were content with a modest increase of rent of fifty per cent or so, and public opinion was strongly on

[3] Cited above, p. 67, fn. 7.
[4] W. S. [?John Hales], *Discourse of the Common Weal,* 1581 (but referring to conditions in 1549), ed. Lamond, Miss E., 1893, p. 19. The Knight is speaking—his remark is a home thrust at the Merchant.

the side of the tenants. More denounced the 'inordinate and unsaciable covetousness' of the landlords, and rejoiced when God sent a murrain which slew many thousands of their sheep, only regretting that the pest had not fallen rather on the sheep-masters' own heads.[5]

Thirty years later Lever restated the old idea that landlord and tenant had mutual duties and responsibilities one towards another.[6]

'The landelorde by lettyng of fermes must dyspose unto the tenants thereof necessary lands, and houses of an indifferent rente . . . so everye man by doying of hys dutye muste dyspose unto other that commodytye and benefyte, which is committed of god until theym. . . .'

He tells with great indignation of the London 'leasemongers' who force up rents, and instances one case near London where land has been enhanced from 2s. 4d. an acre to 'ixs. or as I harde saye xixs., but I am ashamed to name so much.' Those who gamble in real estate will most certainly be damned:

'They do not onelye bye landes and goodes, but also lyves and soules of men, from God and the comen wealth, unto the devyl and theim selves.'

Latimer, about the same time, is equally emphatic.[7] His father, about 1497, had rented a farm in Leicestershire for £3 or £4 a year; when Latimer preached in 1549 the rent was £16.

'My father was a yeoman, and had no lands of his own, only he had a farm of three or four pound by year at the uttermost, and hereupon he tilled so much as kept half a dozen men. He had walk for a hundred sheep; and my mother milked thirty kine. He was able, and did find the King a harness, with himself and his horse. . . . I can remember that I buckled his harness when he went unto Blackheath field. He kept me to school, or else I had not been able to have preached before the king's majesty now. He married my sisters with five pound, or twenty nobles apiece. . . . He kept hospitality for his poor neighbours, and some alms he

---

[5] *Utopia*, edn. cited, p. 41.
[6] *Sermons*, edn. cited, 'A Sermon preached at Paules Crosse', pp. 106, 129. 'A Sermon made in the Shroudes in Paules', p. 29.
[7] *Sermons*, edn. cited, p. 85.

gave to the poor. And all this he did of the said farm, where he that now hath it payeth sixteen pound by the year, or more, and is not able to do anything for his prince, for himself, nor for his children, or give a cup of drink to the poor.'

The *Book of Private Prayer* set forth by King Edward VI in 1553 includes in its *Prayer for Landlords*:[8]

'We heartily pray Thee to send thy Holy Spirit into the hearts of those that possess the grounds, pastures and dwelling places of the earth, that they remembering themselves to be thy tenants may not rack and stretch out the rents of their houses and lands, but so [let them out to others] that . . . after this life they may be received into everlasting dwelling places'.

A few years later this matter of rent crops up again in Thomas Tusser's work. He gives a figure which also is used by some of the other Tudor writers, and which occurs again in the eighteenth century, setting forth that, on an average, land in severalty is worth thrice as much as that in open field:

'More profit is quieter found,
(Where pastures in severall be;)
Of one seelie aker of ground,
Than champion maketh of three.'[9]

Some Seventeenth-century Estimates of Rent Increases

In 1607 John Norden deals with this increase of rent, and in anticipation of what was to become a favourite eighteenth-century argument, he reasons that high rent is a positive benefit to the small farmer, since it is a constant incentive to industry.[10] Samuel Hartlib in 1651 says that on enclosure rent would increase from 6s. to 10s. or 13s. 4d. per acre.[11] Silvanus Taylor, the next year, takes 1s. 8d. as a typical rent for un-enclosed down, 3s. 4d. for enclosed land in severalty.[12] These figures are confirmed by the notebooks of Henry Best, a Yorkshire farmer:

(in 1641) 'The lands in the pasture weere . . . letten . . . for 2s.

[8] This is Tawney's quotation in *Religion and the Rise of Capitalism*, p. 150.
[9] *Comparison betweene Champion and Severall*, stanza 22, edn. cited, p. 145.
[10] *Surveior's Dialogue* . . . 1607.   [11] *Legacie* . . . 1651.
[12] S. T. *Common Good . . . Improvement . . . by . . . Inclosure*, 1652.

a lande, and lastly for 3*s.* a lande, but nowe being inclosed they will let for thrice as much.'[13]

On the whole, perhaps a 200 per cent increase is a fair average of the improvement that was expected. It may be noted, however, that on enclosure the rents of one Cambridge college rose from £140 to £537 p.a.; colleges were then, as they still are, considerate and rather conservatively-minded landlords. As a bridge between the mid-seventeenth century writers on the subject, and those of the eighteenth, we may quote John Houghton, who wrote in 1682. He also justifies rack renting, since 'the racking landlord puts them upon new projects and industry'.[14]

Enclosure and Rent in the Eighteenth Century

A writer for country gentlemen in 1717 says sheep on commons are gysted at 1*s.* per head p.a., in enclosure at 2*s.* 6*d.* per score per week—a sixfold improvement.[15] The eighteenth-century topographers confirm this point. Defoe's *Tour*, which appeared in 1724–6, abounds in instances of enclosed land being worth many times the rent of open land in the same area.[16] The New Forest soil, he says, was virtually worthless in its then state, but on enclosure, after twenty years, it would be cheap at 5*s.* per acre. Half a century later Arthur Young is interested in the rents of land, and his *Tours* give a good deal of data upon them, almost always distinguishing between the rents of open land and those of enclosure.[17] At Offley, near Hitchin, open land averaged 1*s.* an acre, enclosure 4*s.* At Biddenham, near Bedford, the figures are 2*s.* 6*d.* to 3*s.* 6*s.*, and 10*s.* 6*d.* to 12*s.* 6*d.* respectively. There is an absolute concurrence of testimony upon the point; Young and his old rival William Marshall,

---

[13] *The Farming Book of Henry Best* [of Elmswell, Yorks. E.R.], Surtees Soc. 33, 1857, p. 129.

[14] Above, p. 82, fn. 5.

[15] Jacob, G., *Country Gentleman's Vade Mecum*, 1717.

[16] *Tour* . . . 1724–6. I have used the *Everyman* edn. of 1928. It is of course a commonplace that Defoe's special interests make him a sounder guide on urban affairs than rural matters, but where any aspect of business and money-making is concerned probably Defoe may be relied on.

[17] *Southern Tour* . . . 1768, *Northern Tour* . . . 1770, *Eastern Tour* . . . 1771. See also a series of other tours, 1776–91, extracted from (45 volumes of) the *Annals*, as No. 14 in the London School of Economics *Reprints* Series, no editor's name given, 1932.

Sir Frederick Morton Eden, and all the county reporters tell the same tale. It is clear that after enclosure the landlord could reasonably hope for a much bigger net monetary revenue from the same land, even allowing for the fact that he must set on one side a proportion of his gross receipts to cover the interest and sinking fund of the very considerable capital cost—anywhere from perhaps £1 to £10 per acre—which enclosure had involved.[18]

Enclosure and Production

Clearly such substantial increases of rent could be paid only if the net product on enclosure was considerably increased over what the land had yielded in its open state. On this point too there is a general concurrence of testimony. In the early years of enclosure, when it had meant in general the conversion of arable to pasture, or the substitution of enclosed pasture for open common, it is true that the gain in quantity of wool production had been partly offset by a fall in quality. The common-reared sheep produced a fine wool, of much higher quality than that yielded by the flocks kept in enclosed pasture. Even so, however, the net profit was considerable. The profit secured by producing wool instead of corn was handsomer still, probably rather because of reduced labour costs than from a greater monetary value of the product.

In the sixteenth and seventeenth centuries there are numerous descriptions of the poor yield of crops in the open fields, and the miserable quantity and quality of the stock reared on the commons. Probably one or two instances will suffice. It is certain enough that in many places the soil of the open fields was worn out by the continual taking of crops from it. Fitzherbert advises the farmer who has a number of selions lying side by side, and who:

'hath no dung nor shepe to compost nor dung his land withall. Then let the husband take his ploughe, and cast al such landes three or four tymes togider, and make theyre rigge theyr as ye raine was before ... And so shel he finde new moulde, that was not sene in an hundred yeres before, the which must nedes gyve more corne than the other dydde before.'[19]

---

[18] There are some figures on this in an article by the present writer, *Econ. Hist. Rev.* 2nd Ser., 2, 1952, pp. 258–65.

[19] *Surveyinge*, edn. 1567, ch. 24.

According to Tusser also, the need was for laying to grass unproductive corn land:

> 'Land arable driven or worne to the proofe,
> and craveth some rest for thy profits behoofe.
> With otes ye may sowe it, the sooner to grasse,
> more soon to be pasture to bring it to passe.'[20]

All the evidence makes it clear that the open-field farmer who did not practise some such plan as this scratched out but a scanty living from his selions. As a speaker said in the House of Commons in 1597:

> '. . . It fareth with the earth as with other creatures that through continual labour grow faint and feeble-hearted . . . and this did the former law-makers overslip, tyeing the land once tilled to a perpetual bondage and servitude of ever being tilled.'[21]

The Exhaustion of Open-field Soil

Something of this was in the mind of the government in the early seventeenth century, when licences were granted 'for arable lands converted from tillage to pasture'. The government rather optimistically hoped that by a few years' rest the ground would be made fruitful again, and on a rise of corn prices it would be reconverted from pasture back to arable. A memorandum prepared for the Council in connexion with the Midland disturbances in 1607 alleges, apparently with some truth, that open-field agriculture is quite incapable of feeding the population, and compares the position in a few typical open counties with that in some enclosed ones.[22] Particularly interesting is its comparison of Northamptonshire and Somerset, very much to the advantage of the latter. There were occasional voices to the contrary. Joseph Bentham, for example, in 1635 paints an idyllic picture of an open-field village [? in Northamptonshire], and contrasts it with an enclosed township [? where], very much to the disadvantage of the latter in every respect:

> 'Looke into the fields of the one, there shall you see cattell of all

[20] Edn. cited, *Januarie*, last stanza.
[21] *Cf.* above, p. 23. I quote at second hand from Bland, A. E., Brown, P. A., and Tawney, R. H., *Select Documents* . . . 1914, *H.M.C.* VII, pp. 541–3.
[22] Cunningham prints this in full as App. II, Pt. II.

sorts, friendly and familiarly feeding together, not onely the meadowes, but also the slades and lands ends fatted from the land loaden with grasse; the lands loaden and varnish'd with varietie of garnishing and gladding increase; and the people from the new-going stripling to the decrepite and neare-dying old man, in their seedes-time, harvests, and other seasons, like pain-full and industrious pismires, labouring in their severall imploy-ments with much solacing rejoycing and delightsome gladnesse.'[23]

The Agricultural Propagandists

Most of the agricultural writers of the later seventeenth and early eighteenth centuries had something to say of common fields, as of marling, draining, and the sowing of roots, clover and sainfoine. Many of them laid great stress on the enclosure and reclamation of waste. John Houghton in 1682 tried to work out the difference in productivity between open fields and enclosed ones. In Staffordshire he thought twenty bushels to the acre was a fair average wheat crop from open land. Since the land was out of cultivation one year in three this means an annual average of rather more than thirteen bushels to the acre. Houghton 'knew a gentleman near Bristol' who (in enclosed land) had a crop of wheat in enclosures at 30 bushels per acre. Jethro Tull in 1731 had rather less than 32 per acre [which is better than the normal yield as late as 1914].[24]

Young and His Contemporaries

Arthur Young's works are of course a mine of facts and figures (if often of not very factual facts and rather dubious figures), on this point.[25] The enclosed farms he admires so much in general reap anywhere from 28 to 36 bushels of wheat per acre. The open-field farms he rarely describes as yielding as much as 24 bushels—often much less.

Almost any of the hundred-odd volumes of the Board of Agriculture *General Views* . . . taken at random will supply illustrations of this.[26] The only county volumes which do not are those dealing with counties where open fields had long

[23] Bentham, J., *The Christian Conflict*, 1635 (not mentioned in the list of Bentham's works in *D.N.B.*), chap. 13, Duty 9.

[24] *Horse-ho[e]ing Husbandry* 1731. I have used the edn. of 1751. Robert Loder in 1620 (*op. cit.*, passim) had from open-field lands as much per acre as 35 bushels of wheat and 46 of barley. Probably this crop was indeed exceptional.

[25] Above, p. 86, fn. 14.   [26] See the table of these below, App. I, pp. 177–8.

disappeared, and where therefore the matter did not arise. The reader may verify this for himself by turning up the volumes for his own county. In general, then, it seems incontestable that enclosure was quite justified from the point of view of increasing agricultural production in the lands which had been in open field.

The Commons

As to the commons, the evidence is stronger still. Whatever may have been the arguments for commons from the social point of view (and there were many), agriculturally the commons were almost necessarily very much of a blot on the countryside. [Indeed, some (? most) remaining ones still are!] The economic argument for the enclosure of commons is reinforced by another, based on the alleged deleterious effects of the commons upon the morals of the rustic community in breeding idleness and vice. Though in any case, not all of the landed gentry, who gained most by the enclosure of the commons, were particularly shining examples of either industry or virtue! The evidence as to the unproductiveness of the commons, and the small quantity and low value of the stock reared upon them, is even stronger than that as to the depravity of the commoners. Tusser in 1573 gives as reasons for the relative worthlessness of commons in their then state:

> 'Some commons are barren, the nature is such,
>   and some over laieth the common too much,
> The pestered commons small profit doth geeve,
>   and profit as little some reape, I beleeve.
> Some pester the common with jades and with geese
>   with hog without ring and with sheepe without fleese;
> Some lose a daie's labour with seeking their owne,
>   some meet with a bootie they would not have knowne.'[27]

Overstocking

Tusser's two main charges are that the common was generally situated on the least fertile soil, and that it was often overstocked (and, of course, that commons encouraged idleness and theft). These complaints arise time and time again. Many commons were stinted, however, and careful regulations were drawn up by the village community to prevent the surcharging of the limited acreage available. In parishes where there were

[27] Edn. cited, *April*, stanzas 13, 14.

both stinted and unstinted commons the latter were of course in the worse condition. Walter Blith says of these in 1649 'every man laies on at random'; they are abominably overstocked, so that every four or five years 'you shall observe such a rot of sheep' that the commoners lose all their flocks. Child, whose work the *Large Letter* . . . makes up by far the greater part of Hartlib's *Legacie* in 1651 puts seven pointed rhetorical questions concerning the wastes and commons, every one of them directed towards suggesting that the products of the common are worthless cattle and sheep, and a poor and idle peasantry. Silvanus Taylor in 1652 says that people are 'nowhere more penurious than such as border on commons'. This poverty is due to God's displeasure at their idleness—they have no settled industry. Their children are 'brought up lazying upon a Common to attend one cow and a few sheep', and 'being nursed up in idleness in their youth, they become indisposed for labor, and then begging is their portion or Theevery their Trade. . . . The two great Nurseries of Idleness and Beggery are Alehouses and Commons.'

The Alleged Moral Evils of Commons

Joseph Lee takes up the tale. On the enclosure of the commons three or four shepherd boys 'will be necessitated to lay aside that idle employment . . . destructive to the soules of those Lads'. When they should have been at school they are 'playing at nine holes under a bush.[28] Their cattle make a prey on their neighbours' corn, and they themselves are made a prey to Satan.' In 1681 the commons are described as 'a grief and a scandal'. Certainly a large unstinted common had the effect of attracting to the neighbourhood a great many poor—desirable and otherwise—in the hope that they might be able to make a living from it. At least they might hope for the site of a cabin, and with luck for turbary and grazing facilities. The Poor Law of 1662 waxes indignant upon this point.[29] The late seventeenth-

[28] It is, I think, not too fanciful to see a reference to this sort of thing in the nursery rhyme *Little Boy Blue*.

[29] . . . by reason of some defects in the law, poor people are not restrained from going from one parish to another, and therefore do endeavour to settle themselves in those parishes where there is the best stock, the largest common or wastes to build cottages, and the most woods for them to burn and destroy; and when they have consumed it, then to another parish, and at last become rogues and vagabonds . . . (Preamble of 14 Car. II *c.* 12 1662).

and early eighteenth-century agricultural writers are almost unanimous on it; probably it may suffice if one or two eighteenth-century instances are added to those already given.

Marshall on Commons

William Marshall was Young's contemporary and rival. His work on the agriculture of the Midlands appeared in 1790; here, as elsewhere, he has little to say of the value of commons, either agriculturally or socially. To describe land which is quite sterile, he uses the expression 'as bare as a common. They have been continued under the curse of common rights as they are called, but really common nuisances.'

The Board of Agriculture Reporters

All the county reporters go on in much the same strain: John Billingsley, whose report on Somerset appeared in 1794, considered the commons equally wasteful agriculturally, and harmful morally:

> 'Moral effects of an injurious tendency accrue to the cottager, from a reliance on the imaginary benefits of stocking a common. The possession of a cow or two, with a hog and a few geese, naturally exalts the peasant, in his own conception, above his brethren in the same rank of society. It inspires some degree of confidence in a property, inadequate to his support. In sauntering after his cattle, he acquires a habit of indolence. Quarter, half, and occasionally whole days are imperceptibly lost. Day labour becomes disgusting; the aversion increased by indulgence, and at length the sale of a half fed calf, or hog, furnishes the means of adding intemperance to idleness.'

In Gloucestershire, cottages on the commons are 'erected by idle and dissolute people, sometimes from the neighbourhood and sometimes strangers. Their chief building materials are store poles stolen from the neighbouring woods.' In Shropshire:

> 'Let those who doubt go round the commons now open, and view the miserable huts, and poor, ill-cultivated, impoverished spots erected, or rather thrown together . . . which . . . affords them a very trifle towards their maintenance, yet operates upon their minds as a sort of independence; this idea leads the man to lose many days' work, by which he gets a habit of indolence; a

daughter kept at home to milk a poor half starv'd cow, who being open to temptations soon turns harlot, and becomes a distrest ignorant mother instead of making a good useful servant.'

Probably Billingsley, Bishton and Turner, are little more frank here than are some of their colleagues. Many of the commoners were, and could fairly well afford to be, independent of day labour for an employer. From this point of view, as well as from that of agricultural improvement it was desirable, thought the eighteenth-century farmer or landlord, that the commons should disappear.

The Commoners and the Commons

The commoners, of course, were not convinced of this. They clung obstinately to the notion that the common was of benefit to them. They much preferred rearing poor specimens of cattle on the commons for their own benefit, to tending prize stock in enclosures for someone else's. They were not in the least attracted by the prospect set forth by one of the Reporters, seeing the commons 'to wave with luxuriant crops of grain—be covered with innumerable flocks and herds, or clothed with stately timber', since not grain, herds nor timber would be theirs. The commoners of Raunds, Northants, put their case very well when they petitioned (unsuccessfully) against an enclosure bill in 1797:

'That the Petitioners beg Leave to represent to the House that, under Pretence of improving Lands in the said Parish, the Cottagers and other Persons entitled to Right of Common on the Lands intended to be inclosed will be deprived of an inestimable Privilege which they now enjoy . . . that enables them to maintain themselves and their Families in the Depth of Winter . . . in addition to this they can now supply the Grazier with young or lean Stock at a reasonable Price, to fatten and bring to Market . . . which they conceive to be the most rational and effectual Way of establishing Public Plenty . . . a more ruinous Effect of this Inclosure will be the almost total Depopulation of their Town, now filled with bold and hardy Husbandmen, from among whom, and the Inhabitants of other open Parishes, the Nation has hitherto derived its greatest Strength and Glory, in the Supply of its Fleets and Armies, and driving them, from Necessity and Want of Employ, in vast Crowds, into manufacturing Towns, where the very Nature of their Employment, over the Loom or the Forge, soon may waste their Strength, and consequently debilitate their

Posterity, and by imperceptible Degrees, obliterate that great Principle of Obedience to the Laws of God and their Country, which forms the Character of the simple and artless Villager. . . .'[30]

Who shall say that time has not justified some at any rate of such forebodings?

[30] *H.C.J.* 19 June 1797.

CHAPTER 16

ENCLOSURE AND THE PEASANT—THE
SOCIAL CONSEQUENCES OF ENCLOSURE

Enclosure and the Poor

FROM VERY EARLY times the strongest argument levelled against enclosure has been that it affected adversely the interests of the peasant. It was primarily for this reason that Parliament (vainly) legislated against it in Tudor times. It was, one hopes, for this reason that throughout the sixteenth and early seventeenth centuries the great majority of the clergy opposed it. Even in the eighteenth century, it was felt that this argument against the change was a strong one, and that if it could be sustained much of the economic argument for enclosure would be outweighed. Therefore the agricultural propagandists of the period devote many pages to some not altogether convincing counter-arguments, in which they endeavour to prove that in general the poor will gain positive benefits from enclosure, which will more than counterbalance any evil effects it may have upon them.

Depopulation

The manner in which enclosure could harm the poor differed at different times. In the sixteenth century, when, in general enclosure was that of open arable field, enclosed for conversion to pasture, the adverse effect upon the poor was that of de-populating the countryside, because of the scarcity of employ-ment to which the change gave rise. This is the argument set forth by almost all Tudor writers on the subject. Clearly enough there was some justification for it. Rous gives, for example, a list of townships enclosed and depopulated near Warwick,[1] and the reader may satisfy himself as to the disappearance of the places by walking over the Warwickshire countryside, where to this day he will find decayed villages, parish churches with few or no houses near them and pasture fields occupying the sites of what were four or five hundred years ago flourishing village communities. Instances could be given from most counties—certainly from all those in the Midlands—of the

---

[1] *Op. cit.,ff.* 110, 110a, pp. 122–3 in edn. cited above p. 63. *Cf.* Plate IV, facing p. 45.

sweeping depopulation which followed this first wave of enclosure. Contemporary literature already quoted waxes very indignant on the point.

Depopulation in the Midlands

A pamphleteer of 1550–3 gives detailed calculations of the rural depopulation caused in three Midland counties, Oxfordshire, Buckinghamshire, and Northamptonshire:

> 'There is not so many plowes used within Oxforthshire as was in King Henry VII's time and since his first coming there lacketh 40 plowes [elsewhere he says 80], . . . every plough was able to keep 6 persons, down lyinge and uprisinge in his house, the whiche draweth to 240 persons in Oxforthshire . . . whither shall they go—into Northamptonshire, and there also the living of twelf score persons lost;—whither shall then they go—forth from shire to shire and be scattered thus abroad . . . and for lack of masters, by compulsion driven; some of them to begge and some to steale . . .'[2]

About the same time, Becon gives a scathing account of the attitude of the enclosing landlord:

> 'If they once creep into a town or village, they for the most part never cease, till they have devoured and eaten up the whole town . . . Who will be troubled, say they, with such a sort of shake-ragged slaves in a town, which do nothing but burn up our hedges, eat up the common, fill the town with beggars brawls [?brats]?'[3]

Depopulation as a Result of the Conversion of Arable to Pasture

Harrison makes the same point in 1577 and 1587,[4] and the *Statutes* tell a similar story. The depopulation act of 1489 says:

> 'where in some townes two hundred persons were occupied and lived by their lawfull labours; now there are occupied two or three heardmen, and the residue fall into idleness.'

A treatise of (1549, printed in) 1581 continues the old complaint:

> 'Those shepe is the cause of all theise mischeives, for they have driven husbandrie out of the countrie . . . And in stead of some

---

[2] *Certaine Causes* . . . 1550–3.
[3] *The Fortresse of the Faythefull*, 1550, in Parker Soc. edn. (already cited) of Becon, *Works*, p. 599.
[4] Edn. cited, p. 19.

C or CC parsons that had their livinges thereon, now be there but
thre or foure sheppards and the maister only, that hathe a living
thereof.'[5]

Joseph Bentham in 1635 has:

'How much and so many pleasant and commodious habitations
for men, are tragically turned into rude and ruinous heapes, and
the many delicate and delightful fields, plentifully abounding
formerly with folds and flockes, with rich and rejoicing fruits;
deformed and defaced, laid languishing like deplored and desolate
desarts, haunted and inhabited onely by bruit beast and a few
solitary mansions remaining where there is little help in time of
necessity, comfort in time of doubt, or society in time of peace.'[6]

Bentham is quite certain that neither the 'maddened and
irreligious depopulators' nor their posterity will long enjoy
these ill-gotten gains. So strongly did this aspect of the question
impress itself on the propagandists, and through them on the
public mind, that in the eighteenth century when enclosure was
carried on from quite different motives, and with quite different even if equally deplorable results, sometimes writers in
favour of enclosure spend much time in proving that it would
not necessarily involve depopulation. As might be expected, in
general however, eighteenth-century writers view this problem
with complacency. Homer in 1766 says

'there is a natural Transition of the Inhabitants of the Villages,
where the Labour of Agriculture is lessened, into Places of Trade,
where our Naval Superiority, as long as it lasts, will furnish
Sources of perpetual Employment. Whether the Hands, thus
directed from Agriculture to Manufacture, are not in that Station
more useful to the Publick, than in their former, is an Enquiry
which might perhaps be prosecuted with some entertainment to
the Reader . . .'[7]

Goldsmith, the reader will remember, had quite other views
on the subject:

'If to the city sped, what waits him there?
To see profusion that he must not share;

[5] *Discourse of the Common Weal* (cited above, p. 155, fn. 4), pp. 20, 48.
[6] *Op. cit., supra*, p. 161, fn. 23.
[7] *Essay on the Nature and Method* . . . , cited above p. 86, fn. 13.

To see ten thousand baneful arts combin'd,
To pamper luxury, and thin mankind.
To see each joy the sons of pleasure know,
Extorted from his fellow-creature's woe.
Here while the courtier glitters in brocade,
There the pale artist plies the sickly trade;
Here while the proud their long-drawn pomps display,
There the black gibbet glooms beside the way.'[8]

The Social Consequences of Enclosure in the Eighteenth Century

It is beyond dispute that in general eighteenth-century enclosure was not designed to allow the conversion of arable to
pasture. It did not then result in the devastating rural depopulation which certainly followed earlier enclosure movements.
This is a point which has been dwelt on above, and to which we
shall return below. Nevertheless the movement has, not without
reason, been reprehended by writers. Then and now, a great
many charges have been levelled against it, both as to its
method and in its results. It may be said at once that some of
these are demonstrably quite unjustified, others are—to say the
least of it—dubious, while others again are clearly upheld by
the evidence. It will be evident from what has been said above
that no serious historian asserts that private land ownership in
England is a result of enclosure. The land of England was
largely occupied and cultivated in common until relatively
recent years. There is very little historical evidence of communal land ownership in England in even the most primitive
times, much less in the last thousand years or so. Similarly
'class' in rural England was not of course introduced by the
enclosure movement, though it is certainly true that enclosure,
as it was actually carried out, tended to accentuate already
existing social and economic class divisions.

Enclosure and Depopulation

It has been shown that enclosure for improved arable farming
in the eighteenth century did not generally result in the
conversion of arable to pasture as that in earlier centuries
certainly had done. It is indeed an interesting instance of how a
great work of literature can influence subsequent thought that
More's amply justified allegations, especially, for example, his
picturesque phrase about the shepherd and his dog occupying

<hr>

[8] *The Deserted Village*, 1770, ll. 310–19.

the church which has been made a sheephouse, should be repeated uncritically for centuries after his time, long after this particular charge had lost its relevancy. In Tudor times, and in some parts of England during the Stuart period, it is proved up to the hilt; it is quite unhistorical when it is repeated by Cobbett's contemporaries concerning the enclosures of the Georgian era.

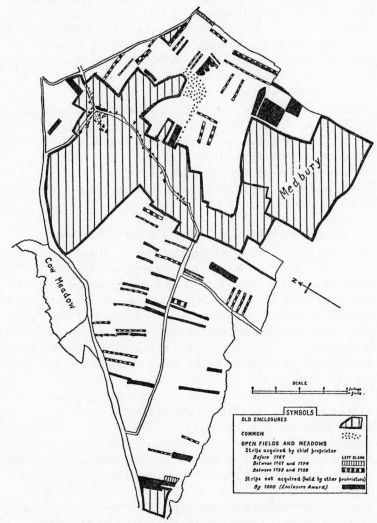

16. The disappearance of the yeoman (1767–99) before enclosure (at Elstow, Beds.), enclosed 1797–1800; *see p. 203*

Enclosure and Consolidation of Estates

Similarly it is quite easy to disprove the assertion that eighteenth-century enclosure was always—or usually—followed by consolidation of estates and tenancies. Indeed in the later part of the eighteenth century, the indisputable evidence of the Land Tax assessments shows that enclosure was often followed by an increase in the number of individual holdings. Even before this, it is clear that consolidation of small holdings often preceded enclosure rather than following it. It was often indeed an indispensable preliminary to the making of enclosure proposals that the promoters should have in their hands a very considerable proportion of the landed property in the parish. But of course whether consolidation followed or preceded enclosure, its social effects were much the same—the (relatively) poor sold, and the (relatively) rich bought. In this way it is certainly true that enclosure had much to do with creating 'the peculiar character of our rural economy, which lies, as everyone knows, in the accumulation of our land in a few hands, and the comparatively small number of our population who own any land at all'.[9]

Enclosure Acts: the Eighteenth Century Legislators

As to the means by which enclosure was carried out in the Georgian era there was, naturally enough a good deal of dissatisfaction at the time. Few of us even nowadays would be happy to have the title to what we regard as our rightful possessions determined by arbitration—especially if the terms of the arbitration and the appointment of the arbitrators were to be decided with little or no regard to our wishes. Traces of this discontent have persisted to the present day, and its influence may be seen in the work of some very reputable modern historians. It is sometimes alleged, for example, though by writers who have very little evidence for their statements, that the parliamentary proceedings on enclosure bills were a mere mockery, gone through by the Members with quite shameless effrontery as a formal preliminary to their helping themselves and one another to handsome endowments of other people's property. A fairly extensive study of the House of Commons *Journal* makes it clear that here again the charge is not borne out by the evidence. Doubtless an eighteenth-century House of

[9] Johnson, work cited in App. 2 below, p. 1.

Lords or Commons was a quite inadequate tribunal for considering matters affecting the existence of a landed peasantry, but of deliberate, persistent misuse by individual Members of their position as legislators, in order to serve their private interests as landlords, there is hardly a shred of evidence which still stands up to fair examination.[10]

Enclosure Awards: the Enclosure Commissioners

Similarly there is some misunderstanding as to the implementing of enclosure acts by the commissioners entrusted with putting them into operation, and in due course executing their 'final award and determination'. It is true of course that these were largely members of the landed classes, or of professions closely allied to these or dependent upon them. It seems to follow that in general sympathies the attorneys, estate stewards, land surveyors and so on, who made up the majority of the commissioners, would be with the landed classes. But members of these professions were clearly the only persons likely to be possessed of the technical knowledge necessary for judicial decisions on the many technical points on which they had to give judgement. Moreover, in the last few years especially, a fair number of minute-books and other working papers of these commissioners have been brought to light—records not previously known to exist.[11] These deserve more exhaustive examination than they have so far received. It may be said at once that a minute scrutiny of a number of them gives no general support to any of the charges laid against the commissioners. Unless the documents are a pack of skilful frauds, carefully designed to deceive posterity (in which case they would, presumably, have been much more carefully preserved and recorded than in fact they have been) they show how very scrupulously and conscientiously the commissioners carried out their duties. They display indeed almost an excessive regard for legality, not to say legalism, and a meticulous attention to the *minutiae* of the business with which the commissioners were entrusted. One finds in the work of some writers who should know better a notion of three or four of the squire's and parson's hangers-on or poor relations descending on the parish, dining and wining there *ad libitum* at the expense of the unfortunate freeholders, then by way of acknowledgement making to their principals a sweeping redistribution of other persons' landed property in the place, with equal disregard of law and justice. Any idea of this kind is wildly unhistorical.[12]

The Expense of Enclosure

Considering the methods by which enclosure was carried out it is certainly true that the process was absurdly expensive. This is, however, because it was regarded as a legal business involving hundreds of thousands of freeholders. It is explanation, rather than excuse, if we note that eighteenth-century English legal proceedings were outrageously costly anyhow. (Even to this day, after all the legal reforms of the last century and a quarter, going to law in England is not to be recommended as an inexpensive hobby!) It throws light, however, on a fact of some importance. Until 1836, when there was relatively little open land left to be enclosed, finding his due (fairly apportioned) share of these excessive expenses may often have been a major difficulty for the small proprietor with little, if any, free capital available. It may well then have been a major factor in inducing him to dispose of his property, before or after enclosure, to one of his neighbours more fortunately endowed.

Enclosure and the Peasant in the Village Community

This then is the real gravamen of the charges levelled against the movement of George III's time, not so much that it reduced the quantity of the rural population, as that enclosure adversely affected its quality. The small farmers disappeared—at any rate as small farmers. The landless labourer had no longer the chance of rising by hard work, abstemiousness, good fortune, a prudent marriage (or a combination of any or all of these) into a social and economic class merging into his own, but in general a shade or two more prosperous. The cottager, even if his cottage was a freehold, was unlikely to receive any substantial allotment of land in respect of it. Any allotment that was made to him was likely to be too small to have economic value, and was subject to heavy legal, fencing and draining charges, which he could not meet save by disposing of it. If his cottage was not a freehold, any allotment to 'it' went to his landlord, not to him. Even if, before enclosure, his common 'rights' had in truth been no rights at all but exercised, in fact as well as in legal theory, by pure usurpation, they had none the less been valuable to him. At enclosure he lost them—he could no longer

[12] *Cf.* Chap. 10.

turn on the common his scraggy cow, his donkey, his few sheep or his poultry and geese. The minor village officials, the viewers of fields, the letters of cattle, the common shepherd, the hayward, the pinder, lost their occupations, and the pay and petty perquisites which went with them. It is from the social point of view, rather than as a matter of pure economics or economic history, that enclosure (carried out as in fact it was) is to be regarded as a major disaster to the village community.

Recent Attempts to Rebuild the Village Community

For more than a century and a half, and especially in the last half-century or so, there have been numerous attempts to 'elevate' the countryman, culturally, socially, economically and morally. A host of institutions and organizations, small-holdings and allotments associations, rural co-operative societies, rural community councils and young farmers' clubs, temperance halls, evening institutes and W.E.A. classes, village 'colleges', farm workers' unions, and parish and rural district councils, mothers' unions and women's institutes have been developed in the attempt to 'rebuild' in the country-side a community to replace the one which had evolved there naturally, and which had been broken up. What results all these will meet with, only time can show—probably very little. There is a melancholy pleasure for the social theorist in visiting the one or two stray villages where the village community has contrived to escape the clutches of the enclosure movements, and to maintain itself as a live and active social organism to this day. Such villages are say Epworth, Haxey, Owston and Belton in the Isle of Axholme in Lincolnshire; or Eakring, or better still, Laxton, both in Nottinghamshire.

A Surviving Open-field Village[13]

Laxton is the solitary example of a village retaining to the present day a great part of its mediaeval village constitution. It is a proud village, a happy one, and a prosperous one. To this day at Laxton nearly everyone occupies land, or at least has grazing rights on the commons. 'Even the largest of the Laxton farmers (with 287 acres) began life at the bottom of the agricultural scale. Every type of holding is represented, from the

[13] The final paragraphs are, by courtesy of the authors, taken almost *verbatim* from Dr. and Mrs. Orwin's book, *The Open Fields*, cited below, App. 2.

cottage with common rights, and two or three acres in the open fields . . . up to the farm of 287 acres, mostly inclosed. The history of the tenants, for the most part, is one of steady progress from the smallest beginnings. A Laxton lad leaves home for employment on one of the big estates of the neighbourhood, or on a farm, and he saves a few pounds. A cottage holding at Laxton becomes vacant, and he applies for it, or it is offered to him. . . . At first, he continues to work for wages, cultivating his holding as a part-time job, and hiring the help of his neighbours for horse labour. So he goes on, supporting himself by his wages, and building up some capital by the profit on his crops and stock. Presently a larger holding falls vacant, and he feels strong enough to apply for it, becoming now a full-time farmer, and giving up his other employment. He may move again, or even more than once, each time into a larger holding, and the most successful of his like may move right away, ultimately, into substantial enclosed farms.

'Nowhere else in England will there be found a village community nearly every member of which is at one stage or other in his progress from the bottom to the top. . . . The opportunity arises solely from the organization of farming in the Open Fields. . . . The government of the Open Fields is a pure democracy, for everyone, sooner or later, has personal responsibility for it . . . the manor court . . . consists of all tenants and freeholders . . . and everyone within the manor has direct personal responsibility, not only for the decisions of the manor court, but also for their enforcement. Thus, both legislative and executive functions are vested in the people themselves. Its people control their own affairs in the daily incidents of their work by a scheme of voluntary administration, maintained by public opinion without recourse to the law of the land, and without the expenditure of a single penny.' It is interesting, and may perhaps not be altogether unprofitable, to speculate upon what might have been were Laxton to this day a typical English village, instead of a rare and precious museum piece.

APPENDIX I*

The Board of Agriculture *General Views* . . .

THE COUNTY *General Views* . . . exist in two forms, the quarto drafts and the octavo finished texts, as follows:

	Quarto Draft		*Octavo Report*	
Bedfordshire	Stone, T.	1794	Batchelor, T.	1808
Berkshire	Pearce, W.	1794	Mavor, W.	1808
Buckinghamshire	James W. &		Priest, St. J.	1810
	Malcolm J.	1794		
Cambridgeshire	Vancouver, C.	1794	Gooch, W.	1813
Cheshire	Wedge, T.	1794	Holland, H.	1808
Cornwall	Fraser, R.	1794	Worgan, G. B.	1811
Cumberland	Bailey, J. &		Bailey, J. &	
	Culley, G.	1794	Culley, G.	1797
Derbyshire	Brown, T.	1794	Farey, J. (3 vols.)	1811
Devonshire	Fraser, R.	1794	Vancouver, C.	1808
Dorset	Claridge, J.	1793	Stevenson, V.	1812
Durham	Granger, J.	1794	Bailey, J.	1810
Essex	Griggs, 'Messrs.'			
	[G. and ? J.]	1794		
	Vancouver, C.	1795	Young, A. (2 vols.)	1807
Gloucestershire	Turner, G.	1794	Rudge, T.	1807
Hampshire	Driver, A. & W.†	1794	Vancouver, C.	1810
Herefordshire	Clark, J.	1794	Duncumbe, J.	1805
Hertfordshire	Walker, D.	1795	Young, A.	1804
Huntingdonshire	Stone, T.	1793	Parkinson, R.	1813
Kent	Boys, J.	1794	Boys, J.	1796
			Boys, J.	1805
Lancashire	Holt, J.	1794	Holt, J.	1795
			Dickinson, R. W.	1814
Leicestershire	Monk, G.	1794	Pitt, W.	1809
Lincolnshire	Stone, T.	1794	Young, A.	1799
Middlesex	Baird, T.	1793	Middleton, J.	1798
	Foot, T.	1794	Middleton, J.	1807
Monmouthshire	Fox, J.	1794	Hassall, C.	1812
Norfolk	Kent, N.	1794	Kent, N.	1796
			Young, A.	1804
Northampton	Donaldson, J.	1794	Pitt, W.	1809

* These are the works referred to on pp. 86, 161, 164, etc. The list is taken from a table in H. C. Taylor's *Decline of Landowning Farmers in England*, itself based on an article by Sir E. Clarke, *Journ. Roy. Ag. Socy. Engl.*, *Ser. III*, Vol. IX.

† Appendix by the Rev. [?R.] Warner on the Isle of Wight, pp. 45–46.

Northumberland	Bailey, J. & Culley, G.	1794	Bailey, J. & Culley, G.	1797
			Bailey, J. & Culley, G.	1805
Nottinghamshire	Lowe, R.	1794	Lowe, R.	1798
Oxfordshire	Davis, R.	1794	Young, A.	1809
Rutland	Crutchley, J.	1794	Parkinson, R.	1808
Shropshire	Bishton, J.	1794	Plymley, J.	1803
Somerset	Billingsley, J.	1794	Billingsley, J.	1797
Staffordshire	Pitt, W.	1794	Pitt, W.	1796
			Pitt, W.	1813
Suffolk	Young, A.	1794	Young, A.	1797
			Young, A. (3rd. edn.)	1804
Surrey	James, W. & Malcolm, J.	1794	Stevenson, W.	1809
Sussex	*Young, A.	1793	Young, A.	1808
Warwickshire	Wedge, J.	1794	Murray, A.	1813
Westmorland	Pringle, A.	1794	Pringle, A.	1797
			Pringle, A. (3rd. edn.)	1813
Wiltshire	Davis, T., Sen.	1794	Davis, T., Jun	1811
Worcestershire	Pomeroy, W. T.	1794	Pitt, W.	1810
Yorkshire				
E. Riding	Leatham, I.	1794	Strickland, H. E.	1812
N. Riding	Tuke, J., Jun.	1794	Tuke, J.	1800
W. Riding	Rennie, G. Brown, R. & Shirreff, J.	1794	Brown, R.	1799

Summaries of these works in convenient form appear in Marshall, W., *Reviews of the Reports* (all published at York), *Northern Department, Western Department, Midland Department, Eastern Department, Southern Department* and *Peninsular and Southwestern Department*, 1808–17.

* Not the celebrated Arthur, but a namesake, a local clergyman.

APPENDIX II

SOME MODERN BOOKS AND ARTICLES ON
OPEN FIELDS AND ENCLOSURE

THERE ARE, OF course, many works on the history of the land
laws, but most of these are, inevitably, full of technicalities and
therefore hard reading. Dr. D. R. Denman's *Origins of Ownership*
(1958 and edns.) attempts rather to survey 'the historical development of the fundamental principles of proprietorship' as Dr. Denman
sees them—that is, from a point of view which differs considerably
from my own. His very interesting and scholarly book, however,
summarizes fairly and dispassionately the differing views of various
historians on aspects of his subject from Later Neolithic times to the
Middle Ages. It is therefore unreservedly recommended as the best
preliminary reading on the subject. The book is furnished with
seven admirable up-to-date bibliographies which, though modestly
styled 'selective', are vastly more comprehensive than I have been
able to make my bibliographical notes below.

The first modern work on field systems is H. L. Gray, *English
Field Systems* (O.U.P. for Harvard, 1915). There is a good biblio-
graphy of some more recent work on the subject in H. E. Hallam,
Settlement and Society (Cambridge, 1965). Both Gray and Hallam should
be read in conjunction with Dr. Joan Thirsk's very stimulating
article 'The Common Fields' in *Past and Present*, 29, pp. 3–29. Dr.
Thirsk's main thesis is that throughout rather more of England than
most students (including the present writer) have realized, the true
open-field (two- and three-field) 'systems' (*a*) never existed in any
degree of completeness, or (*b*) whenever they did so exist, were an
inheritance from early mediaeval rearrangements in land matters
rather than a survival from the primitive days of English settlement
in England.

The first serious modern study of enclosure is T. E. Scrutton,
Commons and Common Fields (Cambridge, 1887). This is written from
the legal point of view, but is very far from legalistic in its tone. It
is still of value as an introduction to the legal aspect of the subject.
G. Slater, *The English Peasantry and the Enclosure of Common Fields*
(1907), has a great deal of useful material, and is very readable. It
contains an (extremely inaccurate) appendix purporting to tabulate
under county heads all English parliamentary enclosures containing
any proportion of the open-field arable land in which Slater was
specially interested. W. Hasbach, *History of the English Agricultural
Labourer* (1894, Eng. trans. 1908), is a painstaking and laborious
work by a German professor, in which enclosure is dealt with as
one of many causes all tending towards the degradation and

impoverishment of the labourer. It is based almost entirely on printed sources, and if only for its careful and comprehensive bibliographies of these it is worth reading—or at any rate having at hand on one's bookshelf.

A. H. Johnson, *The Disappearance of the Small Landowner* (Oxford, 1909), is alleged once to have been bought by a naïve undergraduate, who thought the title indicated that it was a mystery thriller. In fact, it is an attempt to assess the influence of enclosure on the growth of land monopoly from mediaeval times to the 'New Domesday' of 1873. It is, in moderation, on the side of the peasant. E. C. K. Gonner, *Common Land and Inclosure* (1912), is a dull book, ill-written and very difficult to read. The effort to read it is, however, worth making, for Gonner's supposedly 'dispassionate' treatment of the subject serves in some sort as a corrective to the other works noted— Slater, certainly Hasbach, and perhaps Johnson. Another book which is on the whole well-disposed towards enclosure is R. Prothero, Lord Ernle, *English Farming Past and Present* (1912 and edns.). This is natural enough, for Lord Ernle looks at enclosure, quite properly, as a necessary, and indeed inevitable, move towards agricultural improvement.

The one work of outstanding literary merit on the topic is certainly J. L. and B. Hammond's *The Village Labourer* (1912), which contains more distinguished writing than all the other books on the subject taken together. It is usually held, however, to be grossly biased in favour of the peasantry, and against all the other classes of society who were concerned in the movement. It has been described as one of the most brilliant works of historical fiction in the English tongue. At the very least it is to be regarded, to quote a recent writer, as an 'explosive' book, 'to be handled with great care'. No one has yet succeeded in replying to it in a book half as readable. Sir T. Whittaker, *Ownership, Tenure and Taxation of Land* (1914), is heavily outclassed by the adversaries he has rather rashly challenged in his attempt to demolish the arguments of Land Taxers and Land Nationalizers. Much more convincing is another agricultural historian, W. H. R. Curtler. His *Enclosure and Redistribution of Our Land* (Oxford, 1920) is scholarly and accurate, and based on an examination of all the printed sources and some manuscript ones. Perhaps Slater on the one hand and Curtler on the other, taken together, gives as fair and as comprehensive a picture of the whole subject as is possible until much recent and current research on it has been assessed and evaluated, and its results gathered into the corpus of historical knowledge.

The standard economic histories all, of course, make some reference to enclosure. W. Cunningham (1882 and edns.), give it some attention; E. Lipson (1931) is generally held to be better on urban history than upon that of the countryside; P. Mantoux (Eng. trans.

1928) takes the traditional view on the iniquity of enclosure as it was carried out, and its disastrous effect on the peasant. W. H. B. Court (Cambridge, 1954) gives relatively little space to enclosure, in his survey of economic developments from 1750 to the present day. In the little he does say he is as dispassionate as it is possible to be on an aspect of history in which, inevitably, emotional feelings as well as intellectual concepts are involved. A great many articles on various aspects of enclosure history, and detailed surveys of enclosure in specific county or other areas, have appeared in the last twenty or thirty years in the various learned periodicals, the *English Historical Review*, *Economic History*, the *Economic History Review*, the *Agricultural History Review*, with (the American) *Journal of Modern History* and *Agricultural History*. Many of these are listed in an article by W. H. Chaloner in the *Agricultural History Review* for 1954, where they appear under the names of their various authors, especially perhaps M. Beresford, J. D. Chambers, W. G. Hoskins, Dr. J. Thirsk, and myself.

The most recent short introduction to the early history of enclosure is in a pamphlet published by the Historical Association in 1963 (and edns.) as G. 41 in its General Series—Dr. Joan Thirsk's *Tudor Enclosures*. The best short account of the later history of the subject is in another pamphlet published by the same Association in 1960 as No. 7 in its Aids for Teachers Series, Dr. R. A. C. Parker's *Enclosures in the Eighteenth Century*.

Detailed individual studies of the enclosures of Lincolnshire parishes are appearing in an admirable series published by Mr. Rex C. Russell, 11 Priestgate, Barton-upon-Humber, Lincs., and written by Mr. Russell and his W. E. A. and Hull University Extra-Mural students. Each of these is a most interesting and scholarly example of what such a study can be, and the reader thinking of checking or disputing any writer's conclusions by undertaking an inquiry into the history of enclosure in his own parish may well take one of Mr. Russell's booklets as a model for his work.

Since I began the writing of this book, there has appeared an admirable county study—Dr. J. M. Martin's 'Cost of Parliamentary Enclosure in Warwickshire' (*Univ. Birm. Hist. Journ.* IX, 2, 144–62). This is a most scholarly and detailed analysis of enclosure costs in 89 Warwickshire awards, and it makes very generous mention of my own work on this aspect of the subject. Dr. Martin reaffirms the traditional view, which I have ventured on occasion to question, that the admitted adverse social consequences of enclosure were largely due to the grossly excessive cost of the proceedings as they were in fact carried out, and he makes a good and reasoned case for his point of view. I still, however, remain open to conviction on this, as on the other matters of controversy in which the history of enclosure abounds. I suggest above that Ernle, Gonner and Curtler may be read as correctives to Hasbach, Slater, Johnson and the Hammonds. In the same fashion, it may well be that Tate's conclusions on this particular aspect of the matter should be considered in the light of Martin's careful and reasonable criticisms of them.

While this book has been passing through the press, there has appeared *The Agricultural Revolution, 1750–1880* (J. D. Chambers and D. E. Mingay). We have prepared our studies independently of each other, although the subjects overlap (rather than coincide) and the books are written from slightly different points of view. They are essentially complementary rather than competitive, and all three writers trust that students will be sufficiently interested to read both works. On the morning when I am posting my final proofs I have received another work, equally commendable though at a very different level. *The Agrarian Revolution* (John Addy) is essentially a school-book directed at the lower forms in the grammar schools and the upper classes in the county secondary schools. It is an excellent piece of work, based on original research and lavishly illustrated. Probably many readers other than those for whom it is meant will find it of great interest and value.

The long-awaited *Commons and Village Greens* (D. R. Denham *et al.*) is in process of publication while I am correcting the final proofs of this present work. I can, then, do no more than name it here, heartily commending it to the reader who is specially interested in open lands falling into the categories named.

THIS TABLE INCLUDES ALL KNOWN ENGLISH PARLIAMENTARY ENCLOSURES, 1603–1914

Parishes are reckoned in the counties in which they lie now; occasionally these are not the same as at the time of enclosure.

The county numbers refer to the sections of the author's *Domesday of English Enclosure Acts and Awards*. The draft of this has been in course of publication, piecemeal, since 1941. It is hoped to issue the revised text and index as a whole in the not-too-remote future.

Section

A	By private act, etc.	Including open-field arable.
B	By private act, etc.	Common, etc.; not including open-field arable.
C	Under the General Act of 1836	Mainly open-field arable.
D	Under the General Act of 1836 as extended in 1840	Other open lands of any kind.
E(i)	Under the General Act of 1845 and the Annual Enclosure Acts, etc. thereafter	Including open-field arable; award made with specific Parliamentary sanction.
(ii)	„ „ „	Including open-field arable; award made without specific Parliamentary sanction.
F(i)	Under the General Act of 1845, and the Annual Enclosure Acts, etc. thereafter	Not including open-field arable; award made with specific Parliamentary sanction.
(ii)	„ „ „	Not including open-field arable; award made without specific Parliamentary sanction.

(Note: Sections A, C, E—enclosure largely of open fields.

B, D, F—enclosure largely of common pastures etc.)

A Domesday of English Enclosure Acts and Awards, 1603-1914

COUNTY SECTION NO.	A 1603–1845	B 1606–1873	C 1836+	D 1840+	E(i)	E(ii) 1845–1914	F(i) 1845–1914	F(ii) 1845–1914	Total 1603–1914
Bedfordshire (1)	82	4	3	2	1	4	1	1	98
Berkshire (2)	86	9	12		5	4		13	129
Buckinghamshire (3)	102	6	4		1	6		11	130
Cambridgeshire & Isle of Ely (4)	102	12	4		2	8		3	131
Cheshire (5)	1	37		1				18	57
Cornwall (6)		3	3					17	23
Cumberland (7)	6	79	4	6	3			30	128
Derbyshire (8)	72	62	2					7	143
Devonshire (9)		31	1		3			35	70
Dorset (10)	49	19	5	11	11	3		17	115
Durham (11)	6	33	1					2	42
Essex (12)	13	29	5		4	8	2	21	82
Gloucestershire (13)	134	20	13		2	10		24	203
Hampshire & Isle of Wight (14)	58	37	3		2	1+2	+1	58+1	163
Herefordshire (15)	26	22	3	1	2	2	1	16	73
Hertfordshire (16)	27	8	6	1	10	10	1	14	77
Huntingdonshire (17)	68	1	2		2	2			75
Kent (18)		17					3	15	35
Lancashire (19)		69+4	1				1	18+3	96
Leicestershire (20)	148	7	1						156
Lincolnshire (21)	263	53	31		6	1		12	366
Middlesex (22)	25	10	2			1		2	40
Monmouthshire (23)	1	3			3		1	5	13
Norfolk (24)	194	92	2		2	4	2	25	321
Northamptonshire & Soke of Peterborough (25)	193	7				4		8	212
Northumberland (26)	9	19						49	77
Nottinghamshire (27)	116	18	5	5	1	2	1	6	154
Oxfordshire (28)	130	7	13	1	6	19		15	191
Rutland (29)	26		1		1	5			33
Salop (30)	7	42						21	70
Somerset (31)	47	104	3	4	2			18	178
Staffordshire (32)	24	68		1	1			14	108
Suffolk (33)	52	35			2	3	2	22	116
Surrey (34)	23	30	2		5		1	22	83
Sussex (35)	24	17	4		1	1	4	36	87
Warwickshire (36)	125	25	2	1		5	4	13	175
Westmorland (37)	4	45	10				9	28	96
Wiltshire (38)	120	34	10	3	1	5		13	186
Worcestershire (39)	68	35	5	4	2	5		8	127
Yorkshire E.R. (40)	152	21	8	3	3	2		2	191
N.R. (41)	51	72	5	4	1	1	1	20	155
W.R. & Ainsty of York (42)	158	147	7	1	1	3	6	34	357
	2792	1393	183	49	86	121	41	697	5362

GLOSSARY OF TECHNICAL TERMS USED

WHEN THE TEXT explains or, even if only by implication, demonstrates the meaning of any technical term used, the definition is not repeated, but a reference is given to the appropriate page. Terms used in the definitions and themselves defined elsewhere are given in bold type, and should be referred to under their separate headings.

aftermath—herbage remaining after hay harvest.

agistment (gysting, joisting)—the depasturing, on payment, of one's animals on someone else's land.

allotment (in the sense used here)—the allocation of lands parcelled out under an enclosure award.

apparitor—(Chaucer's 'somnour') the official messenger of the archdeacon's or bishop's court, entitled as such to customary fees. These, which had been a grievance for centuries, were regulated by the Canons of 1604.

appendant (**common**)—that attached to an arable holding, and applying only to horses, oxen, cattle and sheep.

appropriator—an ecclesiastical body or person, other than the parish priest, having the right to (usually) great **tithes** in the parish, *cf.* **impropriator.**

appurtenant (**common**)—that (in fact, though not quite in legal theory) attached to a house, rather than to ancient arable land.

assart, essart—enclosure of forest or waste land.

attorney—one of the two types of legal practitioner which coalesced in 1827–31–73 to form the modern profession of solicitor.

award—judicial decision given rather after arbitration than as a result of court proceedings.

balk—an untilled boundary strip, usually between two selions. In Cambs (? only), balk is used to mean **selion.**

beastgate—see **cattlegate.**

Board of Agriculture (*a*)—the first—a voluntary but tax-subsidized body established in 1793 (see App. I), (*b*) the later one, now the Ministry of Agriculture—a Government Department (1889), succeeding *inter alia* to the powers of the (general) Enclosure Commission.

botes (N. Fr. **estovers**), **haybote, housebote, firebote,** etc.— common right of taking wood for hedging, house repair, fuel, etc.

bovate—the law-Latin equivalent of the English term **oxgang.**

brecks (**breaks, breeches,** etc.)—supposedly temporary enclosures (which in fact often became permanent ones), especially from forest land, *cf.* **intakes.**

carr—common, especially marshy common.

cattlegate—the right to graze a single beast on land in the soil of which one has no legal interest.

(**champaign**) **champion**—open field as distinct from enclosed country.

Chancery, Court of—that of the Lord Chancellor, now the Chancery Division of the High Court of Justice.

church ale—the mediaeval to Stuart prototype of the present-day parish tea meeting, garden fête or church bazaar, its degenerate descendant.

Church Commissioners—established 1948 by the amalgamation of Queen Anne's Bounty (1703) and the Ecclesiastical Commissioners (1836).

churchwardens—the annually elected representatives of the parishioners, acting first in ecclesiastical, later in many secular matters.

close—a hedged or fenced or walled piece of land, such as is generally now (incorrectly) styled a **field.**

commissioners—any body of persons given formal authority to act, thus (*a*) Enclosure Commissioners (in the sixteenth century, etc.), those appointed by the Crown to inquire into and/or discourage enclosure; (*b*) enclosure commissioners (especially in the eighteenth century), persons named in an enclosure act, and authorized to carry out its provisions; (*c*) Enclosure Commissioners from 1845 civil servants entrusted with the duty of administering the 1845 Act (these last later the Land Division of the Ministry of Agriculture) presumably now [1967] due for transfer to the Land Commission. **Turnpike** commissioners are usually styled turnpike trustees.

common appendant, appurtenant, see **appendant, appurtenant.**

common lands—a term usually applied nowadays to manorial waste, but applicable also to **open fields** over which common pasture rights existed.

Commonwealth—an incipient Christian-radical party, developing in the mid-sixteenth century.

compost—manure of any kind.

(**parish**) **constable**—a manorial, later parochial, official with many duties in addition to his primary one, that of maintaining the King's peace in the parish.

copyholder—a tenant holding his land by copy of court roll, and belonging to a class deriving from the mediaeval **villeins.**

corn rent—a cash annuity, varying in amount according to the ascertained and vouched price of corn in the area; hence a safeguard against any future fluctuation in the value of money.

cottager—the occupier, sometimes also owner, of a tenement often having attached to it a croft, and usually a common right and a little land.

court baron—the lord's court held in and for his manor, and having jurisdiction in many matters of local concern. Nothing to do with barons or baronies, but the court to which the free *man* of the manor owed suit.

dale (in Westmd., etc.)—**selion.**

demesne—that part of the manor lands which the lord had not granted out, but retained in hands; the precursor of the modern home farm.

Easter offerings—ancient annual payments to the parish priest, now in general quite voluntary, but formerly compulsory under both common and canon law. Usually exempted from the redemption of ancient obligations made under enclosure acts, but commuted under the Tithe Act of 1839. See p. 50, fn. 2.

edge—**balk** or **meer.**

enclosure (inclosure)—the conversion by any means, legal, extra-legal or illegal, of open (common) lands; arable, meadow, pasture or waste into individual ownership, tenancy and use—several(ty).

engrossing—the accumulation in the hands of one man and his family of agricultural holdings adequate to the maintenance of more than one family, and formerly serving for such maintenance.

essart—**assart.**

estovers—the N.F. equivalent of the O.E. term **botes.**

equity—a system of law co-existing with but supplementing or superseding—almost transcending—common and statute law. In England the Chancery administered equity, but the Court of Exchequer had also an equitable jurisdiction.

Exchequer, Court of—a court existing at any rate from Henry II's time, originally concerned with the royal revenue, but later attracting legal business of other kinds. It is now the Exchequer Division of the High Court of Justice.

extensive (cultivation)—see p. 41.

fallow—land ploughed and harrowed, but left uncultivated for a year, so it may recover its fertility.

farm—essentially a landholding held at a rent.

field—(not a modern '**close**' but) a large area of open arable land, divided into furlongs, each again subdivided into selions, all the ss. in a f. being normally subject to the same crop rotation.

field-grass—husbandry, see pp. 41.

fine (and *recovery*)—p. 47, see any work on the history of the land laws.

flat—furlong (*b*).

fother—**gore.**

four-course rotation—such a course as wheat, turnips, barley, clover.

four-field system—the rearrangement of the lands in an ancient two- or three-field area to form a fourth field, so that the occupiers might follow the above, more modern, technique.

free (public) **house**—one whose licensee is not **tied** to a particular brewery company.

furlong (*a*) as a measure of length—220 yards, a convenient length in an average soil for plough oxen to labour on before enjoying a brief respite while they turned on the **headland.**

furlong, flat, shot, etc. (*b*) as a subdivision in an open arable field, —a block of contiguous selions, all more or less the same length and all running the same way. See **field, meer, selion.**

gate—see **cattlegate.**

Gateward's Case—in this (6 Rep. 69, 1603) it was decided, in the first place as to Stixwould, Lincs. (but as a precedent for the country generally) that the word 'inhabitant' is so vague as to be meaningless. This meant that the inhabitants of a rural parish or manor could claim as such no common right. It was subsequently decided that the ruling did not apply when a district had been incorporated or had, as such, received a Crown grant, which was held to satisfy the technical rule as to incorporation. Sometimes, judges interpreted the law fairly generously, justifying an existing custom by the ingenious theory of a 'lost grant'. Inhabitants might —and usually did—in fact exercise 'common rights' while the common remained open, but when it came to be enclosed they had no legal interest which would entitle them to compensation.

gore—a more or less triangular scrap of land, usually in between two neighbouring **furlongs.**

great tithe—see **tithe.**

gyst—see **agistment.**

hade—balk.

half-year land—Lammas land.

haysel—hay harvest.

hayward (no connexion with hay)—a communal officer responsible for the oversight of hedges, etc.

headland (in an open field as in a modern arable close)—land at the end of the furrow, left for the plough to turn on.

high farming—the English translation of such a term as 'intensive cultivation'.

housebote—see **estovers.**

impropriator—a layman having the right to receive (usually the great) **tithes** of the parish, *cf.* **appropriator.**

inclosure—the lawyers' spelling of **enclosure.**

incumbent—the parish priest, whether **rector** or **vicar.**

ings—(usually common) meadows.

intakes—enclosures, especially from moorland or waste.

Lammas lands, half-year land—common land, arable or

meadow, occupied in severalty for part of the year, but after crop taken, pasturable by the severalty owners and others; usually thrown open to pasture on Lammas Day (1 August) or Old Lammas (12 August).

lands (in Notts., Yorks., etc.)—**selions**.

landshares, lantchetts, lawnchers, lynches, etc.—**balks**. The *word* is connected with the 'lynchets' characteristic of 'Celtic' agriculture.

lawn, loon (in Dorset, etc.)—**selion**.

ley—land ploughed for a period, then left to grass for another period of years, *cf.* **fallow**.

loon—see **lawn**.

lot meadow—common meadow in which the mowing rights are annually distributed by an arrangement having some degree of chance in it—often a primitive lottery.

lynches—see **landshares**.

'managed (public) **house'**—one whose licensee is merely the wage-earning or salaried employee of the (brewery) company which owns or leases the premises.

manor—(more or less) the feudal development of the O.E. **township**.

mark—13*s.* 4*d.* (so that an increase in rent from a mark to £1. (p. 155) is one of fifty per cent.

marling—adding to a light soil limey clay by way of manure.

marsh—often a common, swampy or otherwise, not necessarily a mere quagmire.

maslin—mixed corn, properly only styled maslin if a mixture of wheat and rye. Sometimes the grains were grown as a mixed crop, sometimes grown separately, and mixed after threshing.

mear, meer—boundary **balk**, etc. In some counties balk is used for a narrow strip between **selions**, meer for a major boundary between **furlongs** or **fields**, etc.

messuage—not merely a dwelling-house, but essentially a farm-house with land annexed to it.

Norfolk rotation—**four-course rotation**.

Novel Disseisin, Assize of—one of the assizes instituted by Henry II. It provided a summary remedy when a freeholder had been unjustly dispossessed of his holding.

open (arable) **field**—**champion**, see pp. 35–7.

ordinary—the set meal, as it were *table d'hôte*, especially in the inn of a market town.

overlaying (the common)—**surcharging** it.

overseer of the highways—**waywarden**.

overseer of the poor—from Tudor times until after 1834 the parochial officer concerned with the levying of the poor rate, and the administration of the old poor law.

oxgang—half as much as a **yardland,** since two oxen went to a yoke one-eighth of a **ploughland;** on a (very rough) average perhaps something in the neighbourhood of 15 acres.

parish—originally the district assigned to a particular church, later, from Tudor times onwards also a secular unit, entrusted with local administration in many civil affairs. In many (not all) parts of England **township, manor,** and **parish** are often co-extensive.

paulls (in Sussex, etc.)—**selions.**

peasant—countryman of relatively humble social status, but often (?**qu.** usually) having some stake, great or small, in the land.

pightle—**gore;** after enclosure, any small scrap of land.

pike, pyke—**gore.**

pinder—manorial or parochial officer in charge of the **pinfold**—pound—and the detention therein of straying stock.

pismires—p. 161, ants.

plott book—see p. 47.

ploughland—as much open arable land as would keep busy through the year an (eight-ox) plough team, hence a conventional unit of area, varying widely from county to county, and parish to parish, but always containing four yardlands, i.e. eight **oxgangs.** (In some counties perhaps on an average about 120 statute acres.)

raine, reine—**balk, meer.**

raps (in Somerset)—**selions.**

rector—parish priest receiving great and small **tithe** (now tithe rent-charge) from his parishioners.

regulating (a common)—**stinting,** and in other ways securing the proper use of a common, instead of enclosing it.

ridge-and-furrow—often in present permanent grassland, sometime arable, the mark of former open-field cultivation. See Plate II, facing p. 31.

riggs (in Northumberland, etc.)—**selions.**

roots (in this connexion)—turnips, swedes and mangold-wurzels.

selions (dales, lands, raps, stitches, etc.)—open-field 'acre' strips. See pp. 36–8.

several(ty)—the modern system of ownership, tenure and cultivation or depasturing by individuals, as distinct from **champion** (open field), and common pastures, etc.

shot—**furlong** (*b*).

spring corn—barley and/or oats, or (by extension) vetches or peas and beans. See p. 35 and fn. 4.

squatter—one, as it were 'sitting', usually on a scrap of common or waste, especially if he had no legal title to his holding.

squire—technically a man of blood and coat-armour, two degrees above the commonalty (the grades being gentleman, esquire, knight). In fact the principal landowner in any rural village provided that he or his family have been there long enough to establish a customary right to the title. Often the ultimate successor to the mediaeval lord of the **manor**.

statutes—see *Table of Statutes*.

stinting—ensuring that the stock turned on a common are not more than it can feed properly.

stitches (in southern counties)—**selions**.

(**'strips'**) of open land—see **selions**.

surcharging (the common)—turning on to it more stock than it can feed properly, or more than the equivalent of the number of **'gates'** one holds, *cf*. **regulating, stinting**.

'tenanted (public) **house'**—one whose 'landlord' (properly licensee) has a degree of independence in the management of his business, so long as he observes the conditions of his 'tie' to the brewery company.

'tied cottage—one occupied by a farm worker in connexion with, and conditionally upon, his employment. The advantage of the 'tied' cottage is that its rent is (often fantastically) below the economic level. The disadvantage is that on leaving or being dismissed from his employment, the worker may well find himself homeless. See p. 213.

'tied (public) **house'**—one whose licensee, whether 'manager' or 'tenant', is restricted in the purchase of his supplies to an individual brewery company or group which has bought or leased the premises (or occasionally has entered into a covenant with the actual owner).

tithe (now tithe rent-charge)—the ancient obligation of all parishioners to maintain their parish priest from the fruits of the earth in his parish. Great tithe (of corn, hay and wood) was payable to a **rector;** a **vicar,** perhaps in addition to a modest cash stipend, received small tithe on all else (especially wool, and the annual increase of farm stock). *Cf*. **appropriator, impropriator.**

toft, toftstead—originally a homestead, the site of a house and its outbuildings, with its attached land and common right. Hence a farm house having 'full' common rights.

township—the O.E. unit of settlement, often the basis of the later ecclesiastical unit, the **parish**. See also **manor**.

turnpike trustees—local gentlemen empowered, especially in the eighteenth century, to supplement the work of the parish waywardens, by charging tolls for the use of the roads, and expending the proceeds on their maintenance and improvement.

vestry (meeting)—the ancient customary governing body of a parish which all ratepayers might attend, in order to deal with matters, civil or ecclesiastical, of local concern. It still exists, but now it has lost nearly all its civil powers and duties.

vicar—parish priest receiving only small **tithe** (now tithe rent-charge), etc. from his parishioners.

vill—the N.F. equivalent of the O.E. **township.**

villein—the unfree but land-holding countryman of early feudal times.

virgate—the Low Latin equivalent of the English **yardland.**

visitation—official 'inspection' of the parish by or on behalf of the Bishop or his eye, the Archdeacon. See also **apparitor.**

waywarden, surveyor of the highways—parochial official having, from the time of Philip and Mary to that of Queen Victoria, responsibility for the maintenance of the highways in the parish, and the supervision of the labours of his fellow-parishioners in their statutory duty of maintaining and repairing these.

wall—**balk.**

winter corn—wheat and/or rye. See p. 35 fn. 4; 59 and fig. 4 facing.

wong—(*a*) **furlong** in the open fields.

      (*b*) (enclosed) meadow.

yardland (virgate)—as much land as would keep busy through the year a pair of oxen (in a two-ox plough). Its area might vary widely according to local custom, the nature of the soil, etc., 30 acres being a fair general average. Whatever else varied, a yardland was virtually always two oxgangs, one-fourth of a 'ploughland'.

TABLE OF STATUTES, ETC.,
CITED OR REFERRED TO

a.—amended   c.—confirmed   r—repealed

ACTS OF PARLIAMENTS OF SCOTLAND

NOTES ON ILLUSTRATIONS

FIGURE I, PAGE 33

Traditional Mead Marks at Bampton, Oxon and at Alveston, Warws.

(Aston and Cote in Bampton, Oxon, marks used up to 1854. Alveston, Warws. (now in Stratford-on-Avon) marks used in 1772.)

There were numerous customary methods of dividing the meadow each year, usually from Candlemas Day 2 February or St. Gregory's Day 12 March until Lammas Day 1 August (sometimes, of course, after 1752 from old Candlemas . . . etc. . . . eleven days later). Usages varied from parish to parish, manor to manor (really from township to township—see text pp. 33–4 and Glossary). Almost always they involved some form of primitive—but often very complicated—lottery. There is a fair example of this from Brotherton, Yorks. W. in J. A. Venn's *Foundations of Agricultural Economics*. 2nd edn. 1933, pp. 48–51. Here the three major divisions, corresponding to Oxey Mead, Pixey Mead and West Mead at Yarnton, were the Lord, the Bishop and Peter Liberty. The land would remain a private possession until the hay was mown. After hay harvest it reverted to common pasture until it was 'hained'—(closed) again at Candlemas in the succeeding year. The important thing was to mark its temporary ownership February– or March–August, since, acre for acre, it was perhaps thrice as valuable as the best arable land. Such marks as these were sometimes cut on the wooden lottery 'tickets'. Quite often, as each allottee was allocated his meadow strips, he cut in the turf of each of them the mark of his proprietorship for the season.

FIGURE 2, PAGE 51

Parliamentary Enclosure in the County of Nottingham 1743–1868

All kinds of local circumstances may help to account for the early or late Parliamentary enclosure of any particular parish. These may include: (*a*) The nature of the soil, and the extent to which it was 'improvable'; (*b*) the prevalent forms of land tenure, freehold, copyhold (of inheritance or for lives), leasehold, etc., and so on. In some instances this may help to explain the extent to which the villages were still the abodes of organized village communities. Alternatively, they may suggest possible reasons why the land was, or could in the course of time be gathered into, the ownership of a single person, or that of a small group of influential major land-holders. When once this change had taken place, perhaps enclosure would offer fewer difficulties and, in fact, it would occur almost inevitably within a few years from the achievement of any degree of land engrossing or monopoly. Details of the specific categories in which all the enclosures marked are arranged may be found in Chambers, *Nottinghamshire in the Eighteenth Century*, to which I contributed the first draft of this map.

FIGURE 3, PAGE 57

The Main Area of ('Germanic') Open-field Agriculture in England

In detail this rough diagrammatic map (from *English Field Systems*, 1915, Frontispiece) has been superseded by that in Dr. and Mrs. Orwin's *The Open Fields*, 1938, p. 65. The map does not appear in the 2nd, 1954, edition of the book. Gray's map, however, better suits our special purpose. It indicates not every parish for which there is some evidence of open-field cultivation, but rather those parts of England in which the 'organized' 'Germanic' open-field system not only was originally, but also long remained the fundamental basis of agriculture and rural life. Elsewhere the village community seems often to have been but a delicate structure. Here it appears, presumably largely because of its agrarian basis, to have had a degree of cohesion and of resilience which enabled it to survive quite generally into Tudor and Stuart times, often into Georgian days. This often meant that its final destruction could be brought about only under powers specifically given by parliament, *cf.* Plate XIVa, b, and note the very special case of Norfolk, to some extent explained by Slater, *op. cit.*, chap. 8.

Both editions of *The Open Fields*, pp. 59–66 and pp. 63–8 respectively, give clear accounts of the sources other than those used by Gray (his *Introduction*, pp. 13–14 *et passim*) which are most valuable in carrying further the inquiries which he began.

FIGURE 5, PAGE 64

Enclosure and Depopulation in England 1485 (sic)–1607.

After the late Professor E. F. Gay in *Q.J.E.* XVII, 576–97 as adapted by Professor J. B. Black in *The Reign of Elizabeth*.

Especially from 1892 onwards there has been a fair amount of controversy among historians as to the causes and consequences, progress and extent of Tudor (and earlier) enclosures. The classical studies of the problem are those of I. S. Leadam and E. F. Gay. Gay's map reproduced here in Black's recension of it is, of course, subject to much revision in detail. It seems to me, however, still to give a reasonably accurate picture of the movement as a whole, leading to the 1517 Commission, and the 1517 and later returns. It should be noted that the Commission covered all the English counties except the four most northerly ones. So for these four, returns to it, often incomplete and even fragmentary elsewhere, have never existed. Some attempts have been made to minimize the importance of sixteenth-century enclosure on the grounds that the total area involved was relatively small, in all perhaps half a million acres, or $2\frac{3}{4}$ per cent of the gross area of the country. In fact, however, since the enclosure was largely concentrated in the midland counties, it had there most serious adverse social effects. Contemporaries were not exaggerating wildly when they spoke of it as a 'canker, eating away the heart of England'.

FIGURE 6, PAGE 68

Deserted Villages of Northamptonshire (after Allison, Beresford and Hurst)

Deserted villages, whether in the extreme case, 'lost villages', or in the less dramatic form 'shrunken villages', are not of course necessarily identical with enclosed parishes. The first-named are to be reckoned in hundreds, the second in thousands. For the reasons indicated in the text pp. 63–73, 167–71, enclosure, especially in the late seventeenth century and throughout the eighteenth, need not necessarily involve depopulation; the gross population might well increase substantially after the enclosure had taken place (though in spite of rather than as a result of it).

Conversely, a village might be deserted for reasons quite other than enclosure and conversion of arable to pasture. Thus, (*a*) a few villages destroyed by William I seem never to have been resettled with the thrusting forward of the margin of cultivation in early mediaeval times. (*b*) Some secondary settlements were made then, especially on land naturally forest, moor or waste, and these were subsequently abandoned as uneconomic. Soil exhaustion, then explains some losses. (*c*) The Cistercian monks certainly destroyed some settlements in making their grange farms. (*d*) Here and there coastal erosion, or fire, or flood or plague might cause the abandonment of a village site. (*e*) From the fifteenth century onwards, and very notably in the eighteenth century, it was not unusual for a village to be either totally destroyed, or removed piecemeal to another site in order that its proprietor might enlarge his hall or its park, or improve the vista from his mansion.

All the same, especially in late mediaeval and Tudor times, there is a connexion between enclosure and deserted villages, perhaps most marked in the period *c.* 1440–1520 (Beresford, *Lost Villages*, p. 166). This is very evident in the midland counties. The deserted villages of Northamptonshire (so far reckoned at some 82 in number) are distributed very widely through the county.

Apart from a tract of fenland in the extreme N., where villages were always thinly scattered, part of the forest areas of Rockingham and Whittlewood, and a tract of the R. Nene valley, near Northampton, hardly any part of the shire is without them.

FIGURES 7 and 8, PAGES 72, 78

Land without Common or Open Field c. 1600: Land without Common or Open Field c. 1700

These maps are open to the criticism justly advanced against Gonner generally (see note on Plate XIVa) and, for these two periods, to a further one. He plots his data most meticulously according to the areal units he has chosen, but he gives no indication whence his material has been obtained. For the carefully worked out percentages in fig. 7 he gives no evidence whatever, and there seems nothing in his text even to suggest on what he based them. For those in fig. 8 his 'evidence', though still quite inadequate, is at any rate existent.

It seems likely that here (*cf.* notes to fig. 10 below) he has depended (*op. cit.* pp. 170 *et seq.*) almost entirely on inferences drawn from the Ogilby maps of roads passing through the areas. He does not exclude, however, Dorset, where Ogilby shows not a single road, or Sussex, where Ogilby depicts only some eight or ten miles of road in the extreme N.N.W. corner of the county. This does not prevent Gonner from presenting a carefully graded table of counties with open road, ranging from Huntingdonshire with sixty-seven per cent to Essex with three per cent. His elaborate statistical tables for *c.* 1700 seem to me to rest on a very shaky foundation, so they are to be taken for what they are worth. The criticism applies to fig. 8, which is presumably based on much the same material, and with even more force to fig. 7, for which also he gives no indication whatever as to his sources.

FIGURES 9 and 10, PAGES 83, 84

Open and Enclosed Land in Oxfordshire c. 1540, and c. 1700 (based on Leland and on Ogilby)

This is intended to follow up the points made by Slater, pp. 161-2, 314-21 and map facing p. 161, and by Gonner, pp. 170 *et seq.*, and map E, *England in 1675*. These are referred to in my text pp. 83-4.

Leland was a skilled observer, and a most conscientious writer. Enclosure was one of the great political and social questions of his day, and throughout almost the whole of his journeys (whether or not on instructions from the King—the book was to be 'A New Year's Gift' to Henry VIII, 1 January 1545) he takes great care to note whether the land he is passing through is 'inclosed', forest, champion, or 'cultivated' so presumably open. So it is possible with some care to work out (from the better text of Leland now available) for one's own county or district, what is in effect an enlargement of the bit concerning it in Slater's map 4.

In 1675 (my text, p. 128) enclosure was not a main subject of controversy and there can have been no monarch less likely than Charles II to concern himself with the welfare of the poor, or of anyone save himself and his families. So although *Britannia* was dedicated to 'his most Serene and Sacred Majesty', Ogilby was not another Leland. Certainly the country gentlemen and merchants for whose transport inquiries the book catered were not troubled about agrarian reform. But in planning their journeys by any of Ogilby's hundred main roads, and in following these *en route* with an Ogilby in the saddlebag, or open on one's knee in the coach, they liked to know where they were. This would apply whether they were passing along a fairly good road (for 1675!) between hedges and fences, or making their way as best they could over waste land or through dense forest, with the roads such in name only. So Ogilby marked enclosed roads with a solid line, unfenced ones with a dotted one. It seems a sound assumption that open roads led through unfenced country (whether open field or pasture or waste). It does not seem to follow necessarily that fenced or enclosed roads led through a countryside largely enclosed, and in some instances this may be clearly disproved by archival evidence.

When one tries to compare the map based on Leland with that founded on Ogilby (and hence to estimate the land enclosed *c.* 1540–*c.* 1675) other difficulties arise. A principal one is that only rarely do they oblige the present-day historian by following the same road over a long distance. And, of course, we cannot be sure exactly what either of them meant by his conventional terms or symbols, still more can we equate these as has been suggested. The maps of Oxfordshire illustrate both the advantages and the disadvantages, where other material as to enclosure in the late seventeenth century and the early eighteenth is lacking, and where each of the two contains evidence to our purpose, of an attempt to collate the two sources. It may on occasion be possible perhaps to draw an inference from the comparison, and this with some degree of confidence and intellectual honesty.

FIGURE II, PAGE 89

Eakring, Notts. (This Map made by the author in 1936 is based upon ancient plans then in the Rufford Estate Office)

The map makes it quite clear that at Eakring where it chances that we have a succession of accurate surveys, as in a great many other parishes where we have not, a great deal of enclosure had gone on unofficially and informally for centuries. The map is interesting not only as showing a village near the famous Laxton where a little open-field land still survives, but also as indicating roughly to what extent the present enclosed land came into its current state before 1737, from 1737–1840; and since 1840. There is no enclosure act for Eakring and no formal agreement seems to have survived. The whole business was carried out quite legally but without unnecessary formalities.

FIGURE 12, PAGE 97

Constituencies of Members of Parliament concerned in Parliamentary Proceedings on Oxfordshire Enclosures 1696–1853

156 members of parliament were involved in Oxfordshire enclosures on some 796 occasions. Usually (my text, pp. 92–101), in the proceedings on a successful enclosure bill there are three major occasions on which *H.C.J.* records the name(s) of the member(s) concerned. These range from 81 members who acted on only one occasion each, to one (member for the county) who served on 171. It is true that the average eighteenth-century M.P. was profoundly uninterested in enclosure bills relating to lands in someone else's constituency. It has been suggested as a fair inference that in the one or two enclosures—say on four or five occasions—when he did take an active part in the proceedings, it was because his interests or those of his family, his friends or his patron were concerned, so he was active in ensuring that these were not neglected.

The bills were however private bills and the eighteenth century saw no impropriety in persons concerned—sometimes even the petitioners themselves—taking an active part in the proceedings on them, just as they would have done in private bills for divorce, estate settlement, disentailing, etc. The bills were of local interest, so the county members and those for local boroughs were expected to take a special interest in them, as indeed they would be nowadays. Many of the members for distant counties or boroughs were local men with interests in Oxfordshire or the various colleges in the University of Oxford. The matter in Oxfordshire, as elsewhere, lies open to further investigation.

FIGURE 13, PAGE 113

The first folio of a fairly typical bound volume Enclosure Award, Long Crendon, Bucks., Act 1824, 5 Geo. IV. cap. 6, Award 1827

The illustration is from a typical bound copy of the Award (p. 117). This was deposited by way of enrolment with the Clerk of the

Peace for the county, and is still legally in the custody of his successor (pp. 115, 119). Of some 5,400 awards *c.* 500 are enrolled in the
national courts at Westminster (documents now in the P.R.O.)
c. 3,950 with the various clerks of the peace (documents now in the
C.R.O.s). The remaining 950 odd are enrolled either not at all, or in
statutory registries, manorial courts, etc. (p. 118, fn. 15). This does not
really trouble the student, for the C.R.O.s, especially when they do
not hold officially enrolled or deposited copies, have been at special
pains, either to encourage the deposit of original awards, or to have
office copies made so as to complete their collections.

FIGURE 14, PAGE 132

Nottinghamshire Parishes subject to Parliamentary Enclosure 1743–1868

The shading covers the whole area of each parish, etc., concerned.
The actual acreage enclosed was, of course, often much less. Thus,
of a total acreage in the county area of something like 530,000 a.
the enclosure awards covered perhaps 145,000 a. Even so, this kind
of map (*cf.* fig. 15) is perhaps the most useful means available of
indicating generally in any specific area the distribution of enclosure
of any particular type.

FIGURE 15, PAGE 133

Progress of Parliamentary Enclosure in Nottinghamshire

It is possible to reckon the progress of Parliamentary enclosure
on two or three different bases. The diagram illustrates the fact
that, at any rate in Nottinghamshire, whatever the basis of the
reckoning the inferences to be drawn from it are much the same.
There is a marked development in the 1760's and the early 1770's.
It is reasonable to associate this with the general, steady, upward
trend of wheat prices after *c.* 1750. There is an almost complete
cessation of enclosure in the early 1780's. Then comes another
'peak' in the years of war and famine prices, the 1790's and the early
1800's—from 1793 onwards, and during the periods of actual
famine, 1800–1 and 1809–13. After 1815 enclosure falls off—
there is little (cultivable) open land left to be enclosed. This is, in
fact, largely enclosed under the inexpensive and equitable provisions
of the Acts of 1836/40, and the inexpensive procedures of the 1845
General Act. In the period first noted, the 1760's and early 1770's,
enclosure is largely of open field with some waste and common.
In the second it is largely of waste and common (much of it never
cultivated before or since), with occasional odd areas of open
field.

FIGURE 16, PAGE 171

Disappearance of the Yeomen before Enclosure at Elstow, Beds., 1767–99

It is often alleged that in Georgian enclosure, as in that of Tudor times, land engrossing followed enclosure. The point is one of controversy. There is no doubt whatever that some buying out of small freeholders often preceded enclosure. It might, indeed, be a necessary preliminary, so that the proponent of enclosure could safely rely on having a four-fifths majority of property interests in the place in favour of his proposal. The plan illustrates the disappearance of the yeomanry (small proprietors occupying and cultivating their own land) in Elstow, Beds. before the enclosure of 1797.

FRONTISPIECE

The Seventeenth-century Land Surveyor at work in Enclosure (from Norden's Surveior's Dialogue, 1607, 3rd edn. 1617)

There is a close connexion between the enclosure movements of Tudor and Stuart times and the development of the art and science of land surveying. Early surveys and terriers (*cf.* Plates IIIb and VI) depend largely on buttals and boundings (*cf.* Fitzherbert *Boke of Surveyinge*, 1523). This type of survey was quite generally used in conveyancing from the thirteenth century to the eighteenth. Modern accurate surveying comes in about the 1570's, with the growth of mathematical knowledge, and perhaps the more 'business-like' attitude towards land management shown by the rising mercantile bourgeoisie. Methodical inquiries into the extent of landed properties, and the revenues from them gave opportunities to such men as John Norden, 1548–1625, and his son and namesake, and to Ralph Agas, 1540–1621. In a rather different class is the mathematician Edmund Gunter, 1581–1626, whose name is still associated with land surveying in the naming of Gunter's Chain of 100 links = 66 ft. (*cf.* pp. 36–7 and fn. 5). With the development of this, and of the crosshead and ranging rods, and still more with Aaron Rathborne, fl. 1616, and his pocket tables of logarithms, and the use of plane-table and a simple theodolite, surveying became work for a specialist. It is easy to imagine how the art reacted on and was reacted on by the later enclosure movements.

PLATE I (facing page 30)

An Eighteenth-century Surveyor at Work on Enclosure

This is the only contemporary illustration I know of a surveyor, during the Georgian enclosure movement, actually carrying out his duties in the field. (The earlier history of land surveying is touched on in the note above on Frontispiece.) J. G. Maxwell is, I take it, the George Maxwell of Fletton, Hunts., later of Peter-borough, who is recorded quite often in midland enclosures, usually as surveyor, occasionally as commissioner. The land he is dealing with is plainly open field, in ridge and furrow. Here he was first-named of the four commissioners.

Two friends suggest that as clearly the central figure is that of the Surveyor, the two subsidiary ones holding 'arrows' are those of his assistants, so the fourth figure, that of an old man leaning on an inverted staff or shepherd's crook (a practice still not uncommon in rural areas) complete with his stick—is that of an old labourer grinning uncomprehendingly as he watches the queer antics of the strangers. I have wondered rather whether his dress does not suggest a looker-on of more lofty station, perhaps the Rev. Thomas Gregory, Vicar of Henlow, smiling not so much at the thought of his modest allotment of 15 acres, of a total of 200 a., as at thought of the corn rent (text p. 186) which is to replace the tithes and moduses he has had some difficulty in extracting from the lord and ladies of the three manors. These, apart from himself, are the only persons with any landed interest in the parish. Perhaps it may be a self-portrait of Maxwell himself, supervising the work of his underlings.

PLATE II

Grazing Fields at Crimscote, Warws. (facing page 31)

Crimscote is a hamalet in the parish of Whitchurch, Warws., some four miles S.S.E. of Stratford-on-Avon. The aerial photograph is shown here as a very well-known—indeed almost hackneyed—illustration of open-field ridge-and-furrow, with its selions and their ⌒⌣ bends (text pp. 36–7), their headlands and balks and so on, all preserved in some degree of perfection because the land was put down to pasture centuries ago and has been cross-ploughed only within the last decade. It was not technically 'enclosed' in early times, and in fact the enclosure of the open fields of Crimscote and its sister hamlet of Wimpstone in 1867–9 was the latest Parliamentary enclosure in Warwickshire, and one of the latest such enclosures of open field in England. There has in the past been some criticism of the suggestion that ridge-and-furrow is in general a mark of former open-field husbandry a point first made in modern times, I think in 1892 by Sir John Lubbock, I Baron Avebury. For some con-troversy upon it see Beresford in *Econ. Hist. Rev.* II Ser. I., 1948, and Kerridge *ibid.* IV, 1951, with the references in Beresford, *History on the Ground,* p. 83.

Certainly land is still ploughed on occasion in ridge-and-furrow —I have watched a farmer friend doing this, and persuaded him to let me try my hand at 'helping' him. Modern ridges are, however, as straight as may be. The marks of ancient ridge-and-furrow, especially in the Midlands, its characteristic home, are these: (*a*) long narrow strips, (*b*) usually, though not always, following the natural slope of the land, (*c*) 'acres', though rarely approaching anything like a statute acre in area, (*d*) ⁓ shaped, as set out by a two-, four- or perhaps even eight-ox plough team (the leaders of which had to bend a little to the left in order to turn to the right on the headland—an ox team cannot make a neat U turn as can a tractor (on this see Eyre in *Ag. Hist. Rev.* III 1955).

If, in addition, the ridges are set out with entire disregard of such features as roads known to be later in origin, or modern boundary walls or fences or hedges, sixteenth-century manor houses, seventeenth-century farmsteads, eighteenth-century canals or nineteenth-century railways, it is common sense to assume that they preceded all these. They are in general then clearly the marks of mediaeval open-field cultivation, with its furlongs, selions and balks, although the single ridge is rarely to be identified with a single selion.

PLATE III (facing page 44)

(a) *Survey of Open-field Selions in Strettington, West Sussex* (1781) 1781

(a) Strettington is not and never has been a parish. It is a tithing or township (p. 191) and former manor in Boxgrove, about three miles N.E. of Chichester. In the reign of Elizabeth I it was granted to the Morleys, from whom it passed to the Aclands, who sold it in 1765 to Charles Lennox, III Duke of Richmond. (The present Duke is still the chief landowner in the district.) The survey was made in 1781 to the Duke's commission, perhaps as part of a process of stocktaking of recently acquired properties. It was carried out by Thomas Yeakell and William Gardner.*

It is not known exactly when the three open fields of Strettington were enclosed—not in the Boxgrove enclosure of 1845–56, which was a mere tidying up of a few remaining acres of common. Presumably the enclosure was carried out privately by one of the Dukes, at some date at present unknown, but certainly after 1781. The plan is a specially beautiful example of eighteenth-century cartography at its best. It is set more or less E. and W., and it shows clearly the main street of the village, with its tofts and crofts. The larger closes shown already belong to the Duke, but some of the open lands are still in separate ownership. The several distinguishing colours which appear in the reproduction as black and different shades of grey indicate the various proprietors. The very elegant picture frame is in fact engraved, and the plan is drawn within it.

* For other maps and plans by Yeakell and Gardner see F. W. Steer, *A Catalogue of Sussex Estate and Tithe Award Maps* (Sussex Record Society, Vol. 61, 1962).

(b) *First Folio of a Terrier of Open-field Selions in Little Gringley, Notts., 1547 or 1548*

Little Gringley was one of several hamlets in the parish of Clarborough, partly now absorbed in the enlarged borough of East Retford [and, as it happens, my birthplace]. It was not affected by either of the Clarborough Parliamentary enclosures 1776–8, and 1799–1806. The terrier helps to suggest why. The document is 'A terrar [*sic*] made by Sʳ. John Hersye, Nicholas Denman, Sʳ. Steven Pettinger, Sʳ. Seth Godley, John Smyth, Barker, Willm. Cuttys, John Dey and many other mo of all the landes in Gringley fieldes'. Internal evidence helps to date it as no earlier than 1547, and no later than 1548. The text makes it clear that the place had an irregular agrarian structure, based on furlongs rather than on two or three fields. Within this there had plainly been a great deal of interchange of selions, so that individual proprietors had managed to get together two or three or four lands, doubtless with the idea of hedging or fencing them and making convenient closes. Some had been much more successful than others in this. For a detailed statistical analysis of the terrier, with a note of some possible inferences to be drawn from it see (Nottinghamshire) *Thoroton Society Trans.* XLIII, 1939. The terrier of the first furlong noted reads:

Spittle hill furlonge beginninge at the West syde

Impʳimis John Chamberlayne	a Close
the heires of Henrye Smyth	iij lands
John Hercye	iiij lands
The Church of Clarebrough	j lands
Thomas Berrege	ij lands
John Wynbeche	j lande
John Hercye	j lande
John Chamberlayne	ij lands
John Hercye	j lande
Willm Eyre	ij lands
Thomas Berrege	ij lands
Willm Eyre	j lande
The Church of our ladye	j lande
John Cutler	j lande
John Hercye	j lande
John Cutler	j land
Nicholas Denman	j land

PLATE IV (facing page 45)

Two 'Lost Villages, Middle Ditchford, Glos. and Martinsthorpe, Rutland

Each of these aerial photographs shows clearly the site of a former village in the 'heart of England' central area of 'Germanic' open-field agriculture, subjected in early times to the sweeping and disastrous enclosure referred to in the text (Chap. VI).

Middle Ditchford was one of the three Ditchfords (*tres* Dishford) near Warwick, which Rous (p. 63) notes as destroyed within his lifetime. It is now a mere hamlet of Blockley, formerly Worcs., now Glos. In 1299 it had 21 customary tenants, but apparently it was entirely depopulated for sheep grazing in the last quarter of the fifteenth century. The ridge-and-furrow is plain to be seen in the foreground right, and the former common meadow (by the stream with the line of willows) in the foreground left. The level area in the centre of the web of streets probably marks the village green. The deep hollows, top left, appear to be fish ponds, adjoining the stream. In the background the lines of the streets are to be seen, as hollow-ways, worn by the passage of peasants with their carts and their stock from the village to the open fields. The covering of turf has preserved the differences of level among the streets, the houses (toftsteads) and their gardens and crofts. Here and there is a narrow depression—the line of a boundary ditch between a former croft and its neighbour. There seem to be no buried stone foundations. Probably the houses were built entirely of wattle and daub, so they have completely rotted away. The present-day hedgerows are un-likely all to represent the fifteenth-century boundaries. Later farming conditions have caused the subdivision of the extensive pastures. About this place see Beresford and St. Joseph *Mediaeval England*, on which (by permission) this note is very largely based. Middle Ditchford is not now marked on any maps save those on the largest scale, and its existence is not recognized even by its appear-ance as a 'locality' in the census returns. Virtually it has com-pletely disappeared.

Martinsthorpe, two miles S. of Oakham, Rutland, is well recorded from at any rate 1199. It is still a full-scale civil and ecclesiastical parish, with a rector of its own, though the sinecure rectory is always held with the rectory of the contiguous parish of Manton. The last traces of the church disappeared quite recently. During the last century and a half the population of the parish has been returned at figures ranging from one to four. It is now (1961 Census) *nil*. Martinsthorpe seems to have been depopulated quite early. Accord-ing to Beresford (*Lost Villages*, p. 163) its tax assessments were 25s. 6d. in 1327, 40s. 8d. in 1334, and 88 villagers paid to the poll tax in 1377. In the tax re-assessments of 1445 and 1489 it was relieved of half its tax obligations. Even as late as 1534, however, when King Henry VIII's commissioners valued all the major benefices in England, so as to ensure the due payment of his First-fruits and Tenths, it was assessed at £6 0s. 5d. (two other neighbouring rectories are set at only £6 17s. 1d. and £5 4s. 7d. respectively) so it was not quite the poorest rectory in the rural deanery. It seems a reasonable inference that conversion of arable to pasture had led to a great decay in the receipts from corn tithe (pp. 151, 191). The joint benefice is still a miserably poor one.

The photograph (looking westwards) shows plainly the very marked ridge-and-furrow characteristics of the area, stopping dead when it comes to the ?mediaeval moated site to the N. of the former village, and to the village area itself, the 'ring of the town', with its streets and its tofts and crofts. The church site lies S.E. of and immediately opposite the walled garden of the (now empty) farmhouse. The general lay-out of the place is not wholly dissimilar to that of Ditchford. Here, however, the village site is plain to the E. and W., but the markings in its centre have been obliterated by later ones, those of the walls and foundations of the Jacobean mansion built here by the Feildings, Earls of Denbigh ?in the 1620's. It seems clear that they did not depopulate the place, but they built their mansion here on the site of the former village, deserted at some unknown date, but almost certainly before 1589.

PLATE V (a) and (b) (facing page 52)

Frontispieces of Blagrave's Epitome . . . *1669 and* New Additions . . . *1675*

Joseph Blagrave, 1610–82, is neither the most readable nor the most reliable of the writers on agriculture during the Restoration period (text pp. 81–2). His principal notoriety is as an astrologer. The text of his book, which ran into four editions 1669–85, is almost entirely plagiarized from other writers—notably Fitzherbert (text p. 67, fn. 7), a century-and-a-half out of date—an interesting comment on the slowness of changes in agricultural practice. Blagrave does not seem to have been a practical man in agricultural matters and he lacked also the literary skill which might have enabled him to disguise his borrowings. I reproduce his frontispiece rather than the title pages of his contemporaries Meager, Nourse, Yarranton, etc., because of its charming woodcut pictures illustrating various agricultural operations.

PLATE VI (facing page 53)

A Successful Anti-enclosure Petition, Lanchester, Co. Durham, 26 April 1721

Usually (as noted in the text pp. 96–8) anti-enclosure petitions, whether addressed to Lords or Commons, met with little success. Thus, in 144 Nottinghamshire enclosures from 1743 onwards there were eleven counter-petitions. In only three of these instances the petitioners, usually people of influence and substance, succeeded in getting the enclosure deferred for anything up to 39 years. When it was carried out, probably their claims had been met in whole or in part.

Lanchester, Co. Durham, was an enormous parish of some 40,000 to 50,000 acres, and containing four chapelries and fourteen townships. Lanchester proper, the part of it with which we are concerned here, was enclosed more or less in the normal fashion 1773–87, on the petition of several owners of land, tenements and hereditaments and with the concurrence of John Egerton, Lord Bishop of Durham. It is clear that an enclosure proposal half a century earlier, though made on behalf of Lord Crew, Bishop of Durham, and others, had come to nothing, presumably because of the opposition of Thomas and Robert Hunter, and Cuthbert Johnson, Gentlemen, and the Rev. Charles Collinson, Rector, or their predecessors.

PLATE VII (facing page 96)

Exchange of Selions as a Preliminary to Enclosure at Tideswell, Derbys. 1760

In the aggregate many hundreds of thousands of acres of open field must have been subjected to a process similar to that described in the document shown. In the nature of things, however, this was usually done unofficially and informally, and only by the toilsome process of looking through thousands of title deeds can one obtain archival evidence of it. The document is an agreement between Robert Freeman of Wheston, Derbys. and Daniel Taylor of Tideswell. Clearly there had been a great deal of piecemeal consolidation in the Tideswell open fields and this had resulted *inter alia* in Robert Freeman owning a selion in Knowtridge furlong, bounded, at the north side, by the lands of Daniel Taylor. Similarly, Robert Freeman had a close called Luff Flatt consisting, presumably, of half a dozen or so contiguous selions which he had thrown together to make a convenient plot for his purpose. He was, therefore, much inconvenienced by the fact that in the middle of his selions was one only (what would be technically called a quillet—they still survive, especially, in some parts of the counties along the Welsh border) belonging to Daniel Taylor. So very sensibly Taylor and Freeman had agreed to exchange their properties for their common benefit, and this is the document by which they did so.

PLATE VIII (facing page 97)

Popular Reaction to the Enclosure of Commons, Otmoor, Oxon. 1815–29

This paper was found in a copy of Burn's *Justice* . . . , formerly belonging to William Selby-Lowndes, of Whaddon Hall, near Bletchley, Bucks., Member for Buckinghamshire, 1810–20. It is interesting as giving further data concerning an enclosure especially well known to (not to say notorious among) students of agrarian history, because it was described in some detail by the Hammonds (*op. cit.*, pp. 88–96). According to their account it was a fairly scandalous business. Reference to other sources makes it clear that from their point of view it was even more shocking than they supposed.

They are wrong in saying that enclosure was first mooted by the Duke of Marlborough in 1801. An enclosure proposal had been made in 1788. This was rejected because of a counter-petition by the Earl of Abingdon. There was another petition by the Duke in 1801, but this was opposed by influential local landed proprietors, Alexander Croke *et al.*, and came to nothing. Two days later Croke presented his own petition ? doing much more justice to the lord of the manor of Beckley (himself). This again came to nothing, presumably because it neglected the Marlborough interests (not, of course, because of rioting in the area, when indignant peasants tore down the enclosure notices from the church doors). Still more petitions, apparently Croke's, followed in 1814 and 1815, and there was more rioting. Selby-Lowndes, whose draft warrant we have, was one of the two members preparing and bringing in the bill. This time the Duke and the Earl jointly petitioned against the bill, and it was amended to meet their demands. Croke counter-petitioned (apparently to little purpose), and so did the smaller freeholders, cottagers, etc. (to none at all) and the bill duly went through.

The Hammonds have not noticed that the members principally concerned with the various proceedings in the House included Lord Charles Spencer and Lord Francis Spencer. The left-wing historian will recollect that the family name of the Marlboroughs is Spencer (Churchill) and that of the Abingdons Bertie. If he chances to be also a devotee of Debrett, that admirable work of mingled historical fact-and-fiction, he will find therein that Charles was the II son of the II Duke, Francis, his nephew, the II son of the III Duke. Francis appears later in the story as Lord Churchill (he had become I Baron Churchill of Wychwood in 1815), Commanding Officer of the Yeomanry putting down the riots on Otmoor and in St. Giles. The co-signatory of the warrant authorizing him to do so is the Rev. Frederick Bertie, one of the Webbs' much-disliked parson magistrates. As it happened, he was also the IV son of the IV Earl of Abingdon (the petitioner in 1788), and the brother of the IV Earl, who was among the principal beneficiaries when the enclosure at last took place. Our genealogically minded left-winger will find other interesting connexions if he bears in mind that the heir to the Dukedom appears in the House of Commons *Journals* as, by courtesy, the Marquis of Blandford, that to the Earldom as Lord Norreys of Ryecote.

PLATE IX (facing page 128)

Part of a fairly typical Enclosure 'Act' (in fact a Bill) Yaxley, Hunts., 7 Geo. III c. 14. 1767. (text p. 103)

The *arms: or* on a fesse betw. 2 chevrons *sa.* 3 cross crosslets of the field.
crest: a Saracen's head in profile . . . etc. . . . *ppr.*
supporters: an antelope and a stag both *arg.* . . . etc.
motto: FARI QU[A]E SENTIAT . . . . TO SPEAK HIS MIND are nothing to do with either Yaxley or the Probys, Earls of Carysfort. They are those of Robert, Baron Walpole, later, II Earl of Orford (not the great Robert but his son and namesake, granted a barony in 1723, while his father's earldom-and-barony were not conferred until 1742). Presumably the printer (? a local man in Peterborough—there is no imprint) had the block by him and 'used it up' in compliment to Lord Carysfort, not only giving him completely wrong arms, but also incidentally 'degrading' him from earl to baron.

PLATE X (facing page 129)

Yorkshire Freeholders' and Enclosure Commissioners' Inn Bills 1788 and c. 1808–13

It was often held at the time (text pp. 111–12) that much of the admittedly excessive expense attaching to enclosure commissions was due to extravagant fees paid to commissioners, and excessive subsistence expenses, etc., claimed by them. Such commissioners' accounts as survive are rarely detailed enough to enable one to come to a considered judgement on this minor issue. Here and there, however, their miscellaneous papers include a few of their inn bills.

The bill first reproduced is in respect of refreshments at a meeting in 1788 of the freeholders concerned in the enclosure of part of Rumbles (Rombald's) moor in Riddlesden, in Bingley and Keighley (enclosed 1788–90). The purpose of the meeting was to try to ensure that the newly enclosed land should not be subjected to tithe. The total cost of refreshments, etc., at the *Brown Cow* was £1 4s. 0d. (The 6s. was for a stamp on the bond then entered into). This was advanced by the five principal freeholders, who note rather plaintively that they failed to recover any part of it from the other persons present.

The second bill (some date unknown but between 1808 and 1813) is one incurred by ?William Whitelock, ?John Binns and Jonathan Taylor, commissioners for the Chapel Allerton enclosure, at the *Mexborough Arms*, Chapel Allerton. The total, £2 11s. 11d. (even including the interesting 4d. for 'glass brock') does not seem at all excessive for three skilled men, presumably relaxing after a hard day's work on the moor.

PLATE XI (facing page 136)

(*a*) *Leaf in an Enclosure Commissioners' Minute Book, Ulley, Yorks. W. (Enclosure 1798–1800); (b) Original Claim of Thomas Short at Dore, Derbys. 1814 (Enclosure 1809–22); (c) Original Claim of Comfort Clarke at Potter Newton, Yorks. W. 1804 (Enclosure 1803–6)*

(*a*) Enclosure Commissioners' Minute Books as sources of information on the techniques and processes of enclosure have only of late years been seriously studied (text pp. 112–13). Sometimes they are highly formalized, and the student who rejoices because he has come across one will obtain little from it save an admiration of the beautiful calligraphy of the Commissioners' clerk. Occasionally they are really informative, and give a close-up picture of the Commissioners at work, obtainable in no other way. The Ulley book makes it clear that here the Commissioners held what was in effect a court of claims. Unlike many of their fellows, who recorded such proceedings, if at all, in a separate book (now usually lost—perhaps purposely destroyed at the execution of the award) they entered the full details as the minutes of a special meeting of the Commission. Samuel Buck was already the largest owner of land and mineral rights in Ulley. His share of the expenses of enclosure was £600.

(*b*) Original claims for allotments, made by owners of land or common right, have rarely survived. When they have they are sometimes of human interest, as set forth by claimants evidently much more used to handling the plough than the pen. Thomas Short who sets out his claim with some attempt at legal formality, is mentioned in the Award only as one of a group of trustees acting for an infant. Quakers ineligible on various grounds for some of the other professions, were often trusted as commissioners, or clerks or, most of all, surveyors. It is quite usual for the act to contain a reference to their special privileges in respect of exemption from oath-taking. The only *verbatim* account I have seen of every word uttered during the making of a series of claims was recorded, I think, by a Quaker, Sturge of Bath.

(*c*) The enclosure of Potter Newton was essentially that of waste land, subject to various common rights, within the chapelry, in the parish of Leeds, and the 'liberty of the borough' of Leeds, and now a suburban area well within the limits of the enlarged county borough. The sole Commissioner was William Whitelock of Brotherton, a local man much concerned with enclosures in the district. He is known to have acted with some formality in inviting claims, in giving claimants details of any objections raised against their submissions, in hearing his 'cases' and in adjudicating upon them.

There is an interesting personal touch in the record of Comfort Clarke's claim. Presumably she was an old woman, incapable of stating her case formally, and in fact illiterate. It will be seen that the claim is throughout in the handwriting of a third person— Comfort has had no difficulty in finding someone to help her out. The reader may be glad to know that her claim was upheld and Dame Clarke received 30 p. (which she sold to Thomas Ward, who bought up several other small allotments in the place).

PLATE XII (facing page 137)

Ejection of a Farm-worker from a tied Cottage, 1962!

The problem of the tied cottage is one of several rural questions to which the townsman—when he troubles to think about them at all —'knows the answers', but on which the countryman is not so sure. It is one closely connected with the desuetude of the Elizabethan cottage act of 1589 (see Table of Statutes) repealed in 1775; the growth of large scale commercial farming, and enclosure (especially of commons) which had sometimes offered a peasant or farm worker the opportunity of housing himself by 'squatting'.

On the one hand, both in connexion with his arable husbandry and still more for the benefit of his stock, it is desirable that the farmer should have cottages available. Then, if a farm-worker leaves him, as usually nowadays he is entitled to do, with a week's notice, his successor may be offered housing accommodation for himself and his family. The stock cannot wait to be fed while the Rural District Council is deciding whether to build a cottage, and where, and when and who is to have the tenancy. Moreover, the tied cottage is (sometimes) sited with a special view to the convenience of the farm and those who work on it. It is by statute much restricted in rent, and the 'stoppage' made in respect of it may be fantastically below its market value. If the farm worker yields to the temptation to take up better paid employment in the neighbouring town, it would be grossly unjust that his former employer should continue to pay a concealed subsidy towards his wages.

On the other hand, if farm-workers were paid wages fairly comparable with those of skilled men in other crafts, they could (? perhaps would gladly!) pay economic rents. A man may lose his employment for any reason good or bad, for a momentary indiscretion, or a casual peccadillo. He may be dismissed because he has 'had words' with his employer's son, or because the farmer or his wife take exception to his political or religious views, or to his trade union activities. As things are, especially since the farm-worker has been given by law a degree of security of tenure in his home, victimization of this kind happens much less often than it did—though still too often! But the history of the English peasant has influenced the farm-worker's conscious and subconscious attitudes towards his 'betters', so the implicit fear may be there even if it is unjustified. The political and social emancipation of the countryside may well call for further sweeping reforms in the 'tied cottage' system, though it is difficult to see how it can be completely abolished.

PLATE XIII (facing page 152)

Popular Reaction to the Enclosure of Commons:

(*a*) *in Charnwood Forest, Leics., 1753*
(*b*) *In North and South Lopham, Norfolk, 1815*

(The first extract is from a document in my possession: reference to the second I owe to Mr. A. J. Peacock.)

(*a*) Charnwood Forest (always so styled, though technically, as transferred by the Crown to various subjects rather a series of Chases) is an area of North Leicestershire. Its parliamentary enclosure was 1808–29. Probably soon after the Norman Conquest some fifteen parks had been taken out of the Forest, and the process of encroachment and enclosure had continued for centuries. Even so, there was remaining forest, subject, like other land of the same kind, to common pasture rights. The verses are from an unpublished (and rather scurrilous) MS. satire of some merit, *The Charnwood Opera*, 1753, attacking a local 'squire who had encroached on these rights. He is also, alleges the satirist, grossly immoral sexually. In each of these matters, the writer says, the 'squire displays the same weakness, a hankering after other men's 'property', and an inability to be 'content with his own'.

North and South Lopham, Norfolk 1815:

(*b*) One of the few instances of violent opposition to enclosure in East Anglia was at North and South Lopham, Norfolk (enclosed 1812/15) where, as it happens, 200 a. had been allocated to the poor (the present town lands and fuel allotment in the fen). At the trial the four co-defendants were indicted for fence-breaking, the traditional peasant protest against an allegedly unjust enclosure of common. (Under statute law the offence was felony 1769–1827. A more reasonable penalty was fixed by the General Act of 1801, where §28 imposed a fine of £5.)

It will be noted that Mason who 'addressed the court' received four times as heavy a sentence as any of the others. This was presumably upon a principle similar to that shown in our own days towards Mr. Toad of Toad Hall, who, as the student of criminal law will remember, was sentenced to a 'mild' twelve months 'for stealing a valuable motor car', 'a lenient' three years for driving recklessly to the common danger and a 'nominal' fifteen years because on apprehension he was grossly impertinent to a policeman.

PLATE XIV (a) and (b) (facing page 153)

(a) Parliamentary Enclosure of Open-field Arable c. 1700–1870 (after Gonner): (b) Parliamentary Enclosure of Open Fields in England in the Eighteenth and Nineteenth Centuries (after Slater)

It is impossible to show adequately the percentage of the total area subjected to Parliamentary enclosure in the various parts of England. One of several difficulties in the way is in the choice of the geographical units to be plotted. The 42 counties are far too large and heterogeneous in their constitutions. The (10,000) odd (ancient) parishes are far too small. The Hundreds (Wapentakes, Wards) the ancient intermediate units, are much too variable in size— Yorkshire had some 28, Sussex, with an area a quarter as large, had twice as many. (a) Gonner's answer (p. 204) was to take as his areal unit the 'Registration Districts of the Registration Counties', i.e., more or less the 600 odd (now obsolete) poor law unions. These usually dated from the years after 1834 or in a few instances from those after Gilbert's Act, 1782. This had an additional advantage that his 'present day' population statistics were worked out on this basis, so he was able to try to relate enclosure history to population problems. With all its faults his map is well worth comparing with Slater's. It deserves the respect due to any attempt to solve a problem which is, in the nature of things, insoluble (*cf.* caption to Fig. 7 above).

(b) In detail, this map, the classical one on the subject (1907), is incorrect, but in general outline it is sound. There are two or three principal respects in which it is open to criticism. (i) Slater assumed that the collection of private acts in the British Museum Library was a complete one. It is not. Moreover, working as a pioneer, with little help, in what was then a quite new department of historical learning, he made a fair number of errors in transcribing his place names, and identifying his places. (ii) His topographical basis was almost inevitably the English civil parish as existing in 1907, often differing very markedly from the area bearing the same name at the time of its enclosure, a century or a century and a half before. (iii) If he considered that the act covered any area—however small—of open field in the parish he shaded in the whole parish area, so the map makes no distinction between the parishes where open-field agriculture was the foundation of economic and social life, and those where it had long almost disappeared, leaving a few stray relics. Similarly, his map includes some portions on the borders of the open-field area where the 'Germanic' open-field system (text pp. 35–6, map fig. 3, facing p. 57 above) had never had any very substantial existence.

INDEX

The Index is rather more than a mere alphabetical table giving names of persons, places, and books, etc. (but rarely topics or subjects) mentioned. It is intended on occasion to supplement the text as well as serve as a guide to it. I hope the reader will use it fully, and that before doing this he will bear with me in this necessarily somewhat detailed explication of it.

Dates given are normally those of births and deaths, except for Kings and Queens-regnant. For these I give the dates of their reigns. Where extra dates are given for a dignitary in church or state they are those of his accession to and relinquishment of the office with which he is mainly associated. K. signifies king, Q. queen, D. duke, M. marquess, E. earl, V. viscount, B. baron. Members of titled families are indexed under their surnames, and cross-referenced under titles. Nicknames, courtesy titles, etc., are in single quotation marks. Similarly books are dated and cross-referenced to their authors. References are normally given under the author's name. not the book title. Authors' dates are given for early works but not for modern ones. Book titles are italicized.

Parishes, villages, manors, etc., are ascribed to their present-day counties. The page references to places in each specific county are (not repeated but are) summarized, under the name of the county concerned. I think that most of the contractions I have used are generally accepted (like *fl.—floruit*—flourished, where I had an author's approximate date, but not verifiable and accurate ones for his birth or his death). Occasionally I have manufactured or used other contractions, but these are all I think more or less self-explanatory, like, e.g., Abp. for Archbishop, L.C.J. for Lord Chief Justice, L.Ch. for Lord Chancellor, M.R. for Master of the Rolls, P.M. for Prime Minister, etc. If not, a reference from the index to the text will usually make it easy for the reader to expand the contraction. My book is arranged, I hope, with some degree of logic and common sense, both topically and chronologically. So, having to make the most of limited space, I have rarely indexed such topics as the reader will have no difficulty in turning up from the table of contents and the lists of plates and figures. Similarly, I have tried to include in the glossary, not the index, any technical terms which seem to me worthy of notice, and in the table of statutes and acts of Parliament, etc., all those mentioned either specifically or by implication in the text.